CHICKEN SOUP
FOR THE
AFRICAN
AMERICAN
WOMAN'S SOUL

Chicken Soup for the African American Woman's Soul
Laughter, Love and Memories to Honor the Legacy of Sisterhood
Jack Canfield, Mark Victor Hansen, Lisa Nichols

Published by Backlist, LLC,
a unit of Chicken Soup for the Soul Publishing, LLC. www.chickensoup.com

Front cover art by Keith Mallett
Front cover design by Larissa Hise Henoch
Originally published in 2006 by Health Communications, Inc.

Back cover and spine redesign by Pneuma Books, LLC

Distributed to the booktrade by Simon & Schuster. SAN: 200-2442

Publisher's Cataloging-in-Publication Data
(Prepared by The Donohue Group)

Chicken soup for the African American woman's soul : laughter, love and mem-
    ories to honor the legacy of sisterhood / [compiled by] Jack Canfield, Mark
    Victor Hansen, [and] Lisa Nichols.

    p. : ill. ; cm.

    Originally published: Deerfield Beach, FL : Health Communications, c2006.
    ISBN: 978-1-62361-048-7

    1. African American women--Social life and customs--Anecdotes. 2. African
American women--Social conditions--Anecdotes. 3. Anecdotes. I. Canfield,
Jack, 1944- II. Hansen, Mark Victor. III. Nichols, Lisa.

E185.86 .C445 2012
305.48/896073   2012944290

PRINTED IN THE UNITED STATES OF AMERICA
on acid free paper

27 26 25 24 23 22   08 09 10 11

CHICKEN SOUP
FOR THE
AFRICAN
AMERICAN
WOMAN'S SOUL

Laughter, Love and Memories to Honor the Legacy of Sisterhood

Jack Canfield
Mark Victor Hansen
Lisa Nichols

Backlist, LLC, a unit of
Chicken Soup for the Soul Publishing, LLC
Cos Cob, CT
www.chickensoup.com

Contents

v

2. IT TAKES A VILLAGE OF MOTHERS

3. BEAUTIFUL—JUST THE WAY I AM

4. MY SISTER, MY FRIEND

Introduction

Sweat was my great-grandmother's name.
Suffering was my grandmother's name.
Suffice was my mother's name.
Self-Sufficient is my name.

Emma Ransom Hayward

While we were working on *Chicken Soup for the African American Woman's Soul,* two of the most powerful and influential African American women in our history—or rather our *her*story—passed away. Thus, it seems fitting to offer this book as a tribute to their lives and their work. Without Rosa Parks and Coretta Scott King, without their dedication, their courage and their sacrifices, it is questionable whether this book would exist. It is questionable whether many of the story contributors in the book would have had the awesome opportunities and successes that they were able to share in their heartwarming stories.

Sister Rosa Parks was a sweet but powerful lady who spoke softly while making a statement that screamed so loudly. I could see the gentle spirit in her eyes and in her smile, and hear it in her kind words. As I watched Mrs. Rosa's niece speak about her in an interview, I had two reoccurring thoughts: *How proud she must be to have had an aunt like Mrs. Rosa,* and *Mrs. Rosa must have been the most widely adopted "Auntie Rosa" by all of us who are thankful that she took a stand for each of us. We are all proud of her.* Mrs. Rosa took a big stand by taking a firm seat, letting us know that even on our way home from work, on public transportation, in the middle of chaos, if we are willing to pay the price for our convictions, then we are ready to reap the rewards, as well.

When I was blessed with the opportunity to see Coretta Scott King speak, I hadn't before noticed how *really* beautiful she was. Previously, I'd admired her gracefulness, her stand for peace—and her choice in men. But that night, I found myself captivated with her every word, her beautiful disposition, her confidence and her gentle but steady strength. I felt as if I were holding my breath as she told the story of what it was like to actually "be" the stand for truth and justice. As she sat there poised to perfection, I saw for the first time the mother in her, the grandmother, the friend, and I caught a quick intimate glimpse of the solid rock of a wife she must have been. My eyes were fixated on Mrs. Coretta Scott King; my ears were enjoying the melody of her rhythmic and profound words. In the past when I'd heard Mrs. King speak, she had inspired me a great deal, but somehow this moment was different. On this night, she grabbed me; she held my heart, expanded my mind and stirred my soul. I felt her words. I listened as she explained that she was called just as Martin had been, that she was obedient to God in a different way but with equal conviction. She shared that she hadn't sacrificed her life in the same sense that Martin had, but she had definitely offered her life to the cause. For the first time, I did not see Dr. Martin Luther King's wife, I saw Coretta, Coretta Scott, Coretta Scott King, a dedicated, passionate, remarkable African American woman powerful in her own right, not as "the wife of" but as the woman, herself.

The long nights of fear as mothers and wives, the endless organizing and protesting, the ongoing prayer and so much more, were not in vain. Because of Mrs. Coretta and Mrs. Rosa, we stand taller, we breathe deeper, we love ourselves more, and we have bigger convictions to be obedient to our own callings. Many are called but few answer because the price to pay for our convictions is often considered too high of a price. Today we get to be who we are because Coretta Scott King and Rosa Parks had convictions for equality and were willing to pay the price not only for their own sake but for us all.

While the work is not yet done, they have shown us how much one or two people can do in the world. How can we make this world a better place? How can we contribute to the cause? We now know that by sharing our stories of success both large and small, by taking our own stands in honor of our convictions and by rising to the occasion or staying firmly seated as the situation demands, we work every day to live out that answer.

Chicken Soup for the African American Woman's Soul offers a sampling of the stories that each of our lives hold— moments of love, hope, faith, courage, conviction, persistence and inspiration. Sometimes, we just need the inspiration to stop long enough to remember, to find those stories stored within our hearts and hiding within our life's experiences. It is our hope that as you read, powerful, heartwarming stories from your own life will pop into your mind, and you will be inspired to put the book down for a minute and turn to your children, grandchildren, parents, siblings, friends or coworkers and share your magical moments with them. It is our hope that you will take any inspiration this book gives you and share that blessing with someone else. In honor of Rosa Parks and Coretta Scott King, we offer the world this book full of stories by or about women who have benefited from their examples of God's obedience, manifested in the African American woman.

Lisa Nichols

1

THE SHOULDERS WE STAND ON

I am where I am because of the bridges that I crossed. Sojourner Truth was a bridge. Harriet Tubman was a bridge. Ida B. Wells was a bridge. Madame C. J. Walker was a bridge. Fannie Lou Hamer was a bridge. . . .

Oprah Winfrey

A Line in the Sand

On my underground railroad, I never ran my train off the track and I never lost a passenger.

Harriet Tubman

Blue. Once the paint was blue. Weathered, sun tarnished, the house slumped on the sand in the clearing. The door stood open, and though the few windows were without glass, it was dark inside. A roof of rusted tin shaded the front porch and steps, never painted. A shabby cane chair, a broken box of firewood, that's all there was.

She was as weathered as her home, dressed in gray, the blouse darker, but still gray. Gray hair was pulled severely back from her face. Her skirt stopped at bare ankles and cracked, worn feet as she stood on the hot sand and watched me trudge up the road.

The same sand pulled at my low-heeled white shoes making each step a commitment. The runs in my nylons and scratches on my legs were witness to an encounter with a raspberry bush. I'd read books about the sun searing the skin on the desert. Not here. The clouds formed a lid on the pot I'd simmered in since June. Sweat oozed persistently between my breasts, under my arms, down my thighs. Many hand washings had not released a moldy whisper from my cotton dress, which glued itself to my damp body. I yearned to be dry.

What was she thinking as she watched me? White folks drive up in cars; they don't walk up to the house. She went to church regularly, and perhaps she guessed who I was. When I reached her, her eyes were veiled, but not cold. She didn't trust me, but she wasn't locking me out.

"Evenin', Mrs. Crawford?" I asked.

"Evenin'," she answered, her voice almost a whisper as she looked at her feet. She wasn't going to help me.

"My name is Sherie Holbrook, and I am here registering voters for Martin Luther King."

I had said the magic words, *Martin Luther King,* and she looked up at me quickly and then down.

"We're talking to people about going to the courthouse to register to vote. Have you registered yet?" I wished she would offer me a glass of water.

The soft voice answered, "Yes, ma'am." I'm sure she was thinking that perhaps I would go away now.

I didn't believe her. I had been taught to say exuberantly, "Good for you. So few people have. Do you have your registration card?"

"Yes, ma'am." She turned toward the house, limping slightly as she walked up groaning steps and disappeared into the darkness. Time went by. I thought she had decided not to return. Sometimes, that's what folks did. They just disappeared so they wouldn't have to explain they were terrified to vote.

This was the summer of 1965, and waves of change were crashing against shoals of tradition across the American South. The American Negro demanded freedom and the rights that freedom bestows, and they were determined to get that freedom now! For many, the price for that freedom was costly. Some of the people we met told us that Negro votes were not counted, so there was no reason to vote. They knew that some people who resisted the system lost their jobs, like Rosa and Raymond Parks when she refused to give up her seat on the bus to a white man. Some relied on surplus food to feed large families when the income from chopping cotton fell short. With the mere flourish of a pen, this source of sustenance could disappear. There were beatings, lynchings, bombings and burnings. Just having us in the community could have lethal consequences, as it had in Neshoba County, Mississippi, where churches were burned and three civil rights workers disappeared for over a year before their tortured bodies were found buried in an earthen dam. In Birmingham, Alabama, a church was bombed, and four little girls in Sunday school were sacrificed. We represented change, but we also represented danger, and eventually we would leave, and the community would be left with the Ku Klux Klan, the White Citizens' Council and politicians who owed their success to stopping this change at any cost. Terrorism wasn't shipped from afar; it was homegrown and individually specific.

Now I brought that danger into her dooryard. Mrs. Crawford had no job, and her husband could not be fired. He had died long ago. She had no children who could be hurt. They had moved north for jobs in the cities. Her house was all she had, and she knew it could easily be burned to the ground. That's what happened to her church when the "Civil Right" people came and held their mass meetings there.

Her hands were empty except for calluses when she reappeared. She watched the ground as she came closer. "Cain't find it," she mumbled an apology.

"But you don't need it." I didn't want her to get away. "You can help us anyway because you have registered to vote." She glanced up at me for a second.

"On next Monday, we are taking a bus of people down to Monck's Corner to register. If you come with us, you can help them understand how important voting is, and they will see that you have done it."

"Yes, ma'am. I'll come," she said softly.

"We are meeting at Redeemer Church at 10:00 A.M.," I insisted.

"Yes, ma'am," was all she said.

Mrs. Crawford was not there as the old, faded green bus crunched across the church parking lot and rested before the crowd of quiet people. The importance of the occasion was clear that sultry morning: Sunday dresses and suits, fancy hats with feathers and tulle, polished shoes, pocketbooks. They were too quiet, too afraid, but they were there. They deserved more. They deserved to celebrate their courage! Florence began to sing, "Oh, Freedom. Oh, Freedom. Oh, Freedom over me." The crowd began to sing tentatively.

We stepped up the tempo of the singing with "Keep Your Eyes on the Prize." Voices committed a bit more. With "Ain't Gonna Let Nobody Turn Me 'Round" everyone got on the bus, and it slowly whined out onto the road.

Inside the bus fans fluttered like butterflies to beat back the heat. Many had pictures of Martin Luther King on them, others the image of Jesus. Someone else saw her first, walking slowly toward the church, waving her handkerchief. The bus creaked to a stop, and Mrs. Crawford stepped up.

She came down the aisle to the empty seat next to me and smiled as she met my eyes.

"Everyone! We're so lucky. Mrs. Crawford has already registered to vote, and she has come to answer any questions about doing it." Applause. We went on singing.

She sat quietly next to me in her broad-brimmed straw

hat. Five miles went by, and then she whispered, "Chile, I ain't never registered."

I whispered back, "But you will today."

"But I cain't read or write."

"I'll teach you. You just need to sign your name."

"I cain't."

"We have time. I'll show you."

I took a pencil from my purse and turned to the back of the map of Berkeley County. I slowly wrote Rebecca Crawford. It was too much; I could tell as a furrow tightened between her eyes, and her gaze dropped to her lap.

"Wait. Let's start one letter at a time. Here, write over the top of this letter R." I wrote the R and handed her the pencil and paper. Awkwardly, she traced the letter over and over. "Now, write the R fresh here below." Her hand shook as she tried. I couldn't recognize the letter, and we started again.

Fifteen miles is not very far when you're trying to overcome 250 years of defeat. We registered 150 people that day, but Rebecca Crawford was not one of them. She asked me to come and teach her, so she could "regster" next time. I promised I would.

More than a month went by. As much as I remembered my promise, my other responsibilities kept me away. I begged our project director for some time to visit her.

The road was as long and as hot as before. Far ahead, I could see someone moving toward me. I recognized the straw hat first, then a basket on her arm and finally that beaming, delighted face.

"It's you!" She set down her basket in the middle of the road and raised her arms to heaven in thanks. I shook her hand and smiled back into her eyes. Before I could say anything, she said, "Chile, I been wonderin' where you was. Sunday I prayed that you come and learn me how to write."

I explained I had been busy trying to get other folks to

register.

"When I gots up this mornin' I was feeling something extra good was gonna happen today. I cleaned my house real good. I felt so grand I come on down the road. I saw you, and I knew what that good was. Look what I cain do."

She bent down and picked up a stick. With a steady hand she wrote Rebecca slowly and deliberately in the sand.

She was right, good things were coming, but they were much bigger than me.

Sherie Labedis

Legacy

*And so our mothers and grandmothers have,
more often than not anonymously, handed on
the creative spark, the seed of the flower they
themselves never hoped to see—or like a sealed
letter they could not plainly read.*

Alice Walker

Somehow, it just didn't feel right. Maybe it was the way that I was brought up, but it was hard for me to say it. Although I felt blessed and honored to have the opportunity, I just had a hard time saying aloud that I was "a graduate student at Harvard University." After all, *I* know good and well that I'm just a country girl from Sweetwater, Tennessee, who never saw herself as the Ivy League type, but what impression did that title give people who didn't know me?

I was not alone in this dilemma. Many of my black and Latino colleagues in the Graduate School of Education felt the same way. Several of us had to admit that when we told people we were going to graduate school and they asked where, we answered evasively, "Uh, Boston." It wasn't that we were embarrassed about being smart or weren't proud to be there; it was just that the perception people have of "Hah-vahd," conjured up images of privilege and snobbery. Many of us were first-generation college graduates from lower to middle-class families, and most of us were there because we wanted to give back something of educational value to the underserved students of color in America's schools. We actually discussed more than once whether going to Harvard was an asset or liability when our goal was to return to the neighborhoods we came from, "keep it real," and be taken seriously by regular folks. Would we build a "barrier of bourgeoisie" by having a Harvard degree?

Very quickly it was June and graduation day arrived. An incredibly rich year of reading, writing and discussing educational issues had flown by, and I was standing outside in a processional line with my dorm mates and new friends-so-close-we-were-almost-family from the Black Student Union. I sat dazed in my cap and gown on the same lawn where I'd seen Nelson Mandela receive an honorary degree back in September. I sat in a row of brown faces on the lawn with its giant oak trees that had been there since 1636 and tried to comprehend what in the world I was doing there. While the platform dignitaries waxed eloquent, it felt surreal. I snapped back to reality when it was Hazel's turn to take the platform. Hazel Trice Edney, graduating from the Kennedy School of Government, was my friend from the dorm and one of the sharpest sisters I have ever met. She had won the speech contest and was believed to be the first African American woman ever to give the graduate student address at a Harvard graduation. Hazel from Louisa, Virginia, who had grown up in a home with no indoor plumbing and became a single welfare mother at age fifteen, had managed to earn her college degree and risen through journalism in the black press, covering politicians like Governor L. Douglas Wilder. She would soon start a Congressional fellowship in Washington, D.C., in the office of Senator Edward Kennedy. Her delivery of the speech was flawless, and we were all proud to know her.

Suddenly, listening to Hazel, proudly watching her represent all of us, it hit me. This wasn't about me. I was there as a representative. I looked up into the branches of the centuries-old trees and thought about what they would have looked like back in 1636. I thought about where my ancestors would have been in 1636 . . . 1736 . . . 1836 . . . even 1936, and how remote the possibility seemed that any of their daughters would ever be at Harvard. I thought about Grandma Mildred, valedictorian of her Cook High class with her career options so limited. No, this degree was not about me at all. This was about standing on the shoulders of my black grandmothers who scrubbed floors and cared for babies—both theirs and others'. Black women whose potential went untapped and whose intelligence was so long ignored. Women whose great minds could have been idle, except they rerouted genius, pouring it into rearing the next generation. This degree was for my grandma, who was a farmer's wife and a housekeeper, but never just that, like so many black women seen only as the shadow domestic by the outside world but who stood out as pillars of dignity in their own communities. This degree was dedicated to a woman who had to sacrifice many of her personal dreams as a young woman, but made sure all eight of her children had a respect for education and would ascend to the level of their own potential. It was dedicated to a woman who passed on heritage to her numerous grandchildren with old *Ebony* and *Jet* magazines, her gardens and recipes, family stories and photo albums. I was here because she could not be, but had the self-respect and insight to pass something significant on to her offspring.

Sometimes I still have a hard time knowing just what to say when people ask me about graduate school, but right there in Harvard Yard, I made my peace with it. Grandma Mildred didn't know it, but when I walked across that stage, I did not just get my own degree. I held in my hands *her* honorary degree in motherwit, holistic medicine, childhood development, home economics, culinary arts and botany earned by life experience. That degree was about stepping up to accept my responsibility to follow in her footsteps and pass something on. Thank you, Grandma, for your legacy.

Jerilyn Upton Sanders

Letters of Love

Love makes your soul crawl out from its hiding place.

Zora Neale Hurston

The doorbell rang, I moved the curtains back to see who it was and recognized the big brown truck before I even saw the UPS uniform at the door. I hadn't ordered anything, but everyone loves to get packages, so I smiled like a kid at Christmastime as I opened the front door.

"I have a package for this address, will you sign for it?" the deliveryman asked.

I obliged him and said, "Thank you."

As I closed the door, I looked at the package and saw the out-of-state zip code in the upper left-hand corner and knew it was from my mother. I removed the thick brown wrapping paper to reveal a small, simple box with no letter of introduction. That was a strange action for my mother; she always, at the least, attached a letter saying "hello" and giving me the lowdown concerning the lives of the rest of the family. A little bewildered, I opened the box and stared at its contents. There were lots of letters inside, some in the handwriting of a small child, some with a more mature penmanship, but all were from me and addressed to my grandmother. Nearly every envelope was sealed with the phrase *"In God's Care"* written on the back. A tear rolled down my face, and my cathartic journey began.

Grandma had passed three short months earlier. It was a shock to the family, who all seemed to have thought that our "rock" would never leave us, but even more of a shock to me because I was supposed to be on a plane that very morning to go and visit her.

The call came at 6:42 A.M. Central Standard Time.

"Lori, I know you are on your way here, and I struggled with whether or not to tell you now or wait till you got here. I didn't want you to be emotional while traveling, but I could not let you come here and be in a state of shock once you arrived. Grandma is gone. She went quietly in her sleep last night," my mother said. I remember those words as if they are etched inside my eyelids for me to see every time I close my eyes. Those words haunt me.

"Gone, gone where? What are you talking about? I know you don't mean . . . gone as in dead? I'm on my way to see her; she can't be gone!" was my reply. "Mom, this isn't funny. It's a cruel joke, Mom. Why would you say something like that? My grandma isn't dead. I'll see you in a few hours, Mom." My husband heard the back end of the conversation and saw my legs buckle, so he took the phone from me, and he continued the conversation with my mother.

Even though I protested to the contrary, my grandma *was* gone.

I got on the plane and returned to my childhood surroundings. I appeared strong to the rest of the family so that I could hold them all up. That was the way I was raised, taking care of others. As I walked in Grandma's house, the smell was the same, kind of like soap and mothballs mixed

with home cooking. The furniture was in the same spots as
I remembered, and I immediately had visions of myself as
a child running into the kitchen to sit near the stove and
talk to her as she cooked, sing along to the radio and nib-
ble on whatever masterpiece was brewing in the oven.
Grandma was a great cook. The kitchen was always filled
with the smell of fried bologna sandwiches after school and
fried chicken, greens and sweet potato pie at dinnertime.
Everyone in the house sat down together to eat at the
same table and would actually talk to one another without
the aid of the television set. And if the phone rang, it did
not get answered.

That vision was quickly shattered by the reality that the
sound of her beautiful alto voice would never penetrate
those walls again. I fought back the tears and helped with
the funeral arrangements. I allowed my mother to grieve,
and I took care and control of everything else. After all, it
was my mother's mother; I had to be strong for her.
Everyone knew how close I was to my grandma. She was
my world and my inspiration, so the few tears I shed
instead of a more dramatic response was a telltale sign to
all that I was in denial. Everyone knew I had not grieved;
they were all waiting for me to break down, and secretly,
so was I. I just never thought it would be at the hands of
the UPS guy delivering a small box three months later.

My denial seeped out of me as I looked in the box. It was
an exorcism of sorts. The fact that no letter came with it
explaining its contents allowed me to imagine that the box
was delivered from heaven directly from Grandma. I had
been in denial asking myself, *Did you give her enough flowers
while she was here?* I had reassured myself that even though
I lived thousands of miles away, I had showed her love
across the miles, and I had always called a couple times a
month, but a small voice inside me had been questioning,
Could I have done more?

I sat in the middle of my living room floor for two hours or more. As I shuffled through letter after letter, I saw it right there in writing. My whole life was chronicled out in letters that I had sent to Grandma, and now they were sealed within one small box. There were so many of them, and I sat and read them all—each and every letter. I cried, I screamed, I laughed, and I reflected on my life. Middle and high school were in those letters; army life, marriage and motherhood were in those letters. My thoughts, my hopes and my dreams were all encompassed in the words and pages of those letters. I was able to see that even though I was miles and miles away, I had shared it all with my grandma.

There were things there that I had forgotten; thoughts I did not remember having or sharing. Some intimate feelings that most would not expect a young girl to be telling her grandmother, yet I told her. There were letters where I referred to my husband of fifteen years as "my boyfriend." Thoughts of how I was going to get a raise at work and would make $1,000 a month, and how I thought that was a lot of money. There was happiness, fear, sadness, joy and pain, all in black and white and told to the special person in my life.

As I sat there in the middle of my living room reading my life and reintroducing me to myself. I said a thank-you prayer to Grandma, sure that she knew I needed those letters, the letters she had held onto for so many years. She had reached down from heaven and used my mother and the UPS guy to deliver them to me so that I could release my guilt and my grief. It was as if she looked down on me and said, "Child, all is well in my eyes. I've always known that you loved me, and now I rest, as always, *In God's Care.*"

Lorraine M. Elzia

Walking the Lessons of Life

My family directly and my people indirectly have given me the kind of strength that enables me to go anywhere.

Maya Angelou

"Wake up, baby. We need to get ready to go before the sun gets too high up in the sky."

I heard Nanny speaking to me, but I did not want to move. My sheets were freshly washed, smooth and oh so warm against my skin. I tried to ignore her as I snuggled up closer to my Raggedy Ann doll.

"Baby, we have a long walk today to get to cousin Mittie's house. We don't want to get caught out in that hot sun, now do we? Get up, girl, and I mean now, or I'll leave without you!"

At the thought of her actually leaving me behind, I ran to the bathroom and began to brush my teeth. I washed my face and ran to the breakfast table to sit down to eat.

We walked out of the door just when the sun was rising, and our journey down 118th Street began. It was nice walking down the street holding hands. It had been six months since I had seen the person whom I loved most of all in the world.

"So, baby, how is school? Do you like your classmates?"

"Yes, ma'am, I think I like them."

"What do you mean 'you think' you like them?"

"Well there is a girl named Carol who is mean to all the girls. She is really mean to a new girl named Theresa." Nanny took my hand and squeezed it to let me know she was really listening to me and that I could tell her what was on my mind.

"Carol hangs around with a lot of other girls and they follow behind Theresa in the hallways and call her names behind her back. I feel so sorry for her because she looks so sad."

"What are you doing when the other girls tease Theresa?"

"I try to look at her and smile. I even asked her if she needed a pencil one day, because I have a whole bunch of them that you bought me for school."

"That is nice, baby. Always treat people right, and before you say mean or hurtful things to others, remember to ask yourself if you would want someone to hurt your feelings in that way. I am sure your answer will always be that you wouldn't."

Within just a few blocks, Nanny taught me to treat people the way I wanted to be treated.

"Your yard sure looks nice," Nanny said to the lady gardening.

"Why thank you!" said the short, round brown-skinned lady. Nanny walked up to the fence and began carrying on a conversation with her. They talked about flowers and watering grass. Then they started talking about church and shopping. It seemed like she was standing there for hours.

"Well Ms. Rose it was nice to meet you. Maybe I will see you again when I am walking by."

"It was nice to meet you too, Ms. Fannie."

"Nanny," I said as I broke my silence. "I thought you knew that lady already."

"No, ma'am, I didn't know her already, but now she *is* someone I know."

Another block and Nanny taught me to be social, that talking to people makes new friends.

Although I was the younger of the two of us it seemed as though Nanny's energy was endless. She moved each leg back and forth with the strut of a broad peacock and the swish of a runway model.

"Nanny, I'm hot. Can we stop and get some ice cream at the drug store, please?"

"Girl, it is too early to be eating ice cream!"

"I know, but I am hot and tired. Please, Nanny, please!" I begged.

"The last time I bought you ice cream, you didn't even eat the whole thing. You let it melt all over your hands and kept asking me to hold it while you played at the playground. You ended up throwing it away."

My lips began to poke out, and my face turned into the likes of a prune. I let her know that I was not happy with her comments and that I was not going to talk to her the rest of the way. I folded my arms in front of me and walked with my head up in the air. She just looked at me and laughed. She kept right on walking and never said a word for the rest of the block, but during the course of that block, Nanny taught me to waste not, want not.

Finally, we got to a bus stop bench, and Nanny said, "Let's sit here for a while and rest."

"Nanny, can we please catch the bus the rest of the way?"

"Why would we do that?" she asked with a smile on her face. "Exercise is good for your legs and your heart. I have been walking since I was a little girl in Alabama. I used to walk with my Grandma Harriet just like you are walking with me now, and I walked with your mama when she was a little girl just like you. I didn't have a car, but I didn't let that stop me from going where I wanted to go." She sounded so proud and independent. Her life had taught her to stand on her own two feet and not to wait for anyone to take her where she needed to go. In the course of this block, Nanny had taught me those same things and that exercise is important and good for your health.

We sat at the bus stop for about fifteen minutes then we crossed the street to go to the corner store to buy soda pop. Nanny loved soda, and she said that I could have any flavor I wanted for being such a good walker today. This block is where she taught me that persistence brings rewards.

And in the last block she taught me the joy of accomplishing goals.

"Nanny, I think I see cousin Mittie's house!"

"Are you sure? Do you remember what it looks like? You know you were a lot younger the last time we went to visit her."

"I think that is it because there is a lady standing on the porch waving at us."

She laughed at my reasoning, "Well, I guess you are right then."

As we approached the old white house we could see cousin Mittie standing on the porch with a big, loving smile on her face. You could tell that she and Nanny were related because they were both tall, with brown-sugar skin and high cheekbones. She came down from the steps to greet us with her arms stretched open to give us hugs and kisses.

She bent down to me and put her hands on my shoulders. "Did you enjoy your walk today, baby?"

I looked at Nanny, and we smiled at each other. Then I turned to cousin Mittie and said "Yes, ma'am, I sure did!"

These were, literally, the building blocks of my childhood.

H. Renay Anderson

These Precious Hands

Hands the shade of caramel, mocha, honey, chocolate
   and brown
It is in the midst of these precious hands that strength
   can be found.
It begins with Mother's coffee hands that caress me as I
   grow inside
When I am born, these same hands reach out
   and nestle me with pride.
Mother, let me see your hands.
Hands the shade of tan, coffee, beige, pecan and brown
It is in the midst of these precious hands that strength
   can be found.
Look at this grandmother's weathered and calloused
   chocolate hands
Strong enough to work in a factory and field
Yet soft enough to soothe a bruised knee and tender
   enough to heal.
Grandmother, let me see your hands.
Hands the shade of caramel, ebony, copper and brown
It is in the midst of these precious hands that strength
   can be found.
Sister, let me see your hands.

Mocha hands whose fingers skillfully glide over piano
     keys.
Pecan hands strongly clasped together as they pray on
     bended knees.
Nimble chocolate hands that give you that warning tap,
     to let you know that you're still in her sight.
Ebony hands that embrace you to let you know that
     everything is all right.
Hands the shade of honey, mocha, coffee and brown.
It is in the midst of these precious hands that strength
     can be found.
I look at the past and see mocha hands united together
     in the civil rights movement.
I see honey hands sacrificing to bless women in the
     present.
Copper hands that handle the gavel in the judge's seat.
Ebony hands that perform surgery and coffee hands that
     teach.
Nutmeg hands that bake warm pound cakes and sweet
     potato pie,
Served with a heaping side of seasoned wisdom that's
     too delicious to deny.
Hands the shades of honey, caramel, coffee and brown
It is in the midst of these precious hands that strength
     can be found.
Mother, let me see your hands.
I treasure these precious hands that guard and surround
     me
I am here because these precious hands have always
     been around me.
Grandmother, let me see your hands.
These hands are cherished because they are connected to
     the heart
Love is channeled through these hands and fingers with
     tenderness to impart.

Sister, let me see your hands.
Hands the shade of espresso, bronze, ebony and brown
It is in the midst of these precious hands that strength
    can be found.

                                        Sheila P. Spencer

My Mother's Shoes

There were many days when I wanted to walk in my mother's shoes.

On a warm July morning in 2004, I shut and locked the door of my house. As I walked down the multicolored brick sidewalk, I felt uneasy butterflies dance in my stomach. My mother had been having pain in her hip, and my brother and I agreed to accompany her to hear what a specialist had concluded.

Less than an hour later, we were seated inside a cramped office. Although the doctor smiled optimistically, the uneasy feeling returned. With precise words, he explained to us that arthritis was not the cause of our mother's discomfort in her bones—it was a rare form of cancer called multiple myeloma. When the doctor explained that the X-rays also revealed that my mother had a fracture in her back, I felt my courage buckle under the weight of heavy words, and I tried to tolerate hearing more details. I watched my mother take off her glasses, but to my amazement, she appeared unmoved as she listened intently. Feeling as if this were happening to me, I excused myself, in search of a temporary haven. I slowly shut the bathroom door and peered into the mirror. My face was red and the tears in my eyes clouded my vision. I felt an incredible sense of fear grab me, and I could not shake it loose. If I were feeling this, what did it feel like to be in her shoes?

Returning to my mother's home, the car ride was quiet and unnerving. As we paused at red lights, I did not know what to say to someone who just learned that many aggressive approaches would be attempted to slow down the progression of an incurable type of cancer. On the walkway, as we passed a large shrub, I gently grabbed my mother's elbow, helping her up four small steps. She looked at me like a soldier and said, "Andrea, I'm blessed. Something can be done for me." I was amazed that my mother felt blessed in the midst of this storm. By the time we reached her bedroom, I sat on the bed next to my mother, and a rush of honesty invaded my lips. While placing one arm around her, I confessed my sorrow regarding what we found out, thanked her for all of the sacrifices that she made for so many people, and promised to stand by her side, no matter what she would endure. Her shoes and my shoes would remain side by side.

I drove home replaying the day's events in my head, until I reached my driveway. As I placed my feet on the stone-lined driveway, I felt the sun beat upon my back, but the sight of treetops delivered a soothing presence. Feeling defeated, I sighed and walked up the walkway, noticing a large box sitting on the porch. When I stood in full view of it, I read my name and the sender's address. My first box of books had arrived from the printer—I was officially a self-published author. As I lifted the large box and lugged it into the house, I wondered if God was playing some sort of cruel joke on me. I was faced with a difficult decision to devote my full attention to supporting my mother, or divide my time between my literary venture and her needs. After driving to my mother's house the next day, I watched the smile form on her face as she held my book in her hands. Sister soldier did not relent. She never complained about her circumstances—her happiness overshadowed all other issues. Instantly, I made up my mind that I would handle both responsibilities well. If my mother signed up to be a soldier, I did too. Her shoes transformed into army boots, and I went in search of mine.

Although my mother began her treatment, she also collected money for book sales and told me that she would help me make calls when she could. Once again, her resilience amazed me. When she received her first treatment, I sat in the room with her for a while. I placed her tote bag next to the recliner where she sat and noticed the signed copy of my book inside it. Upon leaving the room, she spoke of the other cancer patients' strength. Who was I to feel defeated, if she did not?

Her pride gave me strength, and I pressed forward over many months. To our surprise, I even made the bestseller's list at a popular chain in my area.

Unfortunately, my mother's condition continued to fluctuate, and she ultimately took a turn for the worse. After several blood transfusions, she was scheduled for surgery to install a port in her chest. As I carefully lifted my mother's right foot, to stick it inside her black, slimline Easy Spirit shoe, my spirit revealed that she would not return home again. I spent many nights crying but managed to drag myself out to promote my book. A short time thereafter, a tumor was found on her lung, and the cancer began spreading rapidly. Making my mother comfortable became the only remaining option. I could not imagine what it must have felt like to be in her shoes.

When I entered her hospital room, I asked her to squeeze my hand if she could hear me. Although her pale hand shook, she mustered the strength to greet me. I read the Bible to her and reaffirmed that she was loved and appreciated. Although she could no longer talk, I could feel a sense of unity swirl in the air and felt my strength rise. During this time, I had secured my first radio interview and explained where I was going to my mother. Although her eyes were closed, she smiled, and I knew that I would make it through the interview, despite my jumbled thoughts.

Less than six months after diagnosis, my mother departed to heaven. After her funeral, I found it difficult to do more than sleep or cry. I had written only one chapter of my new book, and I knew that my mother, my best friend, would want me to continue striving to meet my goals. Over time I got stronger. My appetite returned, and I pulled myself together and was able to write the sequel to my first novel.

Almost a year later I helped a delivery driver unload a truck full of boxes. After we finished, I dropped to my knees in my basement and cried tears of joy in thanks to my mother for being my role model. I knew she was looking down smiling.

One day I was unable to find my tennis shoes. My eyes fell on the same Easy Spirit shoes that my mother wore the final time she was dressed to journey to the hospital. In between sniffling, I grabbed the shoes and decided that I would overcome the fear of no longer being able to physically speak to my mother. I put them on and decided that I would wear the shoes to the gym, as a symbolic representation of two soldiers: Mom and me. As I sprinted around the track, with each lap I completed, I felt her strength comfort me.

So this is what it feels like to be in my mother's shoes.

Andrea Blackstone

My "Shero"

Dreams come a size too big so that we can grow into them.

Josie Bisset

All of my childhood and early adult life my mom weighed over 220 pounds. I could feel the pain that my mom experienced with her obesity—not because I had a weight problem, but because our family was so close, and I often watched Mom when no one else was looking. I would see the hollow look in her face as if she lost something a long time ago and was still searching for it. I had no idea that I would soon find out what my mom had actually lost.

She never came to any school events, even though I ran track, swam competition, did water ballet, was a cheerleader, was in student council and many other things. I have no memory of my mother attending anything with me at all. My father made it his responsibility to participate in many of these activities with me, which ultimately led me to forge a greater bond with my dad than with my mom. I often wondered why she chose not to participate in my activities and even wondered if she maybe didn't love me enough to support me. My bitterness and hurt toward my mom's lack of involvement in my life only became heightened as I moved into my later teen years. I found myself resenting her for her choices and criticizing her for her complacency. I looked for female role models elsewhere, away from my mother.

I was never embarrassed about my mother, but I think she was embarrassed about herself, and that feeling was painful for all of us. I would hear stories about when my mother was younger. She used to be the family's number one dancer, dancing all night and lasting longer on the dance floor than all the other guests that came to visit. I longed to know this dancing lady, as I was the dancer of my generation, known for my own smooth moves; I wanted to share that joy with my mom. Maybe the dance floor would be the common ground where we would finally connect! I had never seen this dancing woman, though; the woman I grew up with had traded in her dancing shoes for house slippers.

As I became an adult and interested in psychology and self-development, I began to understand people better. I soon realized that my mom loved me and did for me as much as she could. After a while, I understood that my mom was in pain; however, I did not know how to help her. Fortunately, from somewhere, she found the strength to help herself.

After more than twenty years of battling obesity, my mother completed a vigorous eighteen-month diet that left her ninety pounds lighter than before. A new woman was born! At age twenty-eight, I got a new mom! When I looked at her, I knew she was my mom, but I could not believe that she was real. This jubilant, energetic and lively woman was all mine to call Mom. For the first time, I met the woman my mother truly was, the beautiful little lady underneath the obesity. She now weighed a whopping

125 pounds. It wasn't so much her new body that was the surprise, but rather her new spirit.

To celebrate her new size and to rededicate herself to dance, my mother joined a "Mrs. Forty-Plus" competition, where she would have to model, give a speech and provide a dance performance. She told our family that she did not care if she won—she simply had always wanted to be in a pageant, to walk down a runway and perform on stage.

She told each one of us, "I'm not doing it to win; I'm doing it to dance!"

"I'm not doing it to win; I'm doing it to celebrate."

"I'm not doing it to win; I'm doing it because . . . now I can!"

The competition was intense! Many women—well-seasoned with their elegant salt-and-pepper hair—graced the runway with style and assurance. There were many beautiful women there full of talent and grace, but none had just accomplished the amazing feat my mom had to get herself to this place of confidence. I prayed that my mom would win, but while watching her on stage I was simply overjoyed just by her effort. To me, she had already won. She posed to perfection, her speech brought tears to everyone's eyes, and her performance emulating Janet Jackson stopped the show. She spun, she kicked, and she even danced on the chair like Janet Jackson did in her onstage performances. Who was this lady on stage with black leggings, a rhinestone vest, a head microphone and a Rhythm Nation baseball cap looking like a professional performer?

That night, at age forty-three, my mother was crowned "Mrs. Forty-Plus." She was the first person in our family to ever win such a title. With this new woman, my mother was born again. She gave herself a new chance at life—as a model, a dancer, a mother and a friend. At age twenty-eight, I met my "shero."

Lisa Nichols

What She Said

A successful person is one who can lay a firm foundation with the bricks that others throw at him/her.

David Brinkley

The words Mama flung at me on a summer day in 1978 stabbed me in so many places I figured I'd ache and bleed forever.

"This is what I get," she said, "for working my fingers to the bone raising somebody else's child. You wouldn't have done this if your daddy was still alive."

I was stunned. *Had I heard her right?* "Whose child you raised?" I asked, puzzled.

"Your daddy's. *You.*"

We were sitting outside, lapping up lemonade and sharing a pint of vanilla ice cream. That was the way we communicated in those days, substituting homemade lemonade for "I'm glad to see you," and bowls of ice cream for "I love you." But on this sun-scorched afternoon, Mama, stung by my new, short Afro and sassy ways, finally blurted out what was in her heart.

I could hear the pride in her voice as she talked about how she'd raised me and rescued her marriage. After so many years of living a lie, it seemed to free her to dump our family's secrets on a table and slice them open. But I was angry at her, angry at Daddy, angry at Grandma Eva, angry at Aunt Minnie and angry at anyone else who'd known the truth but kept it buried.

After six or seven months, I finally packed away my anger, dried my tears and began using the journalistic skills I'd learned in the news rooms, hammering Mama with questions about my birth mother. The state of Alabama had never been able to find a birth certificate for Betty Jean DeRamus, the name I'd always believed was mine. However, state workers quickly found one for Betty Jean Nesby, a baby girl born on the same day and year as I was. The story was as true as rain and as real as Grandma's Bible.

Now I understood why Mama had always forgotten my birthdays. Now I understood why her all-consuming love seemed to change at times to resentment once I reached my teens. Her remarks about my long, lank hair, my tan skin and my full lips—all so different from her own—made sense, too. I could even forgive her for once telling one of my friends that it was too bad I lacked her beauty. She'd been watching me become her worst nightmare, a young woman who looked like her rival.

Yet I was still knee-deep in sorrow and still churning with questions. According to my newly acquired birth certificate, my birth mother came from Monroe County, Mississippi, and already had another child when she gave birth to me in Tuscaloosa, Alabama. And according to Mama, my birth mother had willingly handed me over to my dad. I don't think I'll ever know where my father found the courage to bring me home to his wife. Or why Mama, childless though she was, agreed to raise her

husband's love child by another woman. But the two of
them had indeed leaped aboard a train in Alabama and got
off it in Detroit, a city where they created a life for me
without bothering with any uncomfortable paperwork or
truths.

But a funny thing happened while I was packing my
bags for a trip to the South that I hoped would enable me
to pick up the trail of my maternal relatives, including,
perhaps, my biological mother. I woke up that morning
with a familiar phrase dancing in my head—"It takes a
whole village to raise a child."

I recalled that during the slavery era there had been
honorary "aunts" and "uncles" on every plantation, ready
to wrap their arms around youngsters separated from
their parents and school them in the art of survival. Those
traditions endured in the twentieth century and beyond.
My friend's mother raised the daughter my friend had
when she was sixteen. The child grew up believing her
mother was her older sister. And just about every black
family I knew could tell stories about "cousins" who were
actually family friends and "mothers" who were really
open-hearted neighbors.

Mostly, though, I remembered those times when Mama
had shown up at my elementary school in the middle of
the day, bringing raincoat and boots to protect me from a
simmering storm.

I thought about how she used to lean out of windows
to watch me play hopscotch and hide-and-seek, smiling
so much I worried that she would crack her face. I remembered all those pork chops and slabs of chocolate cake
she'd stuffed into my lunch boxes. And the fact that she
and my working-class dad had paid for my weekly piano
lessons and sent me to a tuition-charging Catholic school.

I also thought about all those evenings when Mama had
taken me to the movies, too weary from hours of maid

work to stay awake but determined to give me a shot of joy. Daddy, who read Bible stories to me at bedtime and combed my hair on Sunday mornings, had been my heart. But Mama, I now realized, had been the person who made our little family possible, sheltering a youngster she could easily have despised.

"I'm *your* daughter," I said one day after stopping by Mama's apartment to drop off bags of groceries. She didn't say anything, but her eyes told me that she knew why I'd never gotten around to taking that trip to Alabama to search for traces of my unknown family. My only regret is that I never really thanked Mama, in clear, direct words, for all she'd done.

When she died, I had engraved on her tombstone, "You taught me everything that matters." One of the things she taught me is that life isn't some big-screen drama in which families thrash out all their differences in two hours and then blend their voices in a symphony of joy. Sometimes love is just a lunch packed with extra care, a shared dish of ice cream, a jug of homemade lemonade or a mother who fills her daughter's head with a stream of constant dreams.

And family? I know what that is, too.

It's whomever you're lucky enough to love for a lifetime.

Betty DeRamus

Getting to Know Miss Gladys

It's good when you've got a woman who is a friend of your mind.

Toni Morrison

I recently remarried at age fifty after being divorced for fifteen years. My new husband had been divorced for twenty-five years, so it was not something we entered into blindly.

I married the first time at age nineteen, and my mother-in-law played a very traditional but special role. "Mother," as she was called, was a strong matriarch. She was older and more domestic than my mother. She taught me how to cook, clean, take care of my baby, make herbal potions for everything from colic to cramps, to be a practical, functioning wife and mother at such a young age.

During our courtship, my second husband-to-be took me to his hometown in southern Virginia. He had told me his mother was in a nursing home, but when we arrived, I was emotionally unprepared for what I saw. A very small, frail body in a fetal position, a tiny childlike face with penetrating eyes lying on a pillow with a pink bow in her hair.

She had not spoken in three years. She had recently celebrated her eighty-ninth birthday, and her room was full of balloons and birthday cards. Above her bed was a loving collage of the many people in her life who wanted to acknowledge her and be remembered in some small way. It was obvious that she was loved.

We visited her quite regularly; her eyes followed me wherever I went.

I learned that she was able to communicate her likes, dislikes and even her opinion about things with those deep-set eyes. When my husband-to-be proposed, we went to tell her the news. When we arrived we thought she was napping so we sat, talked and waited for her to awaken. My husband gently stroked her cheeks and hair as you would a sleeping newborn and whispered softly into her ear how much he loved her. Her eyes slowly began to open and look around, and I realized she had not been sleeping but had been playing "possum" to hear what was being said while people thought she was asleep—something she was known to cleverly do.

I walked over to her bed and stood directly in front of her and said, "Miss Gladys, I am going to marry your baby boy, Charlie."

Her eyes widened, and I saw a flash in her stare that only a powerful black mother can give—a look that at once warmed me *and* warned me.

My husband saw it, too, and commented, "Did you see that look Mama gave you?"

I not only saw it, I also felt it; I just wasn't sure exactly how to interpret it. I think it was a dual look of acceptance: "So you are the one that got him—okay, I like you," mixed simultaneously with caution, "You'd better take care of him, 'cause he is *my* baby." She let me know her expectations all in the flash of her eyes.

As we prepared for the wedding, we knew she would

not be able to attend and thought to include her and my deceased mother in our celebration, so we planned to put a picture of each of them and a bouquet of flowers on their seats in the church. Two weeks before our wedding we learned Miss Gladys had taken a sudden turn for the worse. When we got there she was in the hospital surrounded by several noisy machines. Her eyes were closed, her breathing raspy. No "possum," this time. She was passing away. My husband-to-be was shattered and began making arrangements for her funeral, to be held exactly one week before our wedding. While I didn't really know her well, I felt I was losing a wonderful mother-in-law for the second time in my life and wished that I had had the chance to learn from this woman. I knew that to be so obviously loved by so many, she had a wealth of wisdom to share.

For many weeks after our beautiful wedding and honeymoon, my new husband was quiet and withdrawn, had erratic sleeping habits and was always looking for something to do so that he wouldn't have time to think.

One rainy Saturday morning, watching him struggle, I asked, "Honey, what's wrong?"

He replied, "Nothing."

I said, "You are grieving for your mother."

He looked as if it had never occurred to him, "Is that what this is called? I thought that happened at the funeral."

As if we had opened the floodgates, he opened up and started telling me story after story about "Mama," Miss Gladys Gramps, Auntie, Sister Glad—any one of the affectionate names she had earned.

Every story was like opening a present; some were funny and involved him, his brothers and sisters, and her method of discipline. Others were about him and his special love for her as only a son could see his mother. Many were about her wisdom and levelheadedness in dealing in the world without being able to read or write in the Jim Crow South of the twentieth century. Story after story cascaded from him when we were riding in the car, taking our walks, waiting in line at the store, falling asleep, every day some mundane situation would bring a story that started "I remember when Mama . . ." and he would sink into that state of peace and comfort where fond memories take you like a feather bed. I would soak the stories up as I got to know the woman with the penetrating eyes.

Once my husband began sharing his stories, I could see his grief lifting.

I learned that Miss Gladys was born in 1913 in Virginia to a white mother and a black father. She was not schooled past the third grade. In 1931 she married and had eleven children. During the course of their marriage her husband would go back and forth between Virginia and Philadelphia every two years leaving her pregnant after each "homecoming." My husband was "homecoming" number nine, and after number eleven she never let his father return. She did domestic work, picked cotton and tobacco. Her greatest personal pleasure was gardening. She would spend hours tending perfectly straight rows of seasonal vegetables. My husband laughs saying that he was a vegetarian until he was twelve and never knew it.

I learned that Miss Gladys prayed all day on her knees—in the kitchen, bedroom and in her garden. By any account she did an incredible job raising her children. When my husband became an adult, he asked her how she fed, clothed and cared for eleven children with no visible means of support, and she replied, "On the arms of Jesus, son, just leanin' on his arms."

When one of her daughters was murdered by a serial killer, Miss Gladys, age sixty-four at the time, took custody of her four-year-old granddaughter and raised her until she successfully completed college.

In her seventies, my husband asked, "Mama, why are you always so tired?"

She said, "Son, when you climb up to this age you are going to be tired, too." Her journey through life was certainly an uphill climb, and even her valleys were bumpy, not smooth, flower-filled, softly paved paths.

It has been three years since Miss Gladys passed. Still, on Sunday afternoons my husband takes a seat in his favorite chair by the sun-filled bay window and talks on the phone for hours to his sisters. The stories and the laughter start swirling in the room as they reminisce about Mama. I lie on the couch nearby playing possum and listen quietly as I get to know and love him and Miss Gladys a little more with each telling.

Bari-Ellen Ross

The Ring

It was January, and the birthday cards were already starting to arrive. When my mother got the first one, I turned to my sister and said, "It must be from Aunt Kat. You knew she was going to be the first to get her teasing in."

My mother's birthday wasn't until October. As she read the birthday card a full grin broke out on her face. Aunt Kat was well known for sending humorous and sometimes obscene birthday cards. This was the year of my mother's fiftieth birthday, which meant the year of the ring!

My grandparents had eleven children. There was Mary, Kat, Alice, Regina, Elaine (my mother), the twins Joyce and Janice, William Jr., Randy, Pamela, and last but not least, Terri. Yes, I would say my grandparents' quiver was full! Amazingly, over the years they all managed to stay close. They survived trials, fights, different opinions, religions and hundreds of miles between them. Their bond couldn't be broken. When Mary, the oldest, turned fifty, it was a major marker in all of their lives. For her it was like achieving another level in life, a kind of crossing over into ever after. For her younger sibs, it was a milestone of achievement and a cause for celebration. They all got together and bought her a diamond pendant.

Next it was Aunt Kat's turn, and despite the fact that she still claims to be twenty-five (and at first glance you might be inclined to believe her) she accepted her fiftieth birthday with grace and grandeur. The night of her party she was guided in on the arm of her husband, Uncle Joe-Willie. To this day I still say she floated into the room. The evening was perfect, just as long as no one mentioned her age. She was the first to get a ring. A few years later they decided to make the ring a part of the celebration. Aunt Mary traded her necklace in, and it was official. On their fiftieth birthday, each would receive a ring. This year was my mother's turn.

My mother is the mother of four, two boys and two girls. She's always been a single parent, so she worked very hard. I remember there was a time when she worked three jobs. She was a head nurse on the children's ward in one hospital, on call for the emergency room at another, and she did home visits three to four times a week. My mother worked hard all of her life, all just to make sure we had the same chances everyone else had—even when she herself did not always have the best. So after her forty-ninth birthday, my eldest brother had a meeting with us and said that no matter what her next would be a birthday she wouldn't forget. Unlike the sisters before her, she didn't have a husband to throw her a fiftieth birthday bash—we were all she had. So we began planning, sneaking, saving and pooling our resources; her ring year would be her best.

All that year cards came reminding her how old she would be. She would just laugh and light up. Just the thought of getting her ring and joining this "elite" club would tickle her so.

As her birthday neared, there was a light in her eyes and spring in her step, and she always looked like someone had told a joke that no one got but her. Everything was set, even the decoy. Her birthday fell on a Thursday, but the real party was set for Saturday. On Thursday, we had a little party at our house with just her children and their families. It was her fiftieth year, and she was having homemade tacos. She didn't care; my mother never asked for much.

On Saturday, she was still unaware of our plans. I bought her a formal dress to wear to the party. It was a black velvet, two-piece after-five. It had sequins and a split that was a little high, but she could pull it off. After all, the theme of the party was "fifty and fine." The day of the party my sister drove her around pretending to be lost trying to find this new restaurant where we were all supposed to meet. Then they arrived. She started to giggle as she walked down the hall to the surprise party that awaited her; she had started to get suspicious.

"Surprise!!" We all shouted as she looked around the room, amazed to see all of her family and friends smiling back at her. She was speechless with tears as her first born son, now married with four children of his own, led her to the center seat at the head table. My Aunt Kat took the microphone as the emcee, and the roast began.

After the dinner and the dance tribute performed by three of her four granddaughters, a tape recording was played of her youngest granddaughter and namesake, Alaina, who was in Atlanta and couldn't make it, singing "L Is for the Way You Look at Me." Once we had laughed and cried and laughed again, they brought out her ring. It was beautiful and elegant, nothing like anything she would have bought for herself—not that she wasn't an elegant woman; she practiced being a well-rounded lady. She just seemed to always have other priorities when it came to indulging herself. The ring fit her pinky just like everyone else's, and then she began to beam—not just her smile on her tear-stained face, but from the inside. I had never seen her so bright.

Once it was all over and we got home, I asked her, "Are you happy now that you have your ring? That's all you've been thinking about this year."

She said yes, with a smirk and a chuckle. Then she looked at me with glassy eyes and told me what really made her beam with pride was seeing her four adult children, happy, healthy and prospering. She said looking into our faces made her life make sense. "The four of you are the diamonds in my ring!"

That got me thinking; maybe it wasn't the ring after all. Maybe it was that, at fifty years old, she could look back and smile about a life well lived.

Monica Montgomery

Just Like Mom

Inside every older lady is a younger lady—wondering what the hell happened.

Cora Harvey Armstrong

All my life people have told me I "look just like" my mother. When I was young I paid it no attention at all because I simply did not believe it. As a teenager when I heard the words "You look just like your mother," I would respond with "No, I don't. She's an adult and I'm not." After all, what teenage girl wants to be told she looks like her mother? Then, I would run to look in the mirror to make sure I had not changed since the last time I had looked. Relieved that it was still me in the mirror, I'd exclaim, "Whew, that was scary."

When it happened at twenty-five I would respond with, "No, I don't. She is old, and I'm young" and again I would reach for the mirror to make sure things were as they should be. Relieved yet again, I'd mutter under my breath, "I don't know what those people see; they must be blind. I definitely do not look anything like my mother."

By thirty-five, maturity had set in, and I would not

respond at all when I heard those intrusive words, "You look just like your mother," but my thoughts were, *Oh no, you see her hair is thinning and turning gray, her midsection is spreading, and her walk is slowing. That definitely is NOT me. I can walk a fifteen minute mile, I work out every day, and my steps are quicker than they were at twenty-five. No, I definitely DO NOT look like my mother.* I'd still sneak a peak in the mirror, just to be sure.

As I prepared to celebrate my fiftieth birthday, I woke up excited and happy to be alive. As I passed the full-length mirror in the corner of my bedroom I caught a glimpse of a startling figure. I stopped and took a good long look. I could not believe my eyes. There she was staring back at me—my mother. *When did this happen?* As I looked, rather than being upset or in denial over the remarkable resemblance that had somehow eluded me all these years, I found a strange comfort in looking at my mom's and my image comingling in the mirror.

Suddenly, I saw something more than just our physical similarities. I saw beyond the thinning of the hair and the expanding midsection to the strength and courage she had always displayed in the face of tragedy—and that she had given me. I saw the determination that had helped her break free of the shackles of poverty and pain—a determination that she had given me. I saw her spiritual teachings—the ones that helped to shape and mold my own values and beliefs. I saw her commitment to hard work—the commitment that she taught me so that I could achieve my goals and dreams. I saw the love and appreciation that she held for her family that she passed on to me so that I may honor and cherish my own family. Yes, as I looked in the mirror, I realized that it was *her* love of life that taught me to live my life to the fullest and that allowed me to wake up that very day thankful to be alive.

Today, when I look at my mother, I am amazed at how much she looks like her mother and yes, how much I look like her.

Now, when people say to me, "You look just like your mother," a loving warmth spreads through me, and I simply smile, nod and proudly say, "Thank you."

Linda Coleman-Willis

Mama's Hands

When I was a child, I thought that my mama had the prettiest hands. They were brown and smooth, the fingers long and slender. Her nails were always perfectly rounded and polished a bright shade of red. I never once saw her polish them, but I know that she did. Even before the days when there were nail shops in every strip mall, beauticians gave manicures—but not to my mama. She never indulged herself in things just for herself. Her every indulgence was for her family.

Mama still has the prettiest hands. Her nails are still perfectly rounded and polished a bright red—these days by a manicurist. Her hands are no longer smooth. Time has added wrinkles and a spot or two, and veins more pronounced. Hers look like the hands of a fifty-year-old woman—a woman my age. Mama is eighty.

Hands tell tales. Hers tell of sewing countless beautiful dresses with sashes that tied into big bows for her two little girls, bell-bottom pants and prom dresses for her teenagers—until her daughters got too highfalutin to wear "homemade" clothes.

The last dress Mama made for me was a wedding dress. It was not the dress—or the wedding—she had dreamed of for her first daughter. But, I was in *luv*. In the '60s, "living together" was the clarion call of the new women's liberation. It was actually men's liberation, but that's a story for another day. To Mama, it was "shacking up," and no daughter of hers was going to live in sin. She would disown me first. I would become a twenty-one-year-old orphan. So while my beloved and I agreed that we didn't need a piece of paper or a fancy wedding to validate our love, Mama disagreed. She expressed it by refusing to speak to me.

Now to say that Mama and I had had our differences during my adolescent years would be an understatement of gargantuan proportion. Our disagreements were numerous and *loud*. Louder on her part because those were times when "Don't you use that tone of voice with me" meant something—as in something bad was about to happen to one who was heedless. So I made sure to keep my voice several decibels below hers. But our disagreements had never, ever been silent. Hers was a silence I could not bear.

In those days of burning draft cards and burning bras, compromise was a dirty word. But compromise I tried. My beloved and I were married by a justice of the peace. Did this satisfy Mama? Oh, but no. Not even the official marriage license that I brandished would convince her. "Humph" was the closest thing to a word that escaped her lips. Mama was going to have a wedding—or I was going to have no mama. And I was definitely *not* going to sleep with that man under her roof.

Why couldn't she understand about *luv*? She and Daddy had been married for over twenty years. Didn't she even remember what it was like to be young and in love? Apparently not. The deafening silence continued.

In the face of her legendary capacity for persistence, I relented. A date was set—three weeks away. Arrangements were made. Invitations were sent. Flowers were ordered.

Then we went shopping for "the dress." Now a wedding with three weeks' prep time does not exactly scream for a cathedral-length train. That was as much as we could agree on. Mama wanted traditional white, floor length, of course, scaled down somewhat from her original vision. I wanted something African to signify and acknowledge my connection to the Motherland—a place I had never been and still haven't, thirty years later.

After hours of trudging through stores, trying on wedding dresses—always starting with the sales rack—we had not found even one dress that could bridge the gap between us. Tired and exasperated, I said, "Why don't you just *make* the dress?" The scowl that had adorned her face all day—and that matched the one on my own face—didn't turn into a smile, exactly, but it did soften considerably. Off we went to the fabric stores, she fingering the bright white satins and tulle, me searching for something African.

Then I saw it: translucent white voile with thin metallic stripes of gold and silver painted on it, horizontal stripes. (In those days, I was skinny as a rail and could wear horizontal stripes.) It was the most beautiful fabric I'd ever seen. For a hot minute, Mama held out for *real* white, but she saw that I loved that fabric. I can still see her brown hands caressing the cloth, fingering it, draping it over a bolt of white lining. In the end, it was white enough to satisfy her, and even though I wasn't sure about silver, I was pretty sure I'd heard that there were gold mines in Africa. We had found our compromise.

Then I saw the price printed on the end of the bolt, and my heart sank. The fabric was "beyond-our-means" expensive. Mama could squeeze a dollar so hard that ol' George would holler for help. But for once, Mama didn't bat an eye at the cost. I stood by, trying to look stoic and unexcited, as the clerk measured off yards and yards of the fabric. Even before the clerk had rung up our purchase,

Mama had figured the total to the penny—including tax. Like many women of her generation, she claims to not be any good at math, but this is a woman who can multiply a fraction times a decimal in her head (9⅝ yards at $7.95 per yard) with stunning accuracy.

After loading the bags of fabric and notions into the trunk of her car, we headed home. Night and day the sounds of scissors cutting and snipping and the determined whirring of Mama's sewing machine filled our house. Two nights later, Mama had created a dress so beautiful that it took my breath away. When I sheepishly asked her if I should try it on, she answered, "If you think you need to." Then, with a satisfied and confident look on her face, she turned off the light on her machine and went to bed.

You *know* I couldn't resist trying on that dress—very quietly, of course. And I don't have to tell you that it fit me to a tee. As I twirled around and took a deep curtsy in front of the hallway mirror, the dress billowed and settled around me like a cloud. I could almost hear the Motherland calling me home. But at that moment, I also heard another mother—a closer mother—whispering, "I put aside my dream, to give you your own."

Thirty-some years later, I have a daughter the age I was then. I still have a mama—and I still have the dress. Not long ago, I ran across it while cleaning a closet in the guest bedroom, making space for relics from my more recent past. I pulled it out of its heavy plastic bag and laid it across the bed—there not being a hope that it would fit my now "marvelously mature" body. It is still the most beautiful dress I've ever owned. The silver and gold stripes are just as shiny, the lining just as white. I looked down at my brown hands, caressing the beautiful fabric—and saw Mama's hands.

Evelyn Palfrey

The Outfit

Though a person doesn't grow up with a silver spoon in her mouth, she can still taste the good things in life.

Carole Gist

I did not look forward to making the trip back home to my birthplace, San Saba, Texas. I would not be making this trip at all if it were not for my mother's desire to be buried beside my father. And I wanted to make sure her last request was fulfilled. My father, Jabo, was struck by lightning and killed as he was attempting to repair the roof of our modest bungalow. My mother's job as a full-time maid provided our family of one boy and four girls with the bare necessities.

As I drove down the long, winding, lonely highway I was glad I had chosen the top-of-the-line, light blue, four-door, customized El Dorado to make my grand return. It symbolized the changes I had made since living the life of a household domestic cotton picker—and whatever else I could do to make a living back in the late thirties and early forties. Cruising out on the highway, my mind reverted back to the early years in San Saba. For some reason I was drawn to the memory of the first brand-spanking-new outfit that I ever had and never got to wear! I swore out loud as I pushed the pedal farther to the floor.

"Can you keep a secret?" I had asked my little sister. "Sure," she said. "What is it?" "You have to swear you won't tell." "I hope to fall down dead in my tracks and rot," my young sister said. "Okay, Mama said I could get me a whole new outfit, from the dry goods store."

"Brand new things?" she said in wide-eyed amazement.

"Brand spanking new," I declared. "And tomorrow we are going to pick them out. Of course, I'll have to pay it off at the store each Sunday from my fifty-cent earnings, but the main thing I want to do is show Miss Prissy that she's not the only one who can wear new things." I was referring to a snooty classmate I nicknamed Miss Prissy who wore cute little dresses with matching shoes and socks that her adoring grandmother bought for her.

The following Monday after school I met Mama at the dry goods store. After polite exchanges with the store owners, we began searching through racks of clothes. Then, I saw it—a black taffeta skirt with lots of little rubber polka dots, and a shirtmaker blouse. I was thrilled, I could not resist the fashionable snap-brim, black felt fedora hat with a red feather and a pair of two-inch, black patent leather slippers with satin bows.

The shopkeeper showed us the various ways to wear the hat. "To look like Dietrich, you snap it up one side. To look like Garbo, both sides down, and if you wanna look like Gracie, up all around, okay?" she said.

I went to the back of the store to the dressing area. I looked in disbelief at my scrawny frame in the rustling polka dot taffeta skirt. It clung to my waist and ballooned out. The white shimmering satin blouse seemed to radiate near my throat, revealing my long, slim neck.

When my mother saw me she could not hold back the tears. She exclaimed, "Oh, don't Mama's girl look pretty!"

"Thank you, Mama," I squealed as I almost danced back to the dressing room, "Thank you!"

We took the merchandise over to the counter, where the shop owner punched the register keys as he simultaneously announced, "Skirt $4.98, blouse $2.98, hat $1.98, shoes $6.41, stockings no charge, all right?"

The merchandise was to be kept in layaway until half of the $16.35 total was paid.

We left the store with the payment book. According to the book, I would be able to bring my new outfit home the second week in August. Just in time for the jitterbug dance.

That summer was one of the hottest, driest ever. By August, the temperature was soaring near the mid-nineties; myriads of heat waves could actually be seen crisscrossing before the naked eye and into the air.

The school, a one-room, one-story rock building, was located about four blocks from the center of the small community. The student body of San Saba Colored Elementary School fluctuated between forty and fifty students.

The school had no inside plumbing. At recess, students could quench their thirst with a drink of water from the water hydrant near the oak tree in the center of the schoolyard.

One morning shortly after the class sessions began, one of the students was emerging from the boys' outhouse when he noticed puffs of spiraling smoke followed by crimson yellow flames rising from the direction of our neighborhood. He ran swiftly to the classroom yelling, "Fire! Fire!"

"*Berthene,* I think your house is burning!"

The usual silent classroom erupted in chaos! Desks were overturned, paper, pencils and books went flying across the room, and the students were sprinting toward the door. I reached the door first and could see the blazing inferno belching crimson and golden flames from the direction of my house.

Only two weeks before I had brought my new outfit home—my first and only *new* outfit—and I modeled it for the whole family. Then I folded it very neatly and put it in a makeshift suitcase, a hollowed-out portable phonograph case, and placed my treasure beneath my mother's bed for safekeeping.

These were the only thoughts that raced through my mind as I stumbled on the rough, rocky road leading up to my house. I bruised my knee as I fell on a big rock. All I could think about was getting home to save my new outfit. "God," I prayed "please don't let it be my house. But if it is, please save my outfit!"

After an eon, it seemed, I arrived at the burning site. The towering inferno had swooped over and lapped at the dried brush surrounding our house. The house itself was engulfed in flames. Someone cried out, "Berthene, don't go near there! Berthene, Berthene!" I tried to enter the house, but the smoke and the flames were too fierce. There was no way that the volunteer fire department could have reached the burning site in time. There was no running water to supply a fire hose. I stood hopelessly by as the raging inferno tore out every semblance of the former home. The flames were licking more and more at the dried underbrush. Neighbors were emerging with wet rough grass sacks or pieces of dripping wet blankets to fight the spreading flame. Anything that could hold water was used to prevent the fire from spreading.

My mother arrived with terror on her face, screaming, "My children, my children! Where are my children?" It was then that I realized that I had not looked for my brother or sisters! My only thought had been the loss of my precious outfit. Hearing my mother's voice snapped me back to reality and seeing the terror on her face made me realize there was something more important than a new outfit—the safety of my family. Suddenly I felt the same terror she did and began frantically looking for my siblings, trying to account for everyone.

Just then a neighbor arrived with the two younger children. Another sister was sobbing uncontrollably in old Mrs. Ortha May's arms. Bobbie June was crying and running toward our mother. The five of us stood together, hugging, sobbing and staring without speaking. Finally my mother spoke in a low, hoarse whisper, "Children, we may be down, but we are not out."

I heard a fireman say, "Thank God the children were in school." I then realized how truly blessed we were.

Neighbors came one by one to offer their condolences, some offered their services.

The Eagles Foot Lodge sponsored a house-raising fund. A dilapidated storehouse was renovated into a three-bedroom house, with a kitchen with a sink and running water! Several families sent food, bedding, clothing, books and toys. The storekeeper came to the house with bundles of clothing. New clothes! Although I was extremely thankful for them, they weren't what seemed to matter anymore. Thanks to caring neighbors our family's circumstances were better than before. I was transformed. Even now, before retiring at night I bow on my knees and pray, "Lord, thank you for helping me to realize what is really important."

I snapped back to reality as I pulled into the town I had left behind what seemed a lifetime ago. My mother's body had been shipped from Compton, California, to San Saba, Texas. I fulfilled my mother Hallie Mae's desire to be laid to rest by her beloved Jabo, our dad, in the Greenwood Cemetery.

As for me, now that I can buy the things I want, what I treasure most are those precious memories that remind me of the greatest things on Earth. Not things but the love of family.

Berthena Kemp

Birthdays and Blessings

If everyone had a mom like mine, the world would be a better place. I don't know how I got so lucky, but I'm sure glad I did. Some mothers and children slowly drift apart with time, but Mama and I have grown closer over the years. I was the baby in the family, but she was also crazy about my three older sisters and my big brother, Kenny, her only son. Mama's love just seemed to multiply with every child she had. As tired as she must have been, she patiently tolerated my "terrible twos," those "trying teens" and every age in between. Sure, we kids got harsh scoldings when we needed them, but I can't remember when she wasn't there with an endless supply of support, sage advice, encouragement and hugs.

One day, a neighborhood carpool driver picked me up after kindergarten. When he dropped me off in front of my house, there—as always—was Mama, waiting in the open doorway. As we waved to one another, the driver took off, unaware that my coat had gotten caught in the car door. In a split second, I was thrown to the ground and dragged down the coarse cement street until the driver realized what had happened. I can still hear Mama's helpless, blood-curdling wail— "Anesia! Noooooo!" She raced out the door and down the block after us. She scooped me into her arms, cradled me and softly cooed, "It's gonna be okay, baby. Mama's here." For weeks she nursed me back to health. She tirelessly changed my bandages, spoon-fed me homemade chicken soup, helped me walk again as my broken leg healed, and sat up half the night with me when I felt scared.

As a kid, I was sure I wanted to live with Mama forever. It would have been so comforting and safe, but not the "right" thing for me to do. When I was ready to venture into the world on my own, she loved me enough to let me go—even though that meant leaving her and Daddy with a very unwanted "empty nest." Mama never had the opportunity to get a college degree, and she couldn't have been more proud of me for following my dreams. It's not surprising that her gentle, nurturing spirit and compassion for others helped inspire me to pursue a career in nursing. While sitting by the bedside of a frightened or lonely patient, I sometimes hear Mama's soothing words coming out of my mouth. Her ever-present influence on me always makes me smile.

There are lots of mother-in-law jokes, but my husband felt blessed the moment he met my mom. The two quickly formed a mutual admiration society that warmed my heart. Like the rest of the family, my husband was devastated when Mama was diagnosed with pancreatic cancer. With my medical knowledge, I was keenly aware of the seriousness of her condition. Fortunately, though, Mama was still relatively young and in pretty good health otherwise. Plus, she had *always* been a resilient person, physically and emotionally, so we had no doubts that she would beat this challenge, too. Stoic as ever, Mama never asked, "Why me?" But that was just her character. She rarely talked about the difficulties she endured growing up as an African American female before Dr. King and others began the civil rights movement, but I knew that her very birth and early life had been far from easy. Mama didn't dwell on the past or complain about the torment she was going through in the present. She took care of business, did what the doctors told her to do, made the best of every day, and eventually returned to work. Through it all, we never stopped praying. After that horrible scare had passed, life was finally good again.

Shortly thereafter I received some fabulous news that I couldn't wait to share. "Mama!" I gushed excitedly the second I saw her, "We're going to have a baby!" Well, that announcement was better medicine than any radiation or chemotherapy in the world. Even though she already had several other grandchildren by then, Mama's love always multiplied with each new birth. *What lucky little kids to have her as a grandmother*, I thought. I thanked God for creating this amazing woman because I couldn't even imagine what it would be like to experience the miracle of new life without her around. I couldn't even imagine what motherhood would be like without her close by as my role model, my inspiration, my guide. All during my pregnancy, I told my baby how much he would love her and how much she would love him in return.

I suspect that people thought I was crazy when I called out for Mama in the delivery room. "Rashad," I later whispered to my newborn son, "you're such a lucky little boy." Since that day, I've had two more wonderful children, Brandon and Eze. They, too, have grown to know and love the remarkable person who brought me into the world and taught me how to be the best African American woman I can be.

I'm happy to say that I'm still as close to my mom as ever. In some ways, she's my best friend. I still talk with her endlessly about raising my kids, maintaining a happy marriage, coping with stressors at work, dealing with

Dad's worsening health. She listens patiently to every boring detail about my household chores and incessant errands. I seek her advice about my smallest fears and biggest dreams.

"Mama," I gently confronted her one day, "I sure wish you had told all of us sooner that your cancer had metastasized. Did you think that we couldn't handle it? Were you trying to protect us? Don't you know that you taught us to be strong, to focus on the positive, to be grateful for all things, to trust in God's divine plan?"

I close my eyes and wait for a response, but get none. *She is sleeping, Anesia,* I tell myself, then say aloud, so she'll hear me, "I've gotta get home to cook dinner now—and I'm making your special pound cake recipe for dessert. I'll be back soon, Mama, and bring the kids, okay? Brandon wants to tell you all about school, and Eze is painting you the cutest picture."

Before I stand to leave, I adjust the pretty silk flowers in the vase I bought for her last birthday. I glance over toward my brother, Kenny, and then turn my attention back to my mother. "Can you believe that Rashad is almost fourteen now? And he thinks he's 'too old' to have a party! Well, he *is* growing up really fast, but isn't that funny?" I pause and then softly add, "You know, Mama, if only you could have hung on for two more weeks, you could have met Rashad in person. God knows what's best, though. If he had taken Kenny before you, I'm sure you would have died from a broken heart instead of cancer."

I kiss my fingertips and gently touch the headstone on my mama's grave and then the adjacent one where my big brother lies. "Bye-bye for now. I love you both."

Feeling immensely blessed and turning to walk away, I look briefly over my shoulder one last time, then up at the heavens. "Thank you, God," I say aloud with a peaceful smile and a lighter soul. I find myself walking a little

faster to my car. I can't wait to make Mama's pound cake
for my family.

Anesia Okezie
As told to Karen Waldman

Dancing in the Kitchen

I was born in 1946, when Mama was in her early forties and her two other daughters were already adults—what folks called a "change-of-life baby." On my own growing up on Chicago's South Side, I spent a lot of time alone with Mama in the kitchen. I loved to watch and help her prepare great food for the soul like mixed greens and cornbread, sweet potato pies, skillet fried corn, salmon croquettes, biscuits, potato salad, black-eyed peas, red beans and rice, buffalo fish, chitlins, catfish, macaroni, spaghetti, chicken and dumplings, homemade rolls, bread pudding, lemon meringue pie, the best fried chicken in the universe, and my favorite of all, those divine fried pies.

I especially enjoyed holidays and the family feasts Mama created, with turkey and dressing as the centerpiece. We would always get up around four o'clock in the morning. My first duty was to toast slices of bread on trays placed under the broiler, then cut up the slices into cubes for the dressing using scissors. My next duty was to chop up the green peppers, onions, garlic and celery. In the meantime, Mama would start boiling the giblets for stock, fixing the cornbread, melting the butter and beating the eggs. Once the dressing was mixed and seasoned perfectly (with me as official taster) and the bird was stuffed and in the oven (lavishly basted with butter), Mama would put a seventy-eight on the record player or turn up the radio, and we would dance around the kitchen.

"Work a little while and dance a little while, that's what I always say," Mama would announce, starting to sway to the music of Ray Charles, Ruth Brown or Ivory Joe Hunter. This was her philosophy about all household responsibilities. In the midst of cleaning or washing or ironing, Mama would launch into a demonstration of the camel walk or the hucklebuck, with me as her partner. Years later she proudly handed me an article about housework she had clipped from some authoritative magazine like *Woman's Day*. It recommended that you take regular breaks from your chores to dance. "Just like I always said," Mama crowed—and rightly so.

When I took on responsibility for the family Thanksgiving Day dinners in the 1980s, Mama would always come to my house the night before to help. I vividly recall how this tradition started. I was at work late at the local Urban League on the day before Thanksgiving and worrying about how I was going to get everything done in preparation for my first major family dinner. I was tired and particularly distressed about the prospect of having to pick and clean the ton of greens in my refrigerator once I got home from work.

Then the phone on my desk rang, and it was Mama. "I think I'll spend the night with you," she said. "Will you come and get me?"

Hallelujah! In answer to my unspoken prayer, there was Mama in my kitchen that evening, cleaning all those greens and assisting me in every way needed to make our dinner a five-star success. This included helping me master her special technique for tucking the turkey's wings in back so they wouldn't brown too much before the bird was fully cooked.

While we worked together in the kitchen that Thanksgiving and each one after that, I played Mama's favorite music on the stereo in the adjacent dining room. We listened to folks she loved, like B.B. King, Bobby Blue Bland, Gladys Knight and the Pips, Jerry Butler, Dinah Washington and Sam Cooke as we cooked. Every now and then, true to Mama's tradition, we would take a break and dance around the kitchen for a while.

When Mama passed on three days after her birthday in May 1990, I wondered and worried most about how I would get through Thanksgiving that year without her. I arrived home one evening in October to find a letter from my niece Leah, who had moved to Georgia. "I am inviting you to come to Atlanta for Thanksgiving," she wrote. "Your daughters are welcome to come, too," Leah added.

I immediately accepted her invitation—another unspoken answered prayer.

At the time, both of my daughters were away in college—Jacqueline in California and her younger sister, Nikki, in Massachusetts. We decided that, as usual due to the distance and cost, Jacqueline would spend Thanksgiving with friends on the West Coast and come home for Christmas. Nikki, however, was away from home for the first time, and we decided she would meet me in Atlanta to celebrate the holiday with Leah and her family.

Nikki and I arrived on Thanksgiving eve to find that Leah had already done much of the preliminary work—including picking and cleaning the greens. The next morning we got up early, as customary, and started cooking. Leah turned on a radio station that played the dusties—rhythm and blues classics that I had enjoyed all my life.

We were having a wonderful holiday party—cooking, talking, laughing, and yes, taking dance breaks from time to time. I was doing just fine until we came to the part where I needed to show Leah and Nikki how to tuck the turkey's wings in back, just like Mama showed me. Suddenly, a tidal wave of sadness engulfed me, and I felt for a moment like Ray Charles, about to drown in my own tears.

Because I did not want to upset the others, I turned my back and walked over to the open kitchen door leading to Leah's large backyard. I looked at the bright sunlight filtering mystically through the tall Georgia pines and, in a flash, realized that death is not the end.

With that, I returned to our celebration of cooking and music. On the radio, "Mashed Potato Time" by Dee Dee Sharp was playing, and we launched into the dance associated with that early 1960s hit. Then the idea came. We would write a dance-and-cook book, including a song for every recipe. We would call it *Dancing in the Kitchen*. When Jacqueline called from California later in the day, we shared this idea with her. She was equally enthusiastic and started coming up with additional dishes, songs and dances to include.

Over the years since then, we have come back to this project time and again. For our family recipe for black-eyed peas, the song is "Pass the Peas" by James Brown. For our special party punch, it's "You Beat Me to the Punch" by Mary Wells. Fried chicken, "Do the Funky Chicken" by Rufus Thomas, of course. And to start off the dessert section, what else but "How Sweet It Is" by Marvin Gaye?

Whenever we take the time from our busy schedules to complete *Dancing in the Kitchen*, one thing is for sure. It will be a tribute to our mother and grandmother, and the opening selection will be by the Shirelles—"Dedicated to the One I Love."

Barbara Holt

History Through *Herstory*

There is black history untold in the memories of the hundreds of grandmothers, grandfathers, great-aunts.

Alex Haley

Thirty years ago on a hot summer afternoon my mother and I left home early one Saturday morning to spend the day going to tag sales, the New England equivalent of garage sales. My father looked at us with a pained expression on his face and said for the umpteenth time, "Do not bring any more junk in this house." We promptly ignored him and walked out the door. Mom taught me to leave things in the trunk of the car and to bring tag sale purchases in the house little by little.

That bright, sunny day we drifted down winding country lanes stopping at every tag sale we spotted. We stopped at a lovely old country mansion. The woman in charge had lost her mother and was trying to sell a lifetime of her mother's treasures, a yard full of beautiful antiques that I am sure her mother had cherished. A large antique sideboard caught my mother's eye, but we knew we could not get it in the car or slide it past Dad. We went from room to room filled with the flotsam and jetsam of bygone days. It brought tears to my eyes to see those well-loved items scattered about looking a bit lonely and unloved. Just as we were ready to leave empty handed, the owner said, "Did you look upstairs? You might find something you like up there." We ducked our heads and took a cramped staircase up to a stuffy room under the eaves; the room was filled with all kinds of dolls. I stood there simply enchanted.

On a dusty shelf in one corner of the room I spotted two old black composition dolls. It was love at first sight. The girl doll was dressed in a handmade red velvet dress with a beautiful matching bonnet. Alas, the boy doll was naked as a jaybird. I gently picked them up and cuddled them in my arms. Tossed on a table in the corner I spotted an elegant island doll with the name "Cindie Jamaica B.W.I." on her apron. I spotted a tiny hand-carved doll tucked in a basket on the floor and added her to my arms. I quickly paid for all of my treasures. If I had known then what I know now, I would have bought every doll in that room. A lifelong hobby as a black-doll collector was born on that day; I was hooked in a mighty big way.

Somehow, holding these dolls in my hands now, dolls that had dark skin and black hair, dolls that looked like my friends and my family, dolls that were beautiful—beautiful *and black*—filled a void in my heart from my childhood when my mother could not find any black dolls for me to play with. I remember my two Toni dolls, one with blond hair and one a brunette. They did not have a black Toni doll. I did not have any dolls that looked like me.

The next thirty years took me on an endless quest to countless yard sales, flea markets, antique shops and antique malls looking for black dolls. I learned to wheel and deal with the best of them. My mantra was, "Is that

your best price? I must have that doll for my grandbaby."
I had another bargain and another black doll. I had dreams
of one day having a black doll museum.

Over the years I have amassed more than four hundred
black dolls, and I love each and every one of them. Many
times people ask me if I sell any of my dolls, and I tell them
they are all my children; would you sell your children? I
loved each doll I brought home as if I had given birth to it
myself.

My favorite dolls are old black rag dolls. The first rag
doll I purchased was a topsy-turvy doll made with a white
doll on one end, and when you pull her skirt over her
head, the doll on the other side is black, and each doll's
clothing is different. The owner said it was made in the
late 1800s by a little white child who lived on a farm in
upstate New York.

I began to read and research and network with other
doll collectors and discovered that the dolls could retell
history. Rag dolls, especially, have a story to tell. Their
faces are unique and expressive. They speak to me, and
their clothing tells a story, just by the workmanship and
also the patterns and colors in the fabric. You can tell how
old a doll is by close examination of the fabric. Knowing
old patterns and colors is the key.

I determine where each doll belongs chronologically in
the history of the United States—at times a dark history.
As a collector and an African American woman, I had to
get past the negativity of the Jim Crow images of large
lips, side-glancing eyes, pickaninny braids, and just plain
mean characterizations. As I encounter these dolls, I
remember that they represent an important time in our
history, and I am so grateful that I can give them a home
where they can tell their story, be heard and be loved—
perhaps for the very first time.

To slaves and poor African Americans, dolls were a luxury item; therefore I looked for dolls made out of things such as nuts (nut head dolls), cornhusks, rags, fabric scraps and bottles. I even found a tiny, old doll made out of a baby bottle nipple and two graceful dolls made out of tobacco leaves carrying pocketbooks made from chestnuts.

More recent character dolls portray positive images to black children of our culture's many successful people. My collection includes dolls of Diana Ross, Louis Armstrong, Muhammad Ali, Dr. George Washington Carver, Colin Powell, Martin Luther King, Malcolm X, Michael Jackson and my favorites—the Tuskegee Airmen. I also collected many African American sports figures and dolls made by African American doll artists.

Before I knew it I was doing doll displays and lectures at libraries, schools and corporations. I used my dolls to profile the black experience in America from slavery to the present. I liked to encourage young collectors. I tell them to remember the two Rs, "reading and research," and determine where you can place a doll in the history of the United States. I continue to share my collection and my stories about my dolls with young and old alike as I continue on this historic journey. Who would have ever thought that a simple visit to a tag sale would so completely change the course of my life?

As I sit in my grandmother's rocking chair holding my favorite one-hundred-year-old rag doll, I hear a voice that says, "Daughter, thank you for telling our story."

Emma Ransom Hayward

Ninety-Pound Powerhouse

Our scientific power has outrun our spiritual power. We have guided missiles and misguided men.

Martin Luther King, Jr.

As a young African American female growing up in the 1920s, I knew my grandmother had experienced many difficulties being a minority. I never realized the impact those experiences had on her life, until the summer of 2001 when she shared with me the woman she truly was. For years her health had been on the decline, but at times when the family feared she had neared the end, her determination would abound all obstacles in her path. It was amazing to watch this happen time and time again.

During one of my visits to the nursing home in Arkadelphia, Arkansas, which she now called "home," I had an opportunity to sit with her and talk about her life. I had been born in a small town in Arkansas myself, but had been raised mostly in the city. Therefore, I was a city girl at heart. However, I found visiting the country relaxing, and the hospitality people showed was amazing.

Arkadelphia was sixteen miles north of my birth town, Gurdon. Driving down the interstate each day, toward the nursing home, I glanced around me looking at the homes and miles of greenery I passed along the way. The continual flow of hand waves reminded me I had departed the city.

Later that afternoon as I relaxed on the bed beside my grandmother, I asked her to tell me about life during her young years. I knew very little. She had dropped out of school at a young age to work in the cotton fields, so her brothers and sisters would have an opportunity to pursue their education. I admired this, and because of that, the years passed so quickly she never returned to school. Unable to read and write and being elderly now didn't hamper her lifestyle or spirit at all. She claims it has helped keep her stress level down throughout the years. I could only imagine what illiteracy was like considering the fierce competition in the city and the educational credentials required to reach particular advancement levels within corporate America. I listened to and learned amazing details of her journey.

At an age when most women prepared to raise families, she found her marriage crumbling. She and her husband soon parted ways. Granny was left alone with six children, uneducated, and determined to find a way to support them. Cotton fields became her savior. At home there was often a shortage of material items but never love. When the children needed clean undergarments they were hand washed the night before and remained damp in the morning. The children would slip into their damp garments the next morning and proceed toward the school grounds. Granny Martha never received a diploma, but she strove to ensure her children received their opportunities. The older children helped her with the younger ones.

There were times when work was available in the next

town; the next towns in either direction were sixteen miles. Granny Martha had no car to help her reach her destination, but that didn't stop her.

"I had the best car around," she told me as she patted her two feet. I glanced at her, shocked. It was unbelievable that she had walked to the towns of Prescott and Arkadelphia many times. She continued describing how people she knew driving to the same towns drove past her without once stopping to offer her a ride—quite a contrast to the friendly appearance I experienced driving that same route now. Her walks to town would start before the sun rose and end as it settled in its bed.

"Do you think they ever thought about stopping, Granny?" I eagerly asked.

"No," she declared sans any resentment. "They thought they were better than me, but I knew different. I had the Lord on my side," she continued. "That is the only friend I need."

I nodded in agreement. Tears welled in my eyes, as I felt guilty about the anger bubbling in me.

"It would take me all day, honey, to walk up there and back, but I made it every time. Yes, ma'am, I made it. Do you want to know something?" she asked trying to conceal a little smirk.

"What's that?"

"I've outlived most of those folks," she explained in her Southern accent. I smiled back at her listening attentively as the tales continued.

Sometimes she would carry my uncle to town because he was too young to go to school and she needed to work. In the cotton fields, she would carry loads of cotton on her back and drag him around on a sack next to her while she worked, making any money she could. As the day continued I could do nothing but stare in amazement. This little ninety-pound woman was a powerhouse, and I had almost missed out on learning so much about her. I felt proud to call her granny, but I realized my feeling went much deeper than that. Granny Martha became a symbol of strength that African American females have always been known for since the beginning of time.

Swannee Rivers

2

IT TAKES A VILLAGE OF MOTHERS

Next to God we are indebted to women,
first for life itself, and then for making
it worth living.

Mary McLeod Bethune

My Womb's Butterfly

Just don't give up trying to do what you really want to do. Where there's love and inspiration, I don't think you can go wrong.

Ella Fitzgerald

Every time I went to the mall, I would end up in the baby store. What did I need from a baby store? The circle of kids in our family was too old for anything they offered, and there were no little buns in the oven.

As I stood admiring a lace dress, I felt a massive butterfly begin to flap in my belly. (You've heard the phrase, "I've got butterflies in my stomach"—well, that isn't the only place where mine were located.) Placing the dress back on the rack, I picked up a sailor's outfit and reflected on how cute it would look on my son. Then I corrected myself. *Surely, you mean your nephew. Maybe . . . girl, you need to stop tripping.* The butterfly flapped its wings again. Not knowing why the gush of tears was building in the midst of the flapping butterfly, I exited the store quickly, finding refuge in my car four rows away from the mall entrance.

Come on, girl, I encouraged myself, *get this foolishness*

together. You know your motto: Kids should be like soda bottles—
returnable. Why are you about to lose your mind about this?
Where is this coming from?

Where was it coming from indeed? I had always wanted
to be a mother. It's right there in my senior year memory
book. What do you plan to be doing ten years from now?
My response: sitting on the beach, writing my third novel
with my four boys playing all around me. The desire to be
a mother was in the stack of papers hidden beneath my
car's passenger seat: piles of research on fertility clinics,
weight-loss clinics—because one specialist told me I
would never get pregnant as long as I was overweight—a
list of possible donors that I needed to convince and study
notes. I wanted to be somebody's mama. I said it over and
over again, as the butterfly flapped its way from my stomach to the back of my throat. I cried.

Months turned into more months. I made a sizeable
investment in pregnancy kits, ovulation kits and special-
ists—only to suffer from several "almosts." I know, you
cannot be *almost* pregnant, but I refused to tell myself, *No,*
you're not pregnant, AGAIN, and I refused to acknowledge
that the pregnancy misdiagnosis really had anything to
do with a "possibly more serious medical condition." So I
instead believed in *almost* and *maybe next time.* When the
months finally became years, the trips to the baby store
ended, and I tucked the desire to mother my own child
away for the night. I convinced myself that it was not my
role in life to be a mother, and the desire was no more than
fantasy.

Then one spring day, I arrived back at my condo after
dropping off my nephew from a weekend of breaking the
"auntie bank." Turning on the iron to knock wrinkles from
the dress I'd chosen to wear to evening worship, I suddenly felt something that frightened me; my womb's butterfly was back and flapping with a vengeance.

Ignore it, girl. It's the Value Meal. You ate it too fast, that's all. I was clearly trying to convince myself of something that was not true. The butterfly was back. But why? I was resolved. I had accepted what everyone told me—I would not be a mother.

I grabbed my exfoliating scrub and turned on the shower full blast, as hot as possible. Surely, I could scrub away the voice in my head. *It's time for you to be a mother. Your son needs you.*

I lathered. More voices. I exfoliated. More voices—and harder flapping wings. I let suds cover each strand of my natural kinks and felt my sharp nails move along my scalp. More voices. The hot water washed everything away from my body—except the butterfly in my womb. Finally, knowing that this was not a battle I was going to win and knowing that I was not going to birth a child, I decided to ask God, "What are you doing? I've been celibate two years, so I can't be pregnant. I haven't given birth, so I have no 'son needing me.' What are you doing?" Then I added, "Whatever it is, do it quickly, so I don't think I'm going crazy."

The next evening, I found myself sitting in an adoption orientation class. Three months later, on a warm August evening as I rushed home, I got a phone call.

"We have a little one for you. He's just above the requested age range. Only thing is that he has nothing except what he's wearing."

"What do you mean he has nothing? Where is he?"

"He's at our office in Miami Shores. The judge ordered him placed today. Your counselor called this morning and said she had a woman who had more love than any child could take, and your file was on my supervisor's desk. Do you want him?"

"I'm turning around now."

By the time I reached the building I was trembling. That

butterfly was all over the place—my womb, my throat, my heart. When I walked into the office the social worker met me at the door extending her hand. She pointed to a little, thick man asleep behind me. The flapping began to subside. I touched his De La Soul hairdo, and he woke up. Concerned that I had startled him, much as he had startled me, I stepped back. But he reached for me, so I reached for him. He settled, rather peaceably, into my arms, resting his head on my shoulder.

The first few nights I kept staring at him. He didn't seem out of place at all. His first little kiss on my cheek, his bear hugs, his amazing appetite—none of it seemed out of place. Since then we've had our share of tantrums and extreme stubbornness. Did you know a five-year-old could say the word "Mommy" at least a hundred times in a five-minute span? I sure didn't!

I've been like mothers of old, crying and praying during two emergency room visits. We've had mommy-getting-called-to-school days; they discovered his stubbornness as well. We've had our first real report card. Every time I call a friend or my mom in a panic or just to share, I am tickled when I hear the words, "It's called being a mother." Along the way, we've even added a teenager to our divinely appointed family in the form of my nephew. So what do you know—I have two of those four boys I envisioned. Lately, despite losing the physical means to carry a child, my womb's butterfly has been flapping again. While it takes a village to raise a child, I've learned that there are children waiting for the village to come get them; then we raise each other.

E. Claudette Freeman

The Wisdom of Motherhood

*My doctors told me I would never walk again.
My mother told me I would. I believed my mother.*

Wilma Rudolph

We all know it. Whether we decide to articulate it or not—it is one of life's basic truths: Motherhood is sometimes a dirty, rotten, kick-you-in-the-pants, don't-even-think-about-a-reward, thankless job! Yet most of us do it to the best of our abilities (heck, it's not like we can get out of it at this point anyway) and pray that we'll survive the journey—and allow our child to survive it as well.

As the mother of a seventeen-year-old daughter who occasionally thinks the sun rises and sets on her tail, there have been far too many times when I wanted to quote to her my own mother's frequent words to me during my youth. Even though it's been thirty or so years, the threat still reverberates in my head like it was yesterday—"Girl, I brought you into this world . . . and I'll take you out!"

Yep, that whole motherhood thing is sometimes overrated. But, thank God, children grow and mature. And one day, and I must admit it's a really good, even better than chocolate, day, they see us differently. They get their great epiphany. A point comes when they no longer believe we are here to ensure their lives are in a constant state of misery. But they realize that maybe, just maybe, there is a possibility that mothers know a thing or two.

Like most mothers, I'll never forget the most significant of my daughter's brushes with lucidity. It's one of those "it doesn't happen often, so I'll never forget it" moments. She'd been sitting at the computer for a few hours, working on an essay for a college application, when she invited me into the room. As is our usual practice, she asked me to proofread what she had written. I was eager to do so, as usual, but I did notice that somehow this time was different. She had a curious expression on her face—softer, more gentle. And although I couldn't put my finger on when she asked, I knew immediately after I completed the reading. Here's what she wrote. And, oh yeah, check out that "with all of her wisdom" line. It's my favorite!

> *I have always loved the game of basketball. I used to eat, breathe and LIVE the game. I'd go to school, go to practice, do my homework and then go to bed. My goal was to play basketball at a Division I college on an athletic scholarship—and no one would stop me.*
>
> *During my junior year, I really took off. I was the top guard in my area, a key member of the All-Conference team, All-State Honorable Mention and the captain of my high school team.*
>
> *I worked hard the entire summer leading into my senior year. Everyone knew that this was my year—and I was ready. Sports reporters predicted I would lead my team to a league championship—and further. And as the team's captain and only four-year varsity starter, I was eager to deliver.*

The season started well. I was averaging fifteen points per game and frustrating my opponents to no end. And then came the unimaginable. During the first three minutes of the fourth game of my senior year, I took the hardest fall I have ever taken. I came down on my knee and tore a ligament—every athlete's worst nightmare.

It was surreal. As I lay screaming on the hardwood floor, I saw all my dreams for attending college on a Division I basketball scholarship spiral down the drain. I don't know if the tears and blood-curdling shrieks were more about what I knew was a serious injury—or the most cruel pain I have ever felt travel through my body at any one time. But it didn't matter anyway. What I did know was that my life's dream was over. My injury would require major surgery, and my high school basketball career was over. Not in a million years could I even begin to describe the kind of despair that comes along with the decimation of a dream so real, so long-standing, so wanted and so close.

What was I supposed to do? The scholarship offers disappeared and that was the only real plan I had for college. All my hopes and dreams were gone, and I had nothing to fall back upon—or so I thought.

But thank God for mothers. All along, I had counted on basketball for my future. But my mother, with all of her wisdom, had prepared an alternative plan—and I hadn't even known it. For while I was spending so much time over the years practicing my jump shot and ball handling skills, she had encouraged—no demanded—that I spend an equal amount of time on academics. She had always disregarded my school's eligibility requirements and instituted her own: honors courses, National Honor Society membership, volunteer efforts, four years of high school Spanish, and a minimum 3.5 grade point average. Without fulfilling these, there would be no basketball.

So when I blew my knee, she was there to wipe my tears and remind me that everyone has options. I could still achieve my goal of becoming an orthodontist—on an academic scholarship. All I needed was a high ACT score. She also reminded me that over the years, I had always performed better under pressure and responded positively to adversity. All we needed, she said, was a steady plan to rehabilitate my knee, and I would be back on the hard court in no time. After quick consideration, I realized it was a dual plan I could live with. Now let me see . . . I could still play basketball and possibly earn an academic scholarship. It would be hard, but the idea made me smile! My response: "I'm a beast. Sure, why not!"

So I decided to focus even more on academics and study for the exam. At that moment I finally realized the almighty power of academics. I suppose Oprah would call it my "Aha Moment."

So I did it. I buckled down and studied. The result was an ACT score that placed me in the top 10 percent of everyone who took it! It was the best result of the worst experience of my life—and for that I am both proud and grateful.

I'm sure tears were streaming from my eyes when I looked up and saw my daughter watching me for my reaction. Her essay left me speechless. I simply stood up, walked over, hugged her and whispered, "Thank you—and you're welcome."

She smiled and silently hugged me back in what I call one of those special mother-daughter moments. I knew this was her way of thanking me for all those nights of forcing her to do homework, study for tests, and exercise her mind as well as her body. Yes, as a mother, "with all of

my wisdom," I've realized that thank-yous are few and far
between, but when they do come, they last a lifetime.

Lolita Hendrix and Briana Hendrix

One Day, You'll Understand

A mother is not a person to lean on but a person to make leaning unnecessary.

Dorothy C. Fisher

I lay in the hospital bed with my newborn daughter, Jordan, snuggled against my chest. I watched her as she slept, a tiny angel swathed in blankets. Dark locks peeked beneath her sunshine yellow and baby blue knit cap. Her sweet face wore a look of perfect peace. Then her eyelids fluttered and slowly opened. Her big, brown eyes, my eyes, stared up at me. We drank each other in, mother and daughter, sealing our connection. In a rush, I heard my mom's voice, and the voice of my grandmother and her mama, and all the mothers before them saying, "You'll understand when you have kids."

And suddenly I did.

I've heard that saying all of my life, delivered after I forgot to let my mother know I made it somewhere safely or pouted at some rule. It was a cliché, received with an eye roll when mom wasn't watching and relegated to the dusty basement in my mind. But at that moment, gazing at my daughter's face bursting with trust and contentment, I knew just what it meant. Comprehension hit me like a blaring alarm that jars you awake, like a blast of icy air that snaps you to attention. My husband and I are responsible for what happens to this little girl. She needs me.

In my first weeks as a mother, I journeyed from joy to fear and back every day. I delighted in rocking her and singing lullabies passed down through my family like balms. I marveled at how her head fit into the palm of my hand, at how her mouth stretched into a perfect O when she yawned. I memorized her features, her plump cheeks, long fingers, pink heart of a mouth, and the way she felt in my arms. But between the highs, there were the worries: Was she getting enough sleep? Was she eating enough? Would I be a good mom? Then Jordan got sick. Night after night she woke with a wail that pierced my soul. A doctor revealed that she had gastroesophageal reflux, a condition causing frequent and painful spitting up. My stomach twisted into a tangle.

I looked into the mirror one morning and saw my mother. She stood there, beautiful and scared. At eighteen, a child herself, holding baby me. I saw her at twenty-three, screaming when she saw a bloody gash on my forehead caused by my taking a foolish dare to jump down concrete steps. I pictured her at thirty, entering my flu-ridden bedroom with a flowered tray of saltine crackers and ginger ale and soft hands that stroked my face with love. She gazed into my eyes and said softly, "You'll understand when you have kids." And now I did; I felt it right down to my feet.

Nursing an ailing child sobered and terrified me. As stomach acid brought up by Jordan's illness gnawed at the lining of her throat, caused her so much pain that she winced with every suck of formula, and finally she could only be fed when she slept, I rocked her and sang hymns.

Those spirituals I learned in church, "Leaning on the Everlasting Arms," "I Surrender All," and "Precious Lord," were my lifeline. I sang them and felt linked to a legacy of women before me. I saw my mom raising her rich soprano to heaven in the gospel choir at Pittsburgh's Brown Chapel AME, heard my grandmother singing, "His Eye Is on the Sparrow" as she dusted or baked. If I just keep singing, rocking and loving, I thought, somehow we'll make it through this trial. And we did.

Jordan is two years old now and free from the worst of that demon. But I know there are others waiting. I am a sentinel, ready to duke it out and wrestle them away. But in quiet moments, I exult in everyday treasures, like when she runs across the room, arms outstretched waiting to be scooped into my embrace. Or when she says a new word. Or when I do something she thinks is hysterical and she bursts into fits of giggles, her eyes sparkling and her infectious laugh bubbling deep in her tummy and magically gushing out, making me laugh and starting her giggling all over again. There are still times when fear catches my breath. Like when she loses her balance and falls or when she's climbing and seems about to teeter.

"You'll understand when you have kids," I hear my mom and grandma saying in unison.

"I'm telling you," I say back in a soulful way that makes their eyes dance.

Last year, my grandmother died, just four days after Jordan's first birthday. As I mourned and watched my mother, aunts and uncles rally around each other, I considered the circle of life. As loved ones are born, so they pass. One day, Jordan will lose me.

While I'm here, it's my job to teach her to stand on her own, to guide her to make the best choices she can. To instill lessons and values that endure, to fill her with confidence, faith and generosity. To prepare her for a time when she may have children of her own.

"You'll understand when you have kids," I'll say one day and see her teenaged eyes look at me with that "oh, Mom" expression. Standing beside me, I'll feel the presence of a long line of black women who know what it means to be a mother—and showed me the way.

Kelly Starling Lyons

Even a Dancing Time

Periods. Depending on who you were and where you were, it could have meant a thousand different things. In English class it meant punctuation. In history it meant a stage, a moment in time. But in my twelve-year-old existence it meant a turn in the road, a rite of passage, entry into a clan. It meant the end of innocence and the beginning of something evil, disappointing and downright tragic. It meant that like my sisters, my aunts, my mother and her mother and all the mothers before her, I was cursed.

Memories seal firmly in the mind. One I know I'll never lose is the image of my mother on the morning I told her that my period had begun. There I was, so excited, the words pressing against my chest, poised on my tongue so urgent and ready. The morning was fresh with the scent of summer, and the sun hovered over dense green trees, casting long bands of yellow light across the floor of my pretty-girl-pink little room. Here it was, what we girls had been whispering about since the fifth grade: who had gotten "it" and what "it" felt like; who owned the special "belt" and who didn't; whose mother had taken them shopping for special panties and Kotex pads and whose hadn't. For one solid year, I was in the "didn't" and "hadn't" column. But that day, in the freshness of summer, I stood beaming and excited to be in the "had" and "did" corner of the world.

"Ma, I think I have my period," I said, looking to the floor, yet secretly smiling.

I lifted my eyes to check her expression after the words floated from my mouth and wafted along the air to her ears. I imagined her sitting on the edge of my bed, an arm curled around my shoulder. We'd climb into our big yellow Chevy Malibu, just the two of us, and make our way over to Sears where we'd walk hand in hand through the aisles, holding training bras with little pink bows and panties to match. We'd find that special little belt that most of the girls already had and later, at home, I would lower it into my nightstand onto a scented sachet pillow as if it were a treasure made of gold instead of spandex. My little heart felt light and full of song.

It wasn't her arms that curled that day but the corners of her mouth, curling in sheer disgust. Her shoulders slumped. Her eyes were heavy and downcast. The next thing I saw was her back, turning to leave the room and then her words, heavy as bricks, crashing to the floor.

"I guess you'll have to go to the doctor then," she mumbled. And that was it.

The doctor's visit never came. Neither did the sanitary belt or the discussion about what was happening to my body. All that I wanted to know and understand came as whispered misinformation in the coat closet after lunch recess; information that would later be checked and verified against a book I'd found in my older sisters' room.

"Guess what? I heard if a boy kisses a girl on one of those days she can get a baby," wrote a friend in a scribbled note, passed from two rows over in sixth grade class.

"No you can't," I wrote back in big letters.

"Oh, yes you can, too" she insisted, exclamation marks at the end, spikes drawn almost as tall as the paper.

Night after night beneath my covers, guided by a single thread of light from a flashlight no one knew I had, I read. I snuck peeks at pictures of women's reproductive organs and I snickered at images of babies being born. You would have thought I was reading pornography instead of an educational book about the facts of life in an effort to understand what was happening to my body.

For all that I learned from that book and others, I still, for years, held on to the belief that a woman's body—my body—was sinful. As a young teen, I thought breasts were just objects meant for a boy's ogling, wide hips were the result of some girl being "too grown," and menstruation, a word we sixth-grade girls could hardly pronounce, was not natural and life-affirming but dirty, vile and just plain disgusting. Those negative images and beliefs about my body led to years and years of shyness, hiding my changing shape beneath bigger clothing and doing what I could to not "give a man a reason" to violate me. It took just as many years and miles away from that pretty-girl-pink little room to realize that I wasn't alone.

Talking to my girlfriends, we shared many similar stories and came to the conclusion that our African American mothers, aunts and grandmothers came from a generation of women who rarely talked about those things that are inherently female: periods, breasts and vaginas. For many of them, unfortunately, a menstruating daughter only meant the inevitable trouble of an unplanned, unwanted pregnancy they could ill afford; the language and love and support we girls needed was simply choked back in fear.

"Girl, when I told my mother that I had my period, she broke down and cried," one friend said over lunch.

"Hmpf! My mother stopped me from playing with the boys altogether," added someone else, reaching for the sugar.

"Girl, don't feel bad. I'm *just* now learning how to size

myself for a bra," said another, just three years shy of her thirty-fifth birthday.

In sharing our stories, we share our strengths. Somehow, we discover how ridiculous our beliefs can be. The more I shared my story with my friends, the more I learned and appreciated what I now understand as the sacred feminine. Just as the moon makes its way around the Earth every twenty-eight days in a cycle, so, too, does my body cycle to renew and regenerate itself, and what could be more liberating than that? What could be more spiritually freeing than knowing how connected we are, as women, to the divine plan of the universe? What could be more life-affirming than the body of a woman, so fruitful and packed with seeds of possibilities? What could be greater than the stories and poems and music and paintings and the worlds of new ideas all birthed from the body and heart and soul of a woman?

What I know now as a woman that I didn't know as a girl is that not only is my body beautiful and sacred, it is mine to celebrate in the ways that I choose. That "time of the month" is no time for crying or feeling cursed, but for me at least, a time to go within and a reminder to take good care of myself: sometimes a tea time, sometimes a leave-me-alone-for-a-good-long-bath time, sometimes, even, a dancing time. I am science, and I am spirit, but I am nobody's curse.

One more thing I know is this: when that day arrives for my daughter, I *will* curl my arms around her shoulders and welcome her into the fold—the fold of being a woman. I *will* celebrate that milestone with her, not mourn its coming. There we will be, hand in hand, and this time it won't be my imagination.

Angel V. Shannon

Keeping Faith

A doctor . . . a lawyer . . . an actress . . . a queen! That's
what she'll be! I couldn't wait to see what my new daughter would become. As an African American woman, I
wanted to adopt children of African American descent and
raise them to be well-loved, confident, productive members of society. Finally it was happening. My dream was
coming true.

The call came after months of waiting. I was in my office.
It had been so long since I had heard from the Department
of Children's Services, I had almost given up hope. It
seemed as if I was never going to have another daughter.
My biological daughter was eight and had been hoping for
a sister for more than three years. I sipped my coffee and
answered the phone on the third ring. The social worker
on the other end told me that there was a little girl with no
place to go. She immediately aroused every maternal
instinct in my body. Imagine a child not knowing the
warm, constant love and support of a parent. I was ready
to shower her with affection. At the tender age of three,
she had already been in eleven different foster homes. The
worker continued to brief me by explaining that the child
needed to be placed within the hour.

That didn't leave much time to make a decision. Not only was I short on time, I was short on information about this child as well. The only details available were that she was African American and potty trained and that her name was Faith. The social worker wanted to know if I would be interested. Why, of course I was interested! Faith was coming home.

In preparation for my new daughter's arrival, I ran out to buy things for her room, including a beautiful picture of a black ballerina. There was no time to tell my other four children, who were in school, that their new sister was coming home. Alone, I arranged stuffed toys on the bed and hung the picture on the wall. When I thought that everything was suitable, I washed my face, brushed my hair, and headed to the front room to sit down and catch my breath.

Unable to relax, I stood anxiously in the window awaiting Faith's arrival. Finally, after what seemed to be hours, I saw a white van pull up in front of my house. My brown-skinned angel had arrived. But wait! The worker was carrying a small, chubby child with big blue eyes and curly blond hair. She had puffy cheeks and appeared to be very frightened. I was scared, too. I felt her pain deep in my heart but I was still confused. I thought that the child being brought to me was supposed to be African American.

Her social worker explained that although there was some doubt about her paternity, both parents were listed as being African American. Before paternity tests could be run, the father listed died of a heart attack at the age of thirty-eight. What was I going to do? This child would not blend into my existing family. I could not teach this child about a culture that I was unsure of myself. Yet, when I knelt down and looked deep into her piercing blue eyes, my heart told me that none of that should matter. If I turned her away, who would love and care for Faith? Who would encourage, support and be by her side when life got tough? Who would patiently sit with her, night after night, as she learned to read and write? Where would she build her memories? Who would be her "forever family"?

Maybe it was not meant for me to just raise an African American child to be proud of her culture. Perhaps I was to teach this child, who blended into many cultures, how to love herself and others. Perhaps all she required of me was constant love and stability. Then, out of the blue, Faith made the decision for me by saying, "Hi, Mama."

The first few days were hard for Faith. Every night she cried uncontrollably and had violent temper tantrums. I understood her frustration because I am sure that she was afraid of what the next day might bring. In fact, every time we left the house she ran to get her yellow toothbrush, just in case she didn't come back. Her only possessions had been the clothes on her back, a pair of small shoes and the yellow toothbrush.

I began to purchase new things for her. How she treasured the new pink house shoes that made her feel special! She loved the Barbie pillowcase she rested so peacefully on. And she adored the little purple stroller, which allowed her to lavish the affection on her dolls that she had been denied in infancy. One day she came to me and said that she needed more dolls. "Ridiculous," I told her. "You have so many dolls." My three-year-old then explained to me that none of her dolls had social workers. I knew then that it was time for me to move forward and make this adorable little child a legal and permanent member of my family. Until then, she would not be able to move on with her life. Faith had done nothing to deserve being uprooted whenever it was no longer convenient for her to live with a family. I would be sure that she would never have to move again. Instead of getting a child that I thought I could teach about life, she came into my life and taught me many things about myself, my family and what is really important. Yes, this would be her forever home.

What would she be? She would be my daughter.

Tracy Clausell-Alexander

Handpicked to Nurture

Challenges make you discover things about yourself that you never really knew. They're what make the instrument stretch—what make you go beyond the norm.

Cicely Tyson

The fight was on. I was determined to win—determined to hear what the masked figure standing over me had to say. As my eyes focused, my brain connected the dots with what I saw. Bright lights . . . blue scrubs . . . glasses—ah, yes! My doctor.

"Worse case I've ever seen. Stage four."

Too late . . . it won. Without warning I sank back into the hole of unconsciousness I'd fought so hard to leave. I didn't return to the land of the living until the next day when the anesthesia from my exploratory surgery wore off. It was then that I learned my fate—a fate that would make me feel like less than a woman for many years to come.

"Endo what?" I asked the doctor.

"Endometriosis. It's a noncancerous condition in which

pieces of the uterine lining grow outside your uterus and adhere to other pelvic structures, most commonly the ovaries, bowel, fallopian tubes or bladder. It is a common cause of pelvic pain and infertility."

"So what does that mean?" I asked, even though deep in my heart, I knew.

My doctor looked me dead in the eyes. "It means that you will never have children."

Just like that, at the age of twenty-three, all hopes of one day being a mother died.

A month later, my marriage was buried in the same coffin when my husband decided that being a father was more important than being my husband. Much to my devastation, within two weeks he was gone.

It took a while but eventually I got out of bed, put on my clothes and walked out the door with my head held high; carrying a promise with me to never get involved with a man who didn't have children of his own.

Six years and several relationships later, I met Ethan. Immediately, we hit it off. Not only was Ethan a gem, he came with his own kid. Jackpot! It was a dream come true—or so I thought. Unfortunately, I was in for a rude awakening when he called one Saturday, about a month after we'd started dating.

"Tee, I'll be over this afternoon with someone I'd like for you to meet."

"Who?" I asked.

"Someone that I love very much and hope one day you will, too."

Ah, the moment of truth had arrived. I was about to meet Brian, Ethan's son.

As it turned out, Brian was a handful from day one. The second I opened my door, he zoomed past me, jumped over my couch, did a cartwheel and karate-chopped the air with the plastic sword he carried. With wide-open eyes and mouth, I looked at Ethan. *Oh no, he didn't just jump on my new couch!*

"Boy, sit your butt down and act like you got some sense!" Ethan shouted. "This might be your stepmother one day!"

"Umph," I mumbled.

So marked the beginning of my life with Brian. He was a typical three-year-old, running, dashing and jumping constantly—something that I was ill-equipped to handle. As the relationship progressed, and Ethan and I started living with each other, there were times that I wanted to throw in the towel; especially when Brian's mother started dropping him off at our house every weekend.

A couple of hours of dealing with a rowdy three-year-old was one thing, but *every* weekend was a different novel altogether. I tried talking to Ethan, but he was too over-joyed about the time he got to spend with his son. The feeling was mutual as far as Brian was concerned. How was I supposed to fight such a lethal combination?

After some careful strategizing, I decided to speak to Brian's mother. "Look, we have him *every* weekend. Can we please try to work something out so that we can share weekends? You know, you take him one weekend and we'll take him the next?" I asked, with a sugary smile pasted on my face.

Brian's mother smiled back with an equally sugary smile. "I'd love to do that, but I work on the weekends, honey. It's his father's responsibility to keep him when I can't."

Oh, no, she didn't! Girlfriend played me. I knew when I had been trumped, so I shut my mouth and vowed revenge. The fight was on!

Eventually, Ethan and I got married. We decided to spend our honeymoon in New Orleans, and since this included the weekend, Brian's mother was none too happy about the arrangement. *Umm hmmm, things are about to change*, I thought, as I stared into her defeated face.

For seven heavenly days, Ethan and I enjoyed the sights, food and music that comprised New Orleans. On the trip home, something nagged me the entire time, warning me of things to come. As long as I live, I will never forget the sequence of events that followed.

Seconds after we unloaded the car, Brian's mother called to inform us that she would be right over. When she arrived, she politely marched up to the door with Brian in tow. She plopped him down on the doorstep along with a box, which contained all of Brian's worldly belongings as if she were a mail carrier handing us a parcel.

"Your turn," she said, as Ethan and I stood on the doorstep looking at her in disbelief. She turned, and without another word, drove off into the sunset. *Girlfriend won. She blindsided me.*

As I tried to adjust to life with Brian in the house, I realized he had a lot of adjusting to do as well. He needed a mother more than ever. Unfortunately, I was not equipped to give him what he needed at the time. Oh, I made sure all of his physical needs were taken care of, but emotionally something held me back. Perhaps it was my fear that he would be taken from me—that his mother would one day reclaim him. Or maybe it was my insecurity of knowing that I was not Brian's mother—she was. Whatever it was, it kept me from giving him the motherly love that he needed.

I'm not exactly sure when things changed, but somewhere along the line I became his mother and he became my son.

One day, I stood in the hallway ironing.

"Let me ask my mom," I heard Brian tell the neighborhood boy standing at our door.

"Is it okay if I go to Jamal's house?" he asked me.

I was floored. This was the first time I heard him refer to me as his mom. "Yeah, go ahead," I replied. "And Brian . . ."

"Yes," he answered.

"You're the only person in this world that has ever called me Mom—I like it."

He smiled, and so did I.

God has a way of gelling things together, without us ever realizing it. He knew that just because I couldn't physically have children, it didn't mean that I couldn't be a mother. I am humbled that God handpicked me to nurture one of society's most endangered species—an African American child.

As it turns out, I won after all.

T. Rhythm Knight

Single-Mommy Love

If you are a parent . . . what you do every day, what you say and how you act, will do more to shape the future of America than any other factor.

Marian Wright Edelman

Some time ago during one of my pitiful laments over the guilt I harbored for being a single parent, my mother shook me out of my self-centered sobs and said adamantly, "This is not about you. This is about that little boy who is growing more into a young man each day. You have to pray for him daily, like I do. He'll be all right. He reminds me of Daddy. I know he'll turn out to be a good, strong man."

It was then that I noticed three distinct likenesses my five-and-a-half-year-old son has to my deceased maternal grandfather: a fair-skinned, round face; a motor-mouth that runs from coast to coast; and an impenetrable dignity stemming far back into our ancestry. I hoped my mother was right and tried to put a rest to my fears.

Then one day, we were at a typical tee-ball practice on the field of the local elementary school playground. Well, not quite *typical*. My son, Paul, the coach's son, Ian, and another little boy were the only ones present and on time. While we waited for the other five players on the team, the boys played on the slide in the park adjacent to the field.

As an outgoing only child, Paul relished playtime with peers. With twinkles in his dreamy brown eyes, he'd tear away from me in a split second to seek out friendly fun. His boundless energy and youthful innocence were one of my greatest joys in life.

All seemed well until Ian came running full-speed out of the park across the field, yelling, "I don't want to play with you. You're black!"

I know I didn't just hear what I thought I heard!

The coach and I had been engaged in conversation, and we both turned our heads to watch the scene unfold. Paul sprinted up behind Ian, shouting, "Hey, don't call me a color!"

No such luck. I just heard what I thought I heard.

Paul was the only black child on the team, but I never noted a difference between him and the other children.

"Ian, that's not nice. Apologize to Paul," his dad insisted.

Ian threw down his ball cap and stomped his feet in the dirt. "But he is black! He has a black mom!"

I could feel myself controlling my breathing; I noted all of the choice words dancing in my head; I was aware of the pain I instantly felt in my heart for both my son and myself. The only comment I made was, "What's wrong with having a black mom, young man?"

While the coach continued to chastise his son about the remark, I watched Paul's reaction. I waited for him to cry into my arms, to pitch a fit or retaliate. I could feel all my years of hurts wrapped up in this moment waiting to see what he does with his first real experience. He stood before Ian, knock-kneed and all, without shedding a tear.

He spoke calmly, but firmly, "I am a hu-man." His mouth said only those words, but his body posture and his tone said, *See me, respect me and know that I will be counted.*

Ian gave Paul the strangest look, maybe a mixture of shock and admiration that Paul didn't whine or try to fight. Without any further prompting, Ian outstretched his hand to Paul and said, "I'm sorry."

We all could feel his remorse. He realized that he had said something hurtful to a real friend.

Paul lovingly accepted his apology, then looked toward me for the first time since the whole episode had started. He glanced back at Ian expectantly with an unspoken, *Don't you have something to tell my mama?*

Ian walked over to me, head bowed. "I'm sorry, Ms. Smith."

I nodded okay.

Paul marched over to the dugout to retrieve his glove. At first, I thought he was headed for the car to go home. But he jogged to outfield, ready to catch some pitches.

Just that fast, the longest moment in Little League history was over.

Later that evening, I explained to Paul what the "black" race and "white" race meant in simple terms, along with giving some examples of people he knew who were black, white, a combination or another race altogether.

He nodded understanding, but remained quiet.

"I'm proud of you," I told him, kissing the top of his head. "You were very strong today."

"Thanks." He smiled at me. "May I go play a game now?"

"You certainly may."

Tears began streaming down my face. But they weren't the sorrowful droplets of old. These were the moist, jubilant beads of faith, hope and love. For I know that God would not entrust the life of this child to me without empowering and equipping me with the will to succeed. I am no longer crying because I am a single mom, I'm crying because I get to be his mother, and today I was his student.

Dayciaa C. Smith

The Christmas Sparrows

Recently, while driving in the countryside of northwestern New Jersey, I saw a wonderful and rare sight. There were at least a dozen bright red cardinals all perched in a large bush. A childhood memory came flooding back to me. "Christmas sparrows," that was the name Granny gave to these beautiful, red-winged creatures.

The very first time I met Granny, I was about nine years old. I was running home from school, excited to show my art "achievement" to my mother. It was a Halloween decoration, a bat attached to a picture with a pipe cleaner.

As I ran down my street, I tripped and fell on the sidewalk. I tore my pants and had a large scrape on my knee. Of course, I let out a scream. I looked down at my work of art. My heart sank. The pipe cleaner had come off of the colored construction paper. I was extremely upset. But there in a minute was Granny. "Child, child, what on earth?" she exclaimed. I blurted out that I tripped and fell, and ruined my art work.

"Well now, let's see what we can do to make things better," she said with an understanding smile. "What's your name?"

"Joey," I replied as I began to calm down a bit. It was nice to hear a comforting voice.

"Come inside, child. I'll put some medicine on that scrape."

"Yes, ma'am." I said as I followed her into her apartment. Granny lived on the first floor of an old apartment in Perth Amboy, New Jersey, just about a block from our old apartment.

There were just a couple of rooms, sparsely furnished, with a few knickknacks, but a lot of pictures. She gently but very quickly applied some dark-looking salve on my wound. "What's that stuff?" I asked.

"Well child, it's an old family cure, handed down from my grandma. I know it smells kinda bad, but it will work real good." Already I could feel the pain go away. "Whatcha got in your hand?" she asked. "Well, it was supposed to be a Halloween picture for my mom, but it got tore up when I fell," I stated. "Let's take a look to see what we can do to fix this beautiful picture." Granny hunted around in a few drawers and produced some colored construction paper.

"Land sakes, this paper is years old, Joey, but I think it'll do the trick." She made a few drawings of Halloween cats, a big pumpkin and an old witch. Then she let me cut them out. With a little glue and a few finishing touches on the bat—good as new. In fact, it really looked beautiful! I looked up at Granny and she had a big, approving grin. "Child, I have something special for you I think you'd like." The dear lady brought out a plate full of gingerbread men cookies and a glass of milk. I swear, they were the best cookies I've ever tasted.

All of a sudden, I heard my mother's frantic voice calling my name. Gosh, I had forgotten about the time. I went running outside with Granny close behind. I started to explain, but my mom was still justifiably upset. "Your boy fell here on the sidewalk, but he's okay now," Granny explained. "I hope he didn't put you out," my mom replied. "Oh, not at all. He's a nice boy. I did enjoy his company."

"Thank you, ma'am," I said. "Well child, you can just call me Granny," she said with a broad smile. "Okay, Granny!"

Several weeks passed. A November chill was in the air. Granny was sweeping up some leaves on her sidewalk as I was coming home from school one gray afternoon.

"Remember me?" I asked. "I sure do. Say how's the scrape on your knee?" I was impressed that Granny would remember. "It was healed the next day! How about lettin' me clean up those leaves for you?" I asked.

"Well child, how much would you charge me?"

"One gingerbread cookie," I replied as we both began to laugh. "But first I gotta let my mom know," as I started to run down the street. In a few minutes, I was back and in no time the leaves were swept and bagged. "Joey, you can have as many cookies as you want, but don't fill up too much before your supper."

"No, ma'am," I replied.

Sitting there in her kitchen, it was the first time I really took a good look at Granny. She was up in years, but got around very well. She had beautiful dark eyes and a warm-hearted smile. She had a great sense of humor as I would come to know and a hearty laugh that was very contagious. We talked for a long time, getting to know one another. Granny had become a treasured friend. She possessed a great deal of wisdom. One day while talking she asked me what I thought about school. The truth is I did like school and did very well.

"That's so good to hear, child. You know I hardly went to school, but books have knowledge. And knowledge is the key that will unlock many doors in your life as you grow up." I remember asking her how long it took her to get old.

"A long time," was her reply. "But it all happened in the blink of an eye," she said with a hint of sadness in her voice.

I found out that Granny had lived in New Orleans when she was my age. She had twelve brothers and sisters, but she was the only one left. Granny had four daughters, but they all lived down South. Her husband, Jefferson, had died many, many years ago. I asked her about her grandchildren. She told me there were eight of them, and many times she wished she could see them but was "not up to travelin'."

As Christmas approached, Granny received a letter stating that one of her daughters was coming for a visit with her two children for the holidays. What a beautiful sparkle in her eyes as each day went by. On Christmas Eve I stopped by her apartment with a small gift. I had my sister make Granny two red, green and white pot holders. What a fuss she made over them. You'd think I had given her a thousand dollars.

Granny also had two wonderful presents for me, a whole tin of gingerbread men cookies and a red, hand-knit scarf. Her daughter was to arrive that evening. My dear friend was so excited. Suddenly she called out to me. "Joey, come quick!" I ran over to the window.

"See there," she said, pointing to her large holly bush. "The red birds. Some folks call them cardinals, but in truth they are Christmas sparrows.

"You see, when the baby Jesus was born, the Christmas sparrows flew 'round and 'round the manger. The light of the moon and stars reflected off of them, giving a beautiful, warm glow over the Christ child. It's a sign that you will have much joy and peace in the coming year."

With the passing of the holidays, it was decided that Granny would be moving away to stay with her daughter as she began to need help getting around. She gave me her address, and for several years we would send each other a short note or card. Then one day, her daughter wrote that my sweet Granny passed on in peace.

Fifty years later I still cherish her memory, the ginger-bread men cookies, the warm insights into life and the wonderful story of the Christmas sparrows. Granny was a very simple lady with the biggest heart of gold that a person could possess. As we journey through life, we are all gifted in having been touched in heart and soul by the angels that walk among us.

Joe Gurneak

Soul Food Rite of Passage

"Mmm . . . Mommy, this is *all* so yummy!" my five-year-old daughter repeated at least three times while eating.

"Thank you, sweetheart. I was just trying to make it like Bigmamma's."

"You did a good job!" She then walked over to me. And with her sweet, soft voice she said, "Bigmamma would be proud," and she clasped her little arms around my waist.

I had done it. I had finally mastered that delectable pot roast like the one Bigmamma makes. You know, the kind that melts in your mouth and makes you want to sing while you eat. It had taken numerous attempts, but this time I had done it. Seasoned white potatoes, carrots and caramelized sweet onion accompanied the roast—along with golden brown, bubbling-over macaroni and cheese, candied yams and tender collard greens. I had spent most of the afternoon in a hot kitchen preparing this "perfect" soul food dinner, and I was now ready to clear away the dishes so that I could kick back and relax. But wait, something was missing.

"Mommy," my three-year-old said as he gazed up at me from his empty plate with those dark brown puppy-dog eyes.

"Yes, honey?"

"I wanted bread with it."

"Bread?" It took me a few seconds to figure out what he meant.

"Oh . . . you mean cornbread?" I asked.

"Yes," he said.

"I'm sorry, baby. Mommy didn't make any cornbread. I would have to cook some," I said.

"Okay," he said, and he got up and went to play. I thought that because he had already eaten his entire dinner he would soon forget about the cornbread. I continued to clean the kitchen when a few minutes later my son returned.

"Mommy, I said I wanted cornbread!" He was serious.

As I dragged my tired feet to the counter to get back into the cooking mode that I thought I had concluded, I couldn't help but fast-forward into the future sixteen years. *This is what mammas do,* I thought. *They gladly make their children's favorite foods for them.*

"Mom, I'm coming home from school this weekend. Can you make me a roast, macaroni and cheese, candied yams, greens and cornbread?" Yeah . . . I could envision that conversation between me and my nineteen-year-old son. I just didn't think this sort of thing would begin at age three.

And I was tired and wanted to sit down. But there was this voice in my head.

Child, make that boy some cornbread! It was the voice of Bigmamma. Besides, what's a soul-food dinner without cornbread? Bigmamma always has bread. Oven-baked cornbread, hot-water cornbread, homemade rolls, it doesn't matter, but there is always bread.

As I began to stir the egg and pour in the milk, a smile formed on my face. I realized that for hundreds of years African American mammas have taken great pleasure in preparing treasured meals for their children, and now it was my turn—a rite of passage of sorts. I was now the "mamma" whose cooking *her* children would brag about and crave for decades to come.

Truth be told, I'm a grown woman and I *still* like to make food requests of Bigmamma—or at least I did, up until she died months ago. "What you want, baby?" she would ask. And although she was in her seventies, she would spend hours in the kitchen preparing a fantastic made-to-order, home-cooked, soul food extravaganza and drive twenty miles to bring it to us.

Now it's my turn. Bigmamma has passed on. And the next time I get a special food request—even if my feet *are* aching, I will count it a blessing.

The sweet aroma of hot cornbread baking in the oven lured my three-year-old son right back to the table. It wasn't even out of the oven before he was in his seat, ready to eat. The smile on his face made it all worthwhile. "Mmmm . . ." was the only syllable he uttered as he inhaled the bread and filled that tiny tummy of his.

My daughter was right. Bigmamma *would* be proud. She wasn't here to see it, but I had finally had my soul food rite of passage.

Anita S. Lane

Lesson for a New Life

From the moment I found out that I was pregnant at the age of twenty, I placed myself on a self-imposed punishment. I kicked myself over and over for being so stupid and so careless. And to right the wrong, I made a valiant attempt to transform myself into a responsible adult in a matter of months.

It ripped my young, foolish heart in half to learn that my boyfriend, who had just proposed to me weeks before learning we would be parents, decided not to join me in my blind leap into true adulthood. He was not interested in becoming a father again for the second time in two years. I gave him the opportunity to waive his parental rights, but guilt made him stay around for the baby's sake, and he made me miserable. I ended up wishing he had taken the free pass I tried to offer him.

After his swift departure, I immediately took up the cross of being a young, unwed mother and carried it around like a martyr, accepting my impending doom in silence. Though her father and I both shared in the blame of doing what we did to bring the child into the world, I bore the burden for both of us. Because he was no longer around, there was no one else to blame but me. I felt like

Hester Prynne in *The Scarlet Letter*, except instead of a bold red letter emblazoned across my chest, my mark of shame was my huge belly that was increasingly hard to ignore with each passing day.

Ironically, everyone else had already forgiven me. I just could never manage to forgive myself. I asked the Lord for forgiveness as sincerely as I could muster. Even my mother, who was so disappointed that she didn't speak to me for four months, finally came around, flying all the way to California from North Carolina to support me while I brought my baby into the world. But I still felt the need to inflict myself with pain as punishment, almost as if to attempt to purge my sins for the evil I had committed. I wouldn't socialize with my friends or engage in any activities that remotely resembled having a good time. *All of your good times will be spent worrying about somebody else now*, I thought. I wouldn't even afford myself the luxury of screaming out to express my pain during childbirth.

When she finally came into the world six hours and one minute later, my temporary feeling of relief was invaded by more permanent feelings of anxiety and fear. I lacked a significant amount of maternal instincts. And I had no clue what to do with a baby, anyway, especially a girl baby. Heck, I didn't even know how to cornrow. For that matter, I couldn't even do my own hair. I went to the hairdresser every two weeks. Oh well, I guess that forty bucks would be going to something else now.

I was genuinely disappointed that she had not been a boy. *There goes my easy ride*, I thought. Now, on top of everything else, I've got to worry about her doing the same thing I did.

I felt guilty because I couldn't pick up my cross and bear it happily like other mothers, single and married alike. So I begrudgingly began my new life as a young mom with no prospects of being married and no hopes of ever having any fun. With my spirit officially broken I reluctantly settled into single motherhood. My heart was not in it, and I felt like a monster for secretly viewing my child as a burden.

My daughter was always a good baby. She had a serious demeanor and didn't cry much. She became more jovial as she got older and cried even less. She didn't teethe like most babies who run a fever and are cranky when they start to cut teeth. I just happened to notice six little pegs in her mouth one day as I tickled her belly and she threw her head back to laugh. She settled into daycare without so much as a whimper. And she was a breeze to potty train. It was almost like she did everything with minimal supervision because, even as a baby, she was somehow able to sense that my heart really wasn't into raising her, and was afraid that I would leave her, too, if she gave me any trouble. And I felt guilty about that, too.

Oddly enough, with all the guilt, resentment and anxiety I held in my heart, along with the inadequacies I felt about myself as a mom, my daughter either didn't appear to notice all my shortcomings or she didn't care. She actually seemed to like the mom that had been handpicked especially for her. From a baby, she greeted me every morning with a smile when I woke her. And she was always excited to see me when I picked her up from daycare. It seemed that she preferred my company to everyone else's.

And if that wasn't a major ego stroke in itself, as she got older she followed me around imitating my every move. She clomped around in my high heels and mimicked my telephone conversations on an old cell phone that she liked to play with. The funniest thing of all was that she actually liked the way I combed her hair, and to this day she contradicts my story when I tell anyone how much I suck at braiding, even after being parent to a little girl for the last twelve years.

And the fun that I had been so determined to rob myself of has actually been a big hit with my daughter and all her friends. As a younger mom, the music that my daughter likes is not noise to me. In fact, we like many of the same performers, and together we enjoy older groups that I listened to at her age. As a younger mother, I'm able to show her some of the dances we did in the eighties, many of which have come back in style. Just seeing her mouth drop in amazement and admiration at some of the moves I can still pull off is worth the misery I went through to get her here in the first place. We go skating, hang out at the mall together, and even make late night runs to Krispy Kreme on Friday nights to take advantage of the "hot light." I eventually found my maternal instincts and discovered that having my daughter as a companion to share my life experiences has proved to be the best way to live life.

Becoming a mother at the beginning of my twenty-first year did not signify the end of my life, as I had thought, but rather the beginning of a new life for both of us that is rich with fun, opportunity and adventure. And so, twelve years later, I celebrate the realization that I am not stuck raising a child all by myself, but simply savoring every moment of being a parent without having to share.

Evelyn K. Lemar

3

BEAUTIFUL– JUST THE WAY I AM

O, ye daughters of Africa, Awake! Arise!
No longer sleep nor slumber, but distinguish
yourselves. Show forth to the world that ye
are endowed with noble and exalted
faculties.

Maria W. Stewart

Discovering Me

If you're not feeling good about you, what you're wearing outside doesn't mean a thing.

Leontyne Price

I fly a lot but had never flown on a plane looking like such a bum. I wore faded sweat pants and a workout T-shirt that I had torn down the front so that it would not choke me. I was not glamorous, but I was comfortable. After all, this was the red-eye flight, and everything else in my bag was too dressy. I needed to be as comfortable as possible because this flight was all the sleep I was going to get before the big presentation and book signing the next day.

As I boarded the plane, advice given long ago popped into my head to always take a spare pair of black pants, black flats and solid blouse on board a plane just in case my bags got lost. I wondered why that entered my head at that particular moment. While I had not followed that advice, I had traveled to forty-seven cities in ten months and, "knock on wood," I had received my bags just fine each time. I reasoned I was just a little nervous because my plane landed at 9:00 A.M., and I needed to be at Christ Universal Temple by 9:40 A.M. for the 10 o'clock service to deliver the guest message for more than five thousand people. *Well, too late now; I am on the plane and seated. I'm sure it will all be okay—like always.*

"Please fasten your seat belts. We are landing in Chicago, where the local time is 8:54 A.M."

As I waited for my bags, this eerie feeling came over me again. *What if. . . . What if nothing!* I did not have time for issues! There are several thousand people expecting me to speak at one of my favorite places to visit, and I must be dressed for the occasion. After all, everyone who knows me knows that fashion and celebrating my unique style of dress are very important to me.

It is 9:12 A.M. *Where are my bags?! There are only two people left looking for their luggage, and I am one of them. Now there is only one person looking—me!*

It is now 9:20 A.M. and my heart is beating more rapidly than normal as I enter the luggage office. "My bags did not come out; can someone please check outside?" I could hear the urgency in my own voice as my cell phone began ringing.

"Good morning, this is your limo driver. I am outside and we must get going to arrive at services on time."

I explained that my luggage had not arrived. There was a hushed silence on the other end of the line. Her lengthy pause elevated my anxiety. Then she said in a very calm and assuring voice, "It will be fine; let me call the church."

As I hung up the phone, the clerk began his sentence with those dreadful words, "I'm sorry, ma'am, but your luggage did not arrive on this flight." I could feel the pit of my stomach tighten up; my mind was racing as I glanced at the clock.

It is now 9:26 A.M. "I normally dress fashionably casual when flying. What was I thinking? Look at me!" To my own surprise I was speaking out loud, and everyone had heard my thoughts, and they *were* looking at me. In a frantic voice I continued. "You don't understand; in thirty minutes I am supposed to be in front of thousands of people speaking. I cannot go looking like this. Pleeeease check again," I begged.

My head was swimming. I looked down at myself again trying to see how creative I could be with my outfit. Torn T-shirt, faded sweats and a pair of well-used tennis shoes—even Michelangelo needed *something* to work with.

My heart sank, and I began to pray out loud, "Lord, you said that if I work for you that you will never make a fool of me. I need you to show me how we are going to get through this. I need you now, Lord, to give me peace of mind and show me a way out." Everyone was now staring at me, some people obviously uncomfortable with me praying out loud. I didn't care. I had no other choice.

My phone rang again, "Hello, it is your limo driver again." Without thinking, I blurted out, "Let's find a store and I will pick something up quickly." I seemed to have found a flicker of hope in a dismal situation which the limo driver immediately doused. She informed me that it would be impossible to find a clothing store open at 9:30 A.M. on a Sunday morning, and that the church leaders wanted me to arrive as close to 10:00 A.M. as possible. She went on to say that since it was Youth Sunday, the church had requested that I speak in whatever clothes I arrived in. They clearly had not seen my attire.

As we neared the church in the limo, my chest began to tighten. I initially fought back the tears, then they became overwhelming. Tears streamed freely down my face as I surrendered to my fear over what was about to happen. I began wondering why I was so uncomfortable, what was freaking me out this much. I closed my eyes and asked for my concerns and fears to be revealed to me. I stilled myself to hear God, and the answer came barreling down on me like a boulder in an avalanche. I realized in that moment that I have always made a concerted effort to look polished, unique and impeccable. My clothes, my jewelry, my style had become more than optional in my life; they had become my identity. With mocha skin, round hips and full lips—not what society saw as beautiful when I was growing up—I quickly learned to polish my personality and to create a unique dress style as my survival tool. And now, on this day, in just a few minutes I was going out in front of thousands of people without my shield, my safeguard, my protection—*or was it now my crutch?*

In my stillness came something amazing. "It's time you get comfortable with who I have created you to be," God softly whispered in my heart. "Your luggage not arriving was no accident; I needed to get your attention. I know about your mocha skin and your round hips and your full lips. I knew what I was creating when I made you and all of your sisters who look like you. I also knew that no one could wear it quite like you, blended with the character, the love and the humility I gave you. You need to know that you are just fine—even in sweat pants. Wear *you* today—after all, that's who I've been trying to share with the world, anyway."

I was now sobbing uncontrollably, a mixture of thankfulness, conviction, surrender and yes, still some fear. I was hiding my face behind a folder so the limo driver began to speak to me not knowing that I was already in a conversation with God. I was thankful for the interruption.

"There is too much traffic on this route. I am going to have to let you out in the front of the church."

I mumble, "Okay God, you now have my full, undivided, broken-down, surrendered attention, now what?"

As I was escorted to the front door, it swung open and there were three women standing silently, each holding something in her hands. As I neared, Mrs. Helen was holding a dress, another woman was holding a pair of shoes, and the final one was holding a beautiful beaded shawl. Mrs. Helen said, "I'm not sure if this will fit, but it is my dress that has been hanging here for quite some time in case of an emergency." I glanced at Mrs. Helen, noticing that she must have been at least six inches taller and three sizes smaller than me. I forced a polite smile.

I looked at the nice lady carrying the shoes. "These sit under my desk in case my feet hurt." Her feet looked to be about a size seven—a long way from my nine shoe size. Again, I smiled politely. They led me to the bathroom to try on their contributions. I thought that out of respect I would at least try the clothes on, but I was fully ready to grace the stage in sweat pants and a T-shirt if that was God's plan.

Much to my surprise, as if the elegant, cream-colored dress was tailored only for me—it fit perfectly. I was shocked. I hesitantly tried the shoes, which somehow fit my foot better than Cinderella's shoe fit hers. *How is this happening?* My mind began to race. The shawl—which had been on display in the church bookstore the day before— now served as the perfect accent to an amazing outfit, obviously provided by God through his angels.

As I walked on stage, the choir had just sung "God Will Move Mountains for You." With tears streaming down my face and looking more stunning than I could have wearing anything packed in my bags, I began by saying, "God moved some mountains today, just so that you could meet the real me. . . ."

In my heart I knew his even greater intent was for *me* to meet the real me.

Lisa Nichols

Bathed in Love

A necessary act of liberation in myself was to acknowledge the beauty of the black, black woman.

Alice Walker

I was raised in a town called Dix Hills, New York, a town whose borders are formed by Temple Beth Torah to the West and Saint Elizabeth's Catholic Church to the East. The expanse between is filled with wonderful people, my friends, whose ethnic and cultural histories I was delighted to share. My parents taught me the beauty of my own heritage and afforded me the firmament upon which to layer cultural understanding.

My hunger for cultural discovery carried me past my childhood borders to East Asia. As a teacher in Japan I was privy to the personal lives of my students and soon became friends with many of them. They invited me to their homes, filled my stomach with delicacies and my head with their stories, hopes and fears. In spite of our differences, we connected and enjoyed learning from one another.

There were some relationships that did not begin this way, however. I was the first black woman most of my students and friends had ever met. Some were quick to reference the stereotypes they held about black people; to this day my students insist that I am a terrific singer and dancer, though I have never demonstrated my ability. (I refrained for fear that I would be a terrible disappointment.) Other innocent misunderstandings were easily corrected and, to some extent, may have paved the way for our ensuing bond.

Still, while I enjoyed acceptance and kindness from most, there were times when I questioned my pursuit of cultural understanding. The biggest test of my commitment came in Seoul, Korea.

The spring recess of my second year in Japan, a friend and I put the last of our yen together to buy two tour package tickets to Seoul. The tour group was comprised of eighteen people, seventeen Japanese and me, all crammed onto a bus with our cameras around our necks. I soon bonded with my tour-mates to the extent that all considerations of skin color, tongue and nationality melted away. We were unified in our anticipation of spicy food and good shopping.

Our tour bus pulled up to a small leather shop and we all poured out. As my friend and I debated blowing our limited budgets on cute jackets, I noticed the owner walking toward me, a frown on his face. My friend and I approached the staircase to the second floor of the shop when we were stopped.

"Hey, you. Yo. Yo!" An older shopkeeper motioned at me. "Yo. You get out. Yo. No stealing, yo!" His words showered me instantly in fear and shame, and my tour-mates looked equally embarrassed.

I blushed a deep purple as my friend explained to the shop owner that I was part of the tour and had a right to be there. The owner sized me up with narrowed eyes and receded to the back of the shop. I put down the jacket I had been considering and went to wait in the tour bus.

"Don't let that guy get to you," my friend said. It was the first time in my experience in Asia that I felt the sting of racism. My mind raced; what if the entire country was filled with people who felt this way about black people? With fear, disappointment and two days left on my trip, I planned to board myself into the hotel and wait until the flight out on Sunday. I regretted the trip and questioned my goals.

The next day my friend convinced me to emerge from the hotel, reminding me that we had already paid for the trip. My frugality thus appealed to, I timidly strapped on my camera and set out into the streets, waiting for the next attack. Souvenir shops and department stores were sure to hold my next offender, so we steered clear. By the early evening we had walked the streets without accomplishing much more than developing stiff backs and necks.

We walked deep into back alleys and twisted side roads until we stumbled upon a small community spa, and with it the promise of an unparalleled cultural experience. I prayed for the strength to overcome my fear, and entered. Wrapped in a towel, I slid open the heavy door to the main bath. Inside, all conversation stopped, as a bath full of twenty ladies held their breath and watched me cross the floor.

The bath was staffed by an older woman who stood near the massage tables. Again, my mind raced. I feared she would refuse to serve me, that she, too, was tainted by the same racist poison as the shopkeeper. But before I could turn around, she beckoned me over to her table.

The next twenty minutes were a blessing. A warm layer of sesame oil coated my back and shoulders, the rich nutty smell filling my nose and soothing my nerves. She then began working and pounding all my muscles until the very thought of tension slid off the slick surface of my skin. She followed this with a salt exfoliant, rubbed into my skin, peeling off layers of hurt and offense before they hardened and callused. After rinsing off the salt, she splashed on a layer of cucumber cream, the melon-scented wash purifying and sweetening me. She ran her fingers through my hair and washed it, scrubbing deeply, the tips of her fingers caressing my scalp, washing away any residue of negativity. Then she let me rest.

When I stood up again I was refreshed and clean, and my heart was restored to health. The massage woman motioned for me to take a soak in the bath with the on-looking ladies, and I did so with minor hesitation. But as I settled into the water the ladies smiled at me and went back to their soaking, the steam rising from the hot water filling our lungs and wrapping us all together. After a final rinse I left the spa, my eyes red from tears of relief and my hair a giant Afro. That night my friend, my Afro and I hit the town, eating and dancing into the early hours of the next morning, the day of our flight out.

I often wonder about the massage woman. Could she smell the fear and hurt on my skin? I believe she was sent as a representative of all the wonderful people who exist in this world. For every person who fears you and allows racist misconceptions to justify his abuse of you, there is someone far greater who will love you as a human and treat you with kindness. If I hadn't ventured out that day I would never have learned this; I would remain doused in fear instead of the sweet emollient of love.

Adiya Dixon-Sato

My Cup Runneth Over

Once you know who you are, you don't have to worry anymore.

Nikki Giovanni

When I returned from a quick weekend trip to Atlanta, Robin, my youngest daughter who was pregnant with her first child, called before I could get my bags in the door. "Mom! I didn't think you were back yet! I am so glad you're here! We're on our way to the hospital!"

My heart started pounding with excitement. "We" were going to have a baby!

I raced to the hospital to meet her and stayed until I was deliriously tired. After eight months of daily anticipation about this child, my grandson finally arrived around 6:00 A.M. I loved being a grandma the second time just as much as the first. I could not get enough.

When the baby was one week old, the phone rang in the morning and my son-in-law said frantically, "Robin cannot move her left side, and we are on our way to the hospital! Can you meet us there?"

I stopped breathing and went to the hospital on "automatic

pilot." I prayed for my daughter's well-being all the way there. I prayed for the strength to be of help to her and her husband. I prayed for faith that we could see whatever this was through.

After all tests were run, I could see the concern and agony on the faces of the medical team as they approached us. They dropped the news like a bomb. "Robin has had a stroke and is completely paralyzed on one side."

I felt like I had been hit by a ton of bricks! My head was spinning with too many thoughts firing all at once: *Oh my God, it couldn't be! She is only thirty-five years old and never even had high blood pressure! What about the baby? What are we going to do?*

A stroke simply never entered my mind. I had to get myself under control because I knew they would be depending on me to be strong and, as broken as I felt, there was nothing I could do—except pray. I found a quiet place, allowed myself a quick cry to release the intensity of fear and concern I was experiencing, and began to pray. I needed peace of mind so that I could figure out how we were all going to handle this. That was the beginning of my daughter's extended stay in the hospital.

I visited Robin each day, and on her twenty-second day of confinement, a wave of emotion overcame me as I climbed my stairs. I had to hold on to the banister while I staggered—blinded by the flood of tears that came. It caught me completely off-guard. I knew I couldn't visit her that day; all I could do was lay down and sleep. I woke up hours later, and shortly afterward my girlfriend Valerie called and asked "Nik, how are you doing?"

It must have been the manner with which she asked such a simple question, because suddenly the words describing my breakdown came pouring out. She listened carefully and then said, "You know, your cup is running over and you released the excess!"

Surprised by her comment, I asked, "What? What do you mean?"

She replied, "I've always admired the way you handle things when they happen. But I've often wondered what was in your cup! You never talk about anything that bothers you."

I was shocked. We had been friends for more than thirty years. Speechless, I had to wonder whether that was really true. *Naw, uh-huh. Not me. She was wrong! Or was she?*

There was something in what she was saying that captivated me—I just wasn't sure what it was. I was so absorbed in my thoughts I don't even know what I said in response, but within seconds after hanging up from her I had gone from a state of disheartenment to total excitement.

I couldn't stop thinking about it. The next morning I called her to continue the conversation. She had barely answered before I blurted out, "What's in the cup? I can't figure it out?"

She laughed and said, "I don't know exactly, Nik, but it's stress."

I quickly said, "Stress? Well, what's the stress?"

She said, "That's what I don't know—only you know! After all, it is *your* cup."

I knew God was using her to reveal something huge to me. I could feel it, but I could not see what it was. When I hung up, I sat quietly and waited for answers, but they didn't come quickly enough.

I went to the hospital to help pack up my daughter's belongings because she was going home. She had to relearn all the basic things we take for granted—including walking. She had good use of her right side and, incredibly, could hold and take care of her baby. The many prayers of the righteous had truly been answered.

No matter what I did, I continued to think about "my cup." There was a mystique about this that was calling me.

Whenever I asked someone else, each would not hesitate to tell me what was in *their* cup. I heard things like, "I get tired of being responsible for others," "I always put myself last," or "People take me for granted and do not appreciate who I am." The list went on and on, but I knew I was looking for something else; I was looking for what was in *my* cup but still did not know what it was.

I was on a mission. Sometimes God only gives us one piece of the puzzle at a time because that is all we can handle, and that was the case with me.

My "moment of understanding" came in a conversation with my cousin Drina. We used a dilemma that was going on to explore "the cup." We jumped in feet first and started digging like we were searching for gold. She kept asking me questions and I would respond with how I *felt* about whatever we were talking about. I started hearing myself say things I had never said, and I didn't want to stop—and neither did she. All of a sudden I had the epiphany: *Feelings* were what was in my cup!

The puzzle started coming together in a huge way. All the pieces began to emerge. I could see them now. Valerie was right! There was so much I *felt* that I had *never expressed*. Just as I had done when I learned about my daughter's stroke, it was my pattern to "fast-forward" over whatever feelings I had, always thinking I had to be the one to figure out what needed to be done. I had to be the strong one. Then, there was my conditioning to internalize and to please others and be whatever they needed me to be. Usually I was the listener and, for whatever reasons, felt that my own "stuff" was a burden—no matter how much others poured into me. Oh, the cost of that was far too high. I was giving too much of myself away and not honoring my heart and my needs.

This conversation pierced the sludge and sewage in the bottom of my cup—the mass of junk that had been there for years. It came oozing out with every word. I was emptying my cup. What a release!

When we finished talking I felt a freedom—like I had been touched by the hand of God. Now that my cup was running over with something different, rather than stress from stored-up emotions, feelings of being understood, validated and accepted flowed freely. In that moment, I vowed to tell every woman I encountered that we must value and take care of ourselves first and make certain we release the contents of our cups daily. That is what our sister-friends are for. Our feelings shall set us free!

Nikki Shearer-Tilford

Meet Me in the Middle

I used to want the words "She tried" on my tomb-stone. Now I want "She did it."

Katherine Dunham

I'll never forget my first African dance class with the Ko-Thi Dance Company. I was a timid college student and the instructor was a kindhearted, strong-willed woman named Ferne Caulker, who took me under her wing and taught me a thing or two about my culture—and myself.

That very first class is where my schooling began. We learned several dances and just as the class was nearing the end, the instructor moved everyone into a large circle.

Uh oh, what is this? I was cool with the line dances and the group dances—the ones we did in unison—but this dance was different. This dance was freestyle and called for each of us to dance into the middle—by ourselves—to show our own personal moves. As the drummers' pace and volume began to increase so did my anxiety. Ferne explained that in Africa individuality was highly prized, and solo dancing in the middle of the circle was a way to "let your soul out" and "show your own beautiful self—*to shine.*"

Hmmmmm. I don't think so. I was beyond petrified and figured it was time to leave, and that is exactly what I did. I glanced at my watch, acted surprised that time had passed so quickly, grabbed my things and left without even seeing the circle dance and hoping no one was the wiser. I wasn't about to get out into the middle and "shine" or *whatever.* I had spent years perfecting my style of fitting in called "the blend," and I wasn't about to pull out from the crowd and draw attention to myself now.

Of course, Ferne saw it differently. The next time I went to class, toward the end—just when I thought we'd made it through without the circle dance—she made the loud call for the dancers to make a change, "Eh, eh!" Without missing a beat, she grabbed my hand, and circled the dancers up. As I tried to imagine how I was going to sneak out this time, the drummers accompanying the class began to beat the drums even more passionately, and what I saw in that circle took my breath away. Wow! There were several people who were born in Africa taking the class, and you could see that this was truly their favorite part. Before the explanation of solo dancing was even finished, they began taking their moves to the center with wild abandon. I watched in astonishment at their boldness and their beautiful movements done in sync with the drums—and even more so, at their *joy.* They *loved* to "shine," and shine they did. They were sparkling!

It was then that it occurred to me that "the blend" was strictly born of the *American* part of my culture, and perhaps there was something to experiencing this aspect of my *African* heritage. This was an *African* dance class, after all.

Almost as if my hips were willing me forward—I know now that it was my soul—I started to move into the middle. I moved slowly at first, afraid of what would happen when I abandoned my highly perfected ability to blend and discovered what it truly meant to be myself—to sparkle and shine like a brilliant diamond. What would those around me do and say as I stepped out and up? What would they think?

My heart kept beat with the drums, as my head, my thoughts and my fears were simply suspended. My consciousness was entirely in my body—in the way my feet met the earth, my braids jumped with my body, my hips moved seductively to the beat, my lungs took in the air and my brown skin glistened with beads of sweat. Over the frenzy of the drums, I heard my sister and brother dancers shouting their encouragement, yelling my name repeatedly. They whooped and hollered and clapped around me while watching my moves. Even though they surrounded me, forming the circle, I could feel them in the middle *with* me—smiling, laughing, pounding, stirring, planting, harvesting. They shared my joy, while I shared our ancestry.

I moved to the edge of the circle as the next dancer entered, I yelled her name and clapped my appreciation, encouraging her along with the other dancers. As the dance came to an end, I took note of how I felt. It was as if my consciousness just moved back into my head, and I needed to assess any damage I may have endured from this act of boldness. At one with the other dancers, all I felt was joy, power, beauty and strength. Ironically, expressing our individuality seemed to unify us.

That was many years ago, and I have since gone on to become an African dance teacher myself. Following in Ferne's footsteps, I instruct brothers and sisters of all cultures to find their inner beat and share their moves in the center of the circle.

I invite *you* to join us.

I'll turn you away from the mirrors and encourage you to look *inside* at how you *feel* instead of outside at how you *think* you *look*.

I'll grab your hand and call out loudly, "Eh, eh!" to let you know it is time to change. Smiling, I'll pull you and the other dancers into a circle, anticipating what is coming next. I'll move to the center and beckon you to join me, knowing you will never be the same.

"Come," I'll say with my head held high and my hips moving to the beat. "Let your soul out! Show us your beautiful self! Come. Let us shine!"

You'll meet me in the middle—and that is where I'll *truly* meet you, too.

Yes, meet me in the middle and we'll dance. . . .

Connie Bennett

The Dreadful Story

I've *learned to take me for myself and to treat myself with a great deal of love and a great deal of respect 'cause I like me. . . . I think I'm kind of cool.*

Whoopi Goldberg

I vividly recall the first time my mama sat me in a tub to rinse that Ultra Sheen lye-based permanent-relaxer out of my head. "What'cha doin' to the child's head?!" Daddy asked.

"Her hair is too thick and nappy! This'll help me manage this mess!" Mama resolutely responded.

"She's too young for all that in her head!" Daddy pressed.

"No, I got my hair relaxed when I was even younger!" Mama tilted my head back under the tub faucet to rinse out the smelly, caustic gook.

"But—she's fine just like she is, and I. . . ."

"Well, it's too late now," Mama said as she began my lye cleansing–deactivating shampoo. "And I'm the one who has to try to get through this child's long, thick head of hair every day!"

"You gonna do her sister's hair like that, too?" Daddy asked.

"No." Mama lathered my hair. Her fingers stung into my tenderized, chemically softened scalp. I winced silently.

"Good!" Daddy sounded relieved.

"Well, her sister doesn't need it. She has good hair," Mama said matter-of-factly.

"Mama," I whispered having just received the revelation regarding my naughty hair.

"Yes, baby?" Mama answered tenderly as she tilted me back into the cool stream of the tub faucet.

"Am I gonna have *good hair* now, too?" I asked, in search of something "good" out of the strange hair ritual I'd just endured.

"Yes, baby," Mama assured me.

I smiled, squinting my eyes closed to ignore the burning, stinging pain that had been circling the edges of my right ear throughout the process.

The next day all the little girls in my kindergarten class wanted to touch my long silky braids. I felt so pretty . . . despite my scabbing, throbbing ear. My mother had neglected to put enough gel (grease, really) on my right ear before she began relaxing my hair. The lye had been left to sit directly on my ear, causing a nasty chemical burn. I didn't care though. My hair was being so "good."

"Lisa Bartley," my Afro-wearing teacher remarked with a tender smile, "Don't you look pretty today!"

"Thank you, Miss Jackson!" I gleamed.

About thirty years later, I got up one day and looked at the smiling black beauties on my box of Dark and Lovely permanent-relaxer. I looked past their smiles into their eyes, then into the mirror. Those who have known me for a number of years know that I have gone from color to color, style to style, and in and out and back again with my hair. I'm an artist at heart and my head has been a special kind of canvas of self-expression. I've always *loved* trying out different hairstyles. I have sported various relaxed styles, the infamous "flip," braids, the "bone-straight" look, twists, and so on. I was, however, growing weary of the eternal process of trying to maintain so-called "good hair" status.

I began to dread having my hair done . . . when all of sudden it occurred to me, perhaps I *should* "dread" having my hair done! I tossed out my Dark and Lovely, turned up my Bob Marley *Legend* CD, grabbed my beeswax, and went to work on the first step of "locking" my hair. I began by sectioning it into individual single-strand twists of hair that I rolled into separate sections with sticky dollops of beeswax. I was so engaged in what I was doing that time passed quickly, even though it was six hours later when I smiled broadly at the results—a head full of dreads. Of course it would take another six weeks for them to really begin to tighten, get nappy and all "locked up," but in the meantime, as I looked in the mirror, singing right along with Marley (for the hundredth time that day), I nodded my absolute approval.

The next day at work, people kept looking at my hair, but they didn't say much. I chuckled on the inside at their perplexed sideways glances. They were white, mostly middle-aged or older folks. They knew something looked different because I usually wore my hair in relaxed, silky little twists. At this point, my hair appeared basically the same as the twists but subtly different. Things really developed as my hair began to lock up. I could tell that they could not really figure it out. They would look, and some would even make awkward attempts to ask me about it, but I felt *free!* I felt even better than I had felt that first day at school after my first relaxer, and this time there were no burns. Imagine that! I had never been so happy with my hair, my skin and my nature—my authenticity. I felt like a queen . . . a God-crowned queen!

My hair has become my own personal study on culture, on human nature and sisterhood. On a regular basis, I have people of all races stop me and comment on my hair. It's funny sometimes. I never anticipated this. White people don't know what to think—nor do they seem to care all that much. Black people have a more complex reaction. Many are pretty cool about it, even if they would never go "that far" with their own heads. Some are downright hostile. I think it makes them self-conscious or something, but that is their issue, not mine. Many people sport dreads these days, but obviously not so many that they have completely emerged from an enigmatic status.

Recently, I was walking into the grocery store and a sharp sista stopped and said, "GURRRRLLLLLLLLL! I just LOVE your hair! Now, *that* is truly beautiful!"

She was with her man, who was also sharp, and he smiled in agreement.

I said, "Why thank you, Sista! I LOVE your hair, too!"

Now as I look back upon the journey my hair has taken, it seems Daddy knew something about the beauty of African American women's hair that perhaps even we women didn't know—we are naturally beautiful, and we all already have *good hair*. We have the hair that the Creator chose to crown us with. That's good enough for me.

Lisa Bartley-Lacey

Gluttony to Glory

If you want to do better today than you did yesterday, you simply must believe you deserve it.

Iyanla Vanzant

Growing up in the heart of the Midwest, I was always labeled the "fat kid"—the kid with fewer friends, the biggest clothes and always the last to get picked on a team during recess. In every child-oriented social surrounding, whether it was drill team or Brownie troops, I stood out. This had nothing to do with my being black, but everything to do with my corpulent dimension. Things were so out of hand that my family bestowed on me the derogatory nickname "pig" as a way to describe me and my excessive eating habits.

I was raised by my great-grandmother, who would break my sleep on Saturday mornings with the smells of crispy Southern fried chicken, fluffy homemade buttermilk biscuits, dark country gravy and butter-colored rice. This was just breakfast—imagine what dinner was like! You see, Grandma was what you call ol' school; she was not one for a bunch of mushy words, so cooking was one of her many ways of telling me she loved me. I adored this particular type of love, to the point where I allowed it to sculpt my life (and my figure), as if it were my god.

Grandma passed away by the time I reached high school. During my senior year I was weighing way over two hundred pounds and wearing a size twenty-four. I didn't give my size much thought during my last year of high school. I really thought things had turned around for me when the "Denzel Washington" of Central High asked me to the prom. I felt as if I had grown wings and was about to sit beside God on the throne. Unbeknownst to me, I had graduated from the fat kid to the "fat chick." These are the words he heard when he told our peers he was taking me to prom. As I sat at home waiting for him to pick me up, all dolled up and looking as fine as I possibly could look, I watched the clock and waited and waited. With each passing moment my heart cracked a little more. He stood me up, and my emotions were now aflame. It was then that I discovered how much food would ease my pain. With each bite I became numb. Every time I'd chew I'd feel comfort and relief. Food quickly became my best friend, my lover and a way to ease the pain. With each painful experience came a reason to binge. The need to binge would take over if I didn't get a promotion, if someone hurt my feelings, if I had a bad day at work, school, salon—it didn't matter. I would binge at such a high rate, my body would give it back, and I'd see my comfort go down the toilet. Food was something I was sure would never hurt me, so I thought. At the age of thirty I was weighing over three hundred pounds and rocking a size twenty-eight dress.

It was at that point that my best friend, Zelema, who is thirty years older than I, gave me the weight talk. She informed me that there had to be deeper issues that were causing me to eat. In the beginning I didn't want to hear it, because after high school I was sent to what people call a "fat farm," with head shrinks and nurses roaming the floors. In other words, the Eating Disorder Unit at a local hospital. It hadn't worked then, and I didn't want to hear it now. But this was different. The words of wisdom and support were coming from someone who loved me and whom I loved. I pressured myself to stop and listen because she had been my umbrella during many storms and wouldn't lie to me. Zelema is president of a college and has that take-charge attitude, anyway, but she got me when she said, "I'll stick by you every ounce of the way." I knew it wasn't going to be easy because I have the common, black woman's figure—the big hips, legs, breasts and butt . . . all there. All willing to stay!

Over the course of six years I've lost over one hundred pounds and gone down to a size fourteen. I got smaller by eating right, exercising and getting rid of the emotional pain. Though I had lost weight and was looking great, this didn't stop prom night from happening again eighteen years later. I was dumped again by another pretty boy who thought I was too fat, but he added a new twist; he called me ugly as well. Granted, I'm no supermodel, neither am I Medusa. I could feel my heart beating the power of a thousand African drums and my temperature rising to that same number. My big brown eyes were filled with water, and my light brown skin was the color of a beet. Zelema begged me not to resort to food as comfort, but eventually I did. Then the spirits of Mary and Martha came over me, and the weeping ended. I hit the gym harder and cut out even more fattening foods from my diet. I lost another twenty pounds. This enabled me to wear more appealing clothes; my cheekbones became Pikes Peak; my cocoa brown skin became flawless, without a blemish. Five months later, I ran into my second "prom date" in the ritzy part of town. The sight of me brought a hungry gleam to his eyes, and two rows of small pearls appeared across his freckled face. He wants me back; I can see and feel it. However, I won't be having that! I lost the weight and gained a lot of self-dignity in its place! It was then I realized I had fallen in love with myself. Food was no longer my only option to deal with negative situations. I do not cry, nor run to Zelema for cover. I have finally grown into my own.

Lindale Banks

Getting Real

The day I looked at myself with a natural was the first time I liked what I saw.

Marita Golden

I was delighted and relieved when the Afro first became popular. For me, it meant instant deliverance from the tyranny of the straightening comb that had not only pressed my unwieldy hair for years, but pressed me, as well, into believing that I had little recourse except to burn myself often to be beautiful. Finally, I could relax and be my natural black self.

Mother, however, did not share my elation at this new development. In fact, when she came home one day and caught first sight of my woolly head, she dropped both of her grocery bags, and it was not immediately clear if the wail she emitted originated in her throat or from somewhere deep in the recesses of her soul. Even after I had wiped up the last remnants of broken eggs and spilt chocolate milk from the floor, Mother was still fuming well into the night.

At first I assumed that her initial overreaction would be

just a temporary thing, but as time went on, it became increasingly clear that adapting to the new "bush" hairdo was not an item on Mom's to-do list. And when I parted my coarse hair down the middle the next day and wore an Afro puff on each side of my head, it just about pushed Mother over the edge. In fact, she refused to speak to me for several days, and when she did, it was with such an enduring sadness, one might have thought that there had been a death in the house.

"White folks," she murmured one morning, finally emerging from her long silence, "never even knew y'all hair was that bad," as if its true texture was some awful secret that people without color had to be kept safe from. "It's an abomination, and I, Rena Davis Mitchell, will never stoop to wearing my hair like 'that'!" she announced before retreating to her room.

Mother simply couldn't fathom that I had grown tired of living in constant anxiety of drizzly August days, of sudden spring showers. Tired of frying hair late into the night only to sweat it right back to where it started in our un-air-conditioned house, my hair on loan as it were, like Cinderella's pumpkin at midnight. Tired of living out of sync with a universe that had already designed us without flaw, except that no black voice had ever affirmed that to me. Tired of the weekly scalp fry that transformed me into what I was not and could never be, or more specifically, what I could be for a few days or so—provided the humidity didn't rise or, God forbid, the rickety window fan didn't sputter and tap out.

The judging starts very early on when black mothers, grandmas and aunties gather crib-side to gauge the tenuous texture of their newborn's hair on some obscure scale, where kudos are reserved only for the softer-haired ones—hushed silences for all others. It is here that first fears are sealed. To deny the truth about oneself, I thought, was to deny one's own heritage, one's very DNA, the true essence of one's being.

Still, on some level, I couldn't fully blame Mother for her archaic beliefs. After all, in her day, she had few, if any, positive black role models to emulate. She, like most of the black women I knew, lived most of her adult life in hiding.

"We, as women," she often insisted, "must suffer to be beautiful." In her mind, that meant burning the hair to the quick and limiting access to anyone who might see it in its natural state. When I looked around, I observed that many of the women in our family perpetuated the same myth by hiding their hair beneath turbans or wigs.

Then it happened. I came home one day to discover that Mom had done the unthinkable—shaved her head totally bald. When I saw her, I immediately backpedaled, out of the front door, fearful that I had finally pushed my poor mother to the brink. She calmly explained that her childhood friend Eunice had lost most of her hair to cancer treatments. Mother apparently had decided she wanted to be there for Miss Eunice in a big way, so in a drastic move, shaved off her own hair. It was no small feat for a black woman to sport a shaved head in the '60s, least of all for my mother.

Amazingly, through it all, something wonderful began to emerge. By helping her friend, mother was forced to wrestle with her beliefs about her own beauty. I spied her on occasion observing herself in the mirror, slowly coming to terms with the budding, coarse strands she saw there. I took full advantage of this precious time to encourage her. I helped condition and nurture her and Miss Eunice's hair. This was a special time for them and for me. I eavesdropped on their adult chatter, drank from their wisdom, admired the way their heads nodded in loving accord. I was awed by the beauty of Mom's selfless act, but also realized that it was a turning point for her. A confidence

I'd never seen before emerged in her. Even after we lost Miss Eunice, Mother still sported a lovely crop of natural hair, sometimes trimming it down to a regal skullcap. My mother, the eternal poster child for "bone-straight" hair, had become a trendsetter in her own right, instilling confidence among her family and peers, many of whom emulated her and retired their much-used straightening combs as well.

It is a muggy August morning. At daybreak, the same dew that clings to the pebbles scattered at our feet clings to us as well, to our bodies, to our natural hair. My mother and I stride along the silver stretch of beach for our morning walk—a daily ritual. Years ago each of us might have spent these precious moments in quiet desperation rifling through our bags for a plastic rain hat to shield us from the truth we knew would come. Today no such thoughts intrude on our communion with each other. Today we affirm our Creator's knowing hand in his creation. Today we hold our heads high with nothing hampering us, and stride boldly, in our magnificence, into dew-dropping day.

Elaine K. Green

Crown of Splendor

When I look at my mother and her sister-friends
Exchanging their wisdom,
Treasuring their memories,
Laughing so hard,
They end up shedding tears
Entrusting their secrets
Sharing their fears
Becoming wiser more than older
Experiencing new things,
Becoming bolder.

I adore
Their splendor.

This too, is what Solomon must have done,
For he writes in Proverbs 16:31
"Gray hair is a crown of splendor;
It is attained by a righteous life."

As I look at the silver that surrounds my mother's face,
She proudly wears her crown of splendor,
She says, "It's not just gray, it's grace."

It's proof that I've lived and am still living,
Making the most of the life I've been given.
That's why we encourage daughters when
Their faith is shaken.
We know the rewards of the road
Less taken.
We want our daughters to attain their own crown of
    splendor.
We dedicate our lives to be your teacher and defender.
Attaining this crown doesn't come by chance or a whim.
It's a result of a life dedicated to him.
That's why we're examples not in word,
But in deed.
You represent fertile soil into which
We plant our wisdom seed.
Look at your image in the mirror,
And I hope you see me."

As I look at my reflection,
I see my crown of splendor is slowly heading my direction.

As I stroke my few strands of gray,
Or rather grace,
I see my mother and her sister-friend's face,
Exchanging their wisdom,
Treasuring their memories,
Laughing so hard,
They end up shedding tears,
Entrusting their secrets,
Sharing their fears.
Becoming wiser more than older,
Experiencing new things,
Becoming bolder.

They adore
Their splendor.

I adore
Their splendor.

Royalty surrounds me.

Sheila P. Spencer

Birth of a Nappy Hair Affair

We teach you to love the hair God gave you.

Malcolm X

More than eight years ago, I had my first affair for women with nappy hair. It was intended to be a simple hair-grooming session, an opportunity for me and my girl-friends to get together on a Sunday afternoon and do our own hair.

There were some who thought I was trying to revive an African tradition, but as much as I embrace some traditions of the motherland, what I had in mind when I decided to have a gathering wasn't that deep. All I wanted to do was offer a place for my friends who wear African-inspired and natural hairstyles to be among kindred spirits and come get their hair done for free.

At my house their unapologetically nappy heads would not stand out in the crowd. On that one afternoon they could be assured they would have majority status. At my house their royal crowns would be the rule, not the exception.

I also had selfish reasons for sponsoring the gathering. I wanted to take a trip back to my childhood. I missed the moments of bonding when the females in our house got together to do hair.

I am not talking about the traumatic Saturday night rituals when my mother fried our hair in preparation for church on Sunday morning. That's when the sight of her brandishing the hot comb, the hissing sound it made when it came into contact with my grease-laden hair and the peculiar smell of something burning on my head made me wish I was born bald.

What I missed were the more natural moments, when my mother placed her healing hands directly on my head. I remembered how comforting it was nestling between her strong knees as she oiled and massaged my scalp with her fingers before brushing, combing and arranging my hair into a simple style of plaits or ponytails.

I would lean back, close my eyes and surrender to her firm but gentle touch.

Being the eldest daughter, I often did my younger sisters' hair, and when my mother was too tired to do her own, we would do it for her. Those were the times when we were closest. Having the hair affair would give me an opportunity to recreate such moments at my home with my extended family of sister-friends.

I got the idea one day at the office after listening to my friend and co-worker lament about how hard it was to find the right hairstylist to do her locks. As a temporary solution I suggested that she come to my house so we could do each other's hair. I told her I knew other women with similar concerns, so we could make it a communal affair.

I decided to have it on the third Sunday in May. It was an experiment. I didn't really know what to expect. I never imagined that eight years later I would still be having what has now come to be known as Hair Day.

Hair Day has evolved into much more than grooming sessions. At these gatherings my sister-friends and I form a circle of solidarity and support. We celebrate our hair through storytelling and poetry readings and endless testimonials about our journey to appreciate ourselves as we really are. Hair Day is a time when my friends come to relax. They come to talk and sometimes vent about those who have judged them harshly for their choice to be themselves.

Our circle is an eclectic mix of Ivy League pedigrees and sisters with no degrees. We have mothers and daughters, women who work and women in transition. We have artists, writers, teachers and students, African dancers and sisters who drum.

My first hair affair intrigued my friends who wore perms. One even got offended when she didn't get an invitation. It wasn't that I had anything against her— some of my best friends wear perms.

"So is my hair not nappy enough?" Jean asked me. For obvious reasons I didn't think she'd be interested in attending, but she knew that I invited another friend, Karen, who also wears a perm.

"My hair is nappier than hers," Jean whined, and to prove it she proceeded to part her relaxed hair with her fingers to show me her new growth.

I couldn't believe I was actually watching a straight-haired sister trying to out-nap another straight-haired sister.

I was flattered and amused. Jean wanted so much to be invited to my nappy hair affair that she tried to produce enough kinks to qualify for admission. I told her that wasn't necessary and invited her to come anyway.

She never showed up but twenty others did. At three o'clock, women with skin kissed by the sun gathered in my backyard on that warm spring Sunday afternoon and transformed it into a garden of locks and twists, Bantu knots, braids and Afros in full bloom. To set the tone I posted a sign in the kitchen:

"Welcome to my Happy Nappy Hair Care Affair. Make yourself at home."

"Find a seat on a chair on the floor. Help yourself to whatever you brought to eat, but don't bother me because I'm getting my hair 'done.' So you best find someone to do yours."

The message was clear. This was an unstructured, self-serve hair-care affair. My home is a no-shoe zone, and my guests seemed more than willing to shed their footwear and get on common ground. They deposited their potluck dishes in the kitchen then returned to the backyard where they gravitated toward my deck. They briefly exchanged greetings then moved quickly into conversations about hair.

Every conceivable topic was covered. They swapped hair-care recipes, how witch hazel reduces buildup in locks and how lemon juice keeps them tight. They shared hair taboo and superstitions.

Eventually the women got around to what the gathering was all about. They chose partners and got busy grooming hair. We worked to the sounds of reggae, merengue and jazz.

It was beautiful. Some worked while standing, others sat in stair-step fashion, palm rolling, twisting or otherwise fussing over the head of the person in front of them. Their arms were extended like branches of a family tree and moving nonstop. Watching them work reminded me of the painting *Links and Lineage*. The painting by Paul Goodnight, a Boston-based artist, depicts a family tree of black women—from the elderly matriarch to the youngest girl—engaged in the ritual of grooming each other's hair. What was happening on my back deck was like seeing

Goodnight's painting come to life.

Denise, one of the "token permies," was so moved by what she was witnessing that afternoon that she asked for us to take her back to her roots. She asked me for a pair of scissors.

"Does anyone know how to cut hair?" she asked. She insisted that one of us cut away all traces of her relaxed hair.

Annette, a willowy artist, accepted the challenge and took the scissors. Now, the only real experience Annette had cutting hair was when she cut her own locks and used them in her artwork.

Denise wasn't worried. "If there was ever a time to do this, it is today," she said as she settled into a chair.

Annette handled Denise's head like it was a sculpture in progress. For most of an hour Annette meticulously snipped and shaped until all that was left on Denise's head was a short, wooly layer of virgin hair, softly framing her face.

It was a nappy work of art, which drew applause from the sisters who watched from the sidelines and a warm hug from Denise, who was ecstatic over her new natural look.

"I feel good," she squealed as she peered into the mirror. "I feel light. . . . I feel free."

Watching Denise's transformation after Annette's shearing was a powerful moment. I didn't want the evening to end. Apparently my friends didn't either. The last one left at 1:30 A.M.

As I said, I had no grand intentions when I had my first Hair Day. I didn't even think beyond the first one. Yet it evolved into something more than I ever thought it would be.

Now everyone has gotten into the act. Brothers and children also join us for a little nap nurturing and my Hair Day gatherings have spread to many cities in the United States and abroad. My hair affair has become a real family affair. And that's all good.

Linda Jones

4

MY SISTER, MY FRIEND

These women heal us by telling us their stories, by embodying emotion that our everydays can't hold.

Elisabeth Alexander

A Cup of Tenderness

Beloved, you are my sister, you are my daughter, you are my face; you are me.

Toni Morrison

I could feel my cheeks burning a fiery pink in the January wind as I scraped the glacier of ice from my windshield. What was left of the warmth in my hands slowly turned to tingle as the crusty ice chips melted on my gloves. Once I had scraped a few basketball-sized holes to peer out of, I scooted into the driver's seat, grateful to grab my steaming mug of coffee from the roof of the car. I cupped it between my frozen fingers and breathed in slowly. This was the daily moment of truth.

"Come on, gal," I said, touching my hand to the dash and adding a silent prayer for good measure.

Her protests were louder than usual; the Oldsmobile engine sounded more like a horse neighing than any modern mode of transportation. She sounded like I felt. It was clear she needed a cup of tender loving care. *I wish I could afford to give it to you, gal,* I thought. I pumped a little gas and turned the key once again. Again she faltered. Third time's a charm I allowed myself to hope and once again turned the key. The engine growled to life, and I pumped the gas quickly—just enough to keep her hungry engine-belly full, but not enough to kill her.

It was getting harder and harder to hope that she would last.

Hardship, however unwelcome, was not new to me. I grew up in the Appalachian Mountains, a culture of hard knocks, hard work and hard winters. When I was seven my father orphaned the children in our family by killing my mother in an alcoholic rage and then turning the gun on himself. I grew up in my native Appalachia with first one relative and then another, but I learned how to cope. It was a rough place, at times devoid of tenderness, but I had survived it. This year, however, made those times feel like pleasant memories.

My dear husband of twenty-five years, Roger, was fighting for his life in a cold city hospital bed. I wanted more than anything to be able to stay in the hospital with him, to encourage him and to soothe the pain he was enduring daily from his treatments for leukemia. But the illness did not make the pressures of the world disappear. My son was still at home, a senior in high school, and he needed to be fed. The electricity bill had to be paid, the house payment had to be made, and gas had to be put in the tank for my nearly one-hundred mile daily round trip from home to work to hospital. I was beginning to feel the way I had when I was a child. It was all up to me, and I was alone. And so I went to work every day, rolling out of the chair at the hospital where I had spent the night with Roger, or rolling out of bed at 4:00 A.M. at home where I had done some laundry and tried to make time for my son over a dinner of sandwiches. By lunchtime each day I could drop wherever I stood. My body and soul longed for relief, for someone to offer a cup of tenderness to help refresh me.

I splashed water over my pale white face in the rest-room to revive me when I arrived at work; I didn't have to worry about smearing my makeup, no time for such luxuries in my life.

"Brenda."

I looked up to see my co-worker Darlene. Her chestnut-brown skin was furrowed with concern, and there was tenderness in her soft brown eyes. She cast one furtive glance over her shoulder and then she took my hand and pressed some tightly folded money into it. I looked at it in astonishment. I opened my mouth to say something, but she wouldn't let me. "Do not tell anyone I gave you this money," she said. "Just go and get your car fixed, and let me know if you need any more." And then she turned and left.

My astonishment was soon replaced by wonder. I knew very little about Darlene. As so often happens with people from my generation, the few friends I had were white. Darlene and I were from different worlds. I had grown up in the Appalachians where African Americans did not live, and where prejudice and hatred thrived. The high school I had graduated from still carried the mascot name "Rebels" and marched onto the field under a Confederate flag. And although I did not consider myself racist or prejudiced, I became aware of how isolated I was from people who were not like me. Darlene had looked beyond my white skin, beyond my Southern accent and seen the need not just for financial support but the true need I had that lay beneath the surface—she had stepped over the invisible boundary, and she became my friend.

As the months passed our friendship thrived; although I must admit she was the strong one. Her support was unwavering when my beloved Roger died. She offered a cup of tenderness each time I was down, and when the dating scene started calling my name again we shared hours of laughter and a few tears over dates turned sour. Darlene never mentioned the money again and never asked me to repay it. I began to feel like I had known Darlene my whole life. Like an early morning mist, our cultural differences evaporated.

Darlene was my teacher; she educated me about love. Darlene stepped across the chasm of racial prejudice and the unknown that so often divides us to teach me that we have a responsibility to the human race to provide a cup of tenderness when and where it is needed most. And because of Darlene, my cup runneth over.

Brenda Caperton

Sistahood

Family faces are mirrors. Looking at people who belong to us, we see the past, present and future.
                              Gail Lurnet Buckley

When I was a child, I hung onto my big sister's every word. To me, she was Nefertiti, ebony and regal, and I tried to be her kindred spirit at any cost. Recently, I was reminded of that when I saw a copy of the print *Sistahood* by the African American artist Charles Bibbs. It was as if that painting triggered long ago memories, a family wish list that had to do more with emotions than things of materialistic values. It whispered to me thoughts about my own sistahood with my sister, whose love had been signed, sealed and delivered from the time her four-year-old fingers touched the ballooning expanse of our mother's belly to feel me.

When my sister became as "grown as she wanted to be," the term the elder women in the family used to christen teenage girls, words began to latch on to me about our comparison. "She's got some beautiful black skin," or "Those big eyes of hers are gonna make some man walk into a brick wall," or "She's got that fine hair that makes pressin' it a breeze." We were a study in contrasts, but I didn't mind. I was proud that she was my big sister, enjoying running home to our mother to brag about how many fellows whistled, winked, and nearly ran into that brick wall because of their flirting with her.

We lived in a Brooklyn housing project on the fifth floor. We shared a back bedroom with two twin French provincial beds filling up the expanse of the room. As the introverted one, it was more my haven than my sister's. While she seemed to want to escape the confines of our bedroom and our apartment, I longed to be in it with my books and my imagination. When she was not there, I would try on her clothes, her new shades of dime store nail polish and eye shadow, and most of all sneak and read the latest entry in her diary. Her life was more interesting than mine, and I assumed it would always be that way. She was the one who took modeling classes and drama classes and joined all of those black awareness clubs in the community. She was the one who wrote about Afro-wearing boys walking her home from school and giving her a tender kiss. It didn't matter, though, because I knew that even if my sister's life dared her to journey in a different direction, she'd never abandon me. Our sistahood was nonnegotiable, or so I thought.

When I finally caught up with my sister and became the woman that I now am, I realized that we had done nothing to safeguard our sistahood. Somewhere between our marriages, our children, our careers and even our painful storms, we lost track of each other. We came together for family functions or other social occasions, but we seemed to do a dance of pretense. "She's the writer in the family," my sister would often brag to one of our long-time-no-see relatives or a sister-friend she happened to bring with her. But she often only heard about what I had published through the grapevine, through our mother who made a point of calling each of us each day. We sidestepped the fact that sometimes we didn't speak to each other for six months at a time. We shrugged it off to being busy that neither of us knew the color schemes of each other's living room, what photos were in each other's family albums, or what home-cooked aromas filled each other's kitchen on a Sunday afternoon.

Other women had become our sisters throughout the years. Other women had begun to fill up those sisterly spaces once reserved for each other. We shared our tumultuous storms with those sisters we had adopted along the way instead of letting each other's arms be the familial balm that they were intended to be. It was my sister's adopted sisters who were there to help her heal after years of domestic abuse at the hands of her ex-husband. It was my adopted sisters who helped me heal from the pain and the shame after my two sons, her nephews, were incarcerated. Wasn't it our mother who instilled in us that blood was thicker than water? Didn't movies like *Soul Food* inspire us to renew and rekindle what we once shared because we were all we had?

It would have probably remained that way, our sistahood fragmented, if our mother hadn't become critically ill. She had been suffering from a debilitating heart condition for years, and her prognosis wasn't good. When the doctors finally told us that our mother had only days to live, my sister and I began a vigil in her hospital room. We talked about everything, but it was talking about childhood memories that lessened our pain. We talked about those times that we wished could have lasted forever, knowing that we were beginning a new chapter in our life, life without our mother. "You remember when . . . Girl, I will never forget the time! . . ." our words long held began to freely tumble out. As our mother drifted off into a deep sleep, our conversations continued in the near-empty hospital cafeteria over a late meal that always ended with a piece of cake as we laughed about having our mother's sweet tooth. We began to realize how much we missed each other and how this was the best send-off we could give our mother.

After our mother died and we buried her beside our father, my sister and I knew we had an unfinished painting to complete, and we finally understood the process. True sistahood was an art. Its canvas had to be brush-stroked with the vibrant colors of our presence, the deepest hues of our forgiveness, and most of all the fiery splash of our love in order to become a masterpiece so aptly entitled, "Sistahood."

Jeanine DeHoney

Who Is Helping Whom?

How far you go in life depends on your being tender with the young, compassionate with the aged, sympathetic with the striving, and tolerant of the weak and strong. Because some day in life you will have been all these.

George Washington Carver

The apartment door unlocked as usual, I let myself in. Viola was not there, at least not where I typically found her, in her wheelchair in the living room. I followed the light through the half-opened bedroom door. There she sat on the floor beside her bed—with no way to get back up.

"Are you hurt?" I asked.

"No," she replied with a smile, "just my feelings."

I thought of my first visit as her physical therapist. She had been propped up in bed with a thick crocheted blanket over her two short stumps of legs. But no one would have noticed, she postured herself with such dignity.

I learned she had been the pastor of a church while she raised two girls and stood by an alcoholic husband. At night while her family slept, she remained on her knees. In the end they all prospered and called her blessed.

Years later, cut down by diabetes, her stature remained just as tall. In contrast, I had recently experienced my second divorce and the weight of it had bent me over. As I trudged along inner-city streets to provide home health care, seldom did I look up to smile at passersby. I felt more worthless than the local drug addicts.

"I'm so embarrassed," said Viola, bringing me back to her present needs. "Somehow, I just slipped off the side of my bed, but I'm fine, really I am," she said, her eyes bright. Despite her words, I knew she had landed with a terrible bump. Her hospital bed stood high off the floor, and she had had no way to break her fall.

I reached in her direction. "Let me help you."

"It might hurt your back to pick me up," she said, "and I don't want to be a burden to you." She seemed like Joan of Arc in the flames, more concerned about her executioner being burned than herself. "My son-in-law will soon be here to lift me."

Although my eyes gazed downward at her, my heart looked up to her. I realized she was debilitated in body, certainly, but not in spirit.

For many weeks I continued to provide therapy. As I exercised Viola's muscles, strength not only flowed into her body but into mine as well. Eventually she met all her treatment goals and the sessions ended—but not the friendship.

Like a moth around a Tiffany lamp, I was drawn to her radiant pecan-colored face. She spoke of her life and her family. When she spoke of her Lord, it was not as a preacher would, but as one who had had a personal encounter. I visited her often and even brought my children to absorb her light.

"What did you think about Viola?" I asked them.

"She is a lady without legs—but with love that can't be taken away," said Karin, my daughter, who liked to "sit at her feet" and listen to her talk.

"It wasn't what she said, Mom, it was how she said it," my son, Norm, added.

"Yes, I know," I said quietly. She called Norm "her boy." He brought her gifts and she served him lunch. Together they chatted like family.

In time the call came—Viola had passed away. It seemed as if the entire city turned out for her funeral service.

As they carried her casket past, I remembered the day she lay on the floor, from her operation only four-feet tall, but through her strength and conviction she was a giant in spirit. If this fine woman accustomed to preaching from a lofty pulpit could maintain her self-respect from a fallen, demeaning position, then surely so could I.

Imagine, I was hired to help assist and strengthen her when it was *my soul* that needed help, and *my strength* that was weak. As I sat with the seemingly thousands of lucky people who got to be in Viola's presence, I realized, that in her passing she gifted me with her faith, conviction and independence. She had opened the door of my caged soul and set me free.

I dried my tears and left the church ready to start again—it was in that moment that I noticed that I had already begun to stand up and stand out again, especially because I had the only white face in the congregation, and I felt right at home.

Margaret Lang

Merry Christmas, Emma

It's so clear that you have to cherish everyone. I think that's what I get from these older black women, that every soul is to be cherished, that every flower is to bloom.

Alice Walker

Emma was a seventy-year-old patient who received home care from our nursing agency. She lived alone in a three room, unpainted and uninsulated house that sat in the middle of a pasture just west of Shreveport, Louisiana. Six of the biggest, ugliest, hungriest mongrels in west Louisiana stood guard around her. Inside the pasture there were several cows and a bull, which all ran to the gate whenever we approached to make our weekly visits. The roads leading to the gate were unpaved, and the gate was made of logs and barbed wire. Opening the gate, driving through and closing the gate without letting the bovines loose was as great a challenge as finding the house in the first place! For this reason, we usually went in pairs.

Emma, who had no telephone, always tried to come out onto the porch when she heard us approaching. She warned us not to get out of the car until she got the dogs settled down. Emma would say, "That one there, that Jake, he'll eat you right up if you get out of that car before I tell you to!" We never tested the truth of that statement.

Once the dogs calmed down we could begin whatever work we intended to do. We visited every week or two to draw blood samples for lab work and to evaluate the status of her condition, multiple myeloma.

One of Emma's three rooms was a huge kitchen, housing a massive wooden table and nothing else. All her cooking was done on a potbellied stove in the living room. This little black, cast-iron heater was fueled by coal or with logs from nearby woods. Every time we visited her, whether in the scorching heat of August or in the chilly damp of December, she had a pan of cornbread cooking on top of that little stove. "That is for the dogs," she always said. Her bed had no sheets and only one rough blanket with U.S. Army stamped on it. She was tall and thin, as brown as chocolate and as imperious as a queen. Visits to her were the highlights of our weeks, and we watched helplessly as her health and strength waned.

When Thanksgiving came she was admitted to the hospital for blood transfusions. We visited her every day, as our office was on the ground floor of the hospital. Her Thanksgiving dinner was almost untouched, but she ate what she could.

After the transfusions she went home again, and our first December visit found her rolled up in that one blanket in that cold and drafty little house. The little stove would never be enough to keep her warm, especially with the blood condition she had.

We nurses chose her as our Christmas Angel that year, the one whom, out of our many patients, we most wanted to recognize. We all chipped in and bought her a set of flannel sheets and another blanket and pillow, planning to take them out on the next visit. However, the following week she called us from the doctor's office and told us not to come as he was drawing blood for the lab work for that week. She wept as she told us that she had paid someone half of her monthly check to take her to the grocery store and to the doctor, and that somewhere between the two places she had lost her purse and what was left of her money. We decided then to make a special trip right before Christmas to take the gifts.

The week before Christmas we wrapped the things we already had and added a flannel gown, a woolly robe, some fuzzy slippers, a nightcap, a pair of gloves and a pretty book. The day before our planned visit her doctor called and said he had received her lab report and was going to readmit her to the hospital and try to keep her through Christmas.

On Christmas Eve we decided to take her gifts upstairs to her hospital room rather than wait till Christmas Day, as most of us would be off duty then. We filed into her room singing "We Wish You a Merry Christmas," and laid the gifts on her bed.

As she opened the first one she said, "Y'all don't know this, but this is the first wrapped-up present I ever got." She lingered over each pretty package and caressed each item as she unwrapped it, trying on the ones she could. She kept the nightcap on.

Before we left one of the nurses asked about the care of the dogs. Emma said her landlord was throwing food over the fence for them, she guessed. The nurse who lived nearest to Emma said, "I'll send my husband out with some food for the dogs if you think they won't eat him up!"

Emma grinned and lowered her eyes. "Aw, them dogs wouldn't hurt nobody. I just tell folks that. Keeps the bad peoples away." As we left she said, "Merry Christmas, y'all."

When we came back to work the day after Christmas we were glad we had given Emma her gifts when we did, for we learned that during the night on Christmas Eve, she had gone home—to her final home.

Emma lived her life standing tall on her feet in the face of adversity, and she died with great dignity, without a whimper. Never once during our service to her did she utter a word of complaint about her feelings, her living conditions or her station in life. Her gracious acceptance of her first wrapped-up presents and her last words to us, "Merry Christmas, y'all," were gifts far more precious than anything we could have bought for her in her last days with us.

Mary Saxon Wilburn

Elegant Ladies . . . Again

The kind of beauty I want most is the hard-to-get kind that comes from within—strength, courage, dignity.

Ruby Dee

When we were young, my sisters and I used to leaf through magazines choosing outfits for ourselves and each other. We loved pretty clothes. I have a hazy memory of taking an oath over cherry Kool-Aid and brownies to become elegant ladies when we grew up.

Now, years later, I was returning home, a divorce statistic at thirty-four. I had a résumé patched with a fragmented college education and dead-end jobs. I also had two little girls to support and two suitcases between us. Dreams of elegance had been long forgotten.

Except for the occasional phone call and one brief get-together, my younger sisters and I were well-intentioned strangers who'd led separate lives for almost thirteen years. They didn't know that I still cried at sappy movies. I didn't know if one still had a childlike delight in wishing upon stars or if the other still loved to lounge in a hot tub like an undiscovered pearl. My sisters had stepped forward with their hearts open and arms outstretched when I called home.

They bought our eastbound train tickets and promised to be waiting. As my daughters and I traveled through golden California, I tried to remember what my sisters and I used to talk about. As the scenery gradually passed from arid to the wildflower-dotted fields of Pennsylvania, I wondered what we used to laugh about. I couldn't even remember how to laugh.

They had told me to send my clothes ahead, but I couldn't bear for my sisters to unpack my meager wardrobe. My secondhand jeans and T-shirts represented how I felt about myself: too tired to care, struggling to hold my girls and myself together by mere threads.

As we stepped off the train, Jan and Sue were there. Glowing. Beautiful. Perfect.

"Kar! Look at how much those little girls have grown! Give me some love!" Well, some things hadn't changed. As my sisters swooped on my little family, tears and laughter intermingled as easily as clouds drifting across a summer sky.

"Wow! Do you two dress like this all the time?" Their carefully accessorized outfits awakened a twinge of pure feminine longing. My confidence waned a little bit more.

No husband. No money. No style. Jan and Sue didn't seem to notice. They hustled the girls and me to the car and into our new lives. During this difficult transition period, they helped me cobble together a suitable wardrobe for job interviews. I, who was accustomed to drying children's tears and holding their hands, needed my hand held and my tears dried as I stumbled into a new womanhood. And, gradually, I remembered how to laugh.

One Saturday night, their heads popped into the bedroom.

"We're going out. Secret mission. We're not taking 'no' for an answer."

The kids were fine with a babysitter, so I reluctantly accompanied them. I loved my sisters, but I felt awkward compared to their casual chic. They took me to a mall, straight to a trendy women's boutique, the kind I'd avoided for years. Who had money for the latest fashion when invariably a child needed money for a class trip or a classmate's birthday gift? I dutifully followed in their wake, sighing at the prices. They stopped in front of a sweater rack.

Jan held out a pink sweater. Sue draped a blue one over my shoulders. I frowned at the beautiful garments and batted them away.

"Stop it! Buy something so we can go." If I'd wanted to be embarrassed, I could've stayed home and studied my checkbook. They barricaded my exit, one on either side. Jan took my hands.

"Listen, Kar, if you don't start loving yourself enough to buy something new occasionally, how are you going to teach those daughters of yours to love themselves?"

Well, damn! Knock me over with a steamroller, why don't you? Even as I opened my mouth to say something really nasty, I realized she was right. Sue nodded in agreement. As tears welled in my eyes, I realized that my sisters loved me enough to do this.

I bought a midnight-purple sweater swirled with different colors—one that made me feel elegant and beautiful. Even more surprising, I felt a twinge of worthiness creeping over me.

I hugged them both, gratefully, for a feeling that had long eluded me.

Jan whispered, "Elegance is an inside job; the outside stuff is how you *celebrate* your elegance." I nodded a silent understanding.

When we got back into the car, they had one more surprise for me. They reached into a bag in the back seat and emerged with Cherry Cokes and fudge brownies.

"It is clear we need to renew our vows!" Giggling just like we did as kids, they led me through the same oath we had taken more than twenty years earlier.

Sue smiled and said, "Now, about those girls of yours. It is time to get them some magazines, so we can initiate them into the club."

Karla Brown

Friday Afternoon at the Beauty Shop

Each moment is magical, precious and complete and will never exist again.

Susan Taylor

The sound of women's voices could faintly be heard over the hum of the hair dryers. As clients waited for their turn to be pampered, they watched one court show after another on the small television set at the front of the shop. Occasional laughter erupted from various conversations around the room.

It was an array of washing, drying, cutting, styling, weaving and braiding—your typical Friday afternoon at the beauty shop.

At least it started out that way.

As my stylist was braiding my hair, a few women behind me near the wash bowls began conversing about the music playing on the shop's portable boom box.

The song "In the Sanctuary" by Kurt Carr and The Kurt Carr Singers was brought in by one of the clients,

unconsciously welcomed by all. Without much notice,
the gospel CD replaced the old-school music that had
played most of the morning.

The music had a contagious rhythm to it. Its lyrics drew
you in, and before you realized it, you were humming
along, tapping your foot, snapping your fingers.

Before long, a few of the patrons began harmonizing,
as the others listened with interest. Toward the front of
the shop, clients stopped their gossiping long enough to
take note of the sweet sounds emanating from the back
of the salon.

I quietly watched and listened to the transformation
taking place. A peaceful calm settled over the room. It was
as if someone new had entered the shop; a presence who
didn't need a door to make an entrance.

For the next two hours, the song played nonstop.
Giving little thought to their actions, the clients would
take turns pressing "play" whenever the song ended.
Occasionally other songs from the CD would play, but
someone would always return it to the first track.

I continued to observe the diverse group of women
with interest. Gossip turned to stories of spiritual discovery and enlightenment. Conversation about trivial matters was replaced with tales of hope and dreams. The
presence even took my thoughts of responsibilities waiting for me outside the shop's doors and replaced them
with wonder and praise for this day, for this moment.

Before long, one of the stylists recruited several patrons
to join the others in song. Some could sing, some could
not, but that didn't matter. What mattered was joining
together to give thanks.

The afternoon reached a climax when the same stylist,
using a comb as a conductor's stick, gathered the women
and led them through a final playing of the song.
Resembling a church choir, clapping hands and stepping

from side to side, eight to ten patrons stood facing their director to sing one last time. It didn't matter that people walking by the storefront could see them draped in towels and capes, hair in rollers, weaves half-finished. The only important thing was that they sing this song.

For a journalist, watching the celebration was similar to "getting the story." What I was witnessing was unique. We were experiencing a moment that would never be repeated in this manner again.

The song ended, everyone clapped and hugged one another. The CD's owner took her music and left. And as quickly as the transformation began a couple hours earlier, the activity in the shop reverted back to what one would expect on your typical Friday afternoon at the beauty shop.

Women's voices could faintly be heard over the hum of the hair dryers. Clients waited for their turn to be pampered. Occasional laughter erupted from various conversations around the room. The washing, drying, cutting, styling, weaving and braiding resumed as if it had never stopped.

On the outside, it was as if nothing had ever happened.

But on the inside, we all knew it had.

Michelle Fitzhugh-Craig

Sisters' Song

It is singing with soul that counts.

Sarah Vaughan

The Oklahoma City bombing had devastated our community; but just six weeks later the largest high school in Oklahoma City was having the baccalaureate service as usual in a neighborhood church. There was still a heartfelt obligation to affirm this end-of-year ceremony for our students. At our "Little United Nations," as I liked to call it, we were a strong community of faith, and our young Vietnamese Catholics would worship beside our African American Baptists, in this, their next to the-last ceremony before they danced off into the world of college and jobs.

Court rulings involving separation of church and state meant the students and parents were totally in charge of this event. The students had to meet on their own for the rehearsal and to set the tone of the program. Even though it was difficult to "let go" of a service of this nature, as the principal I had done just that. From past history I knew that this release of responsibility had normally worked out fine, but this year was a difficult time for everyone. Several students had loved ones injured and killed in the bombing.

As the principal, my role was minimal, but I was able to participate in helping students pin collars on their robes in the waiting area, help quiet the nervous jitters and supervise as they lined up for this most important event—which many viewed as a dress rehearsal for commencement.

Finally, all was in readiness, and I slid silently into a back pew as the students began to proudly march down the center of the sanctuary. Many a parent's eyes dripped tears as a son or daughter quietly walked in line with their classmates to the front rows of the church, which had been reserved for the graduating class of 1995.

The program began normally with a routine of introductions and speeches. Finally, it was time for one of the most coveted parts of the ceremony—the senior solo. Several students each year would try out for this honor, but only one was chosen.

One of our beautiful young ladies walked proudly to the lectern and prepared to sing. Her song was an old hymn and one that seemed especially appropriate after this recent tragedy—"His Eye Is on the Sparrow." However, as she began to sing, something appeared to be wrong. She began to stumble through the first verse of the song, and tears started running down her face. Suddenly from the back of the church, the song echoed from another voice. Her older sister had seen her distress and had come to her aid. She calmly walked down the center aisle of the church, keeping her eyes steadfastly on her sister, as she continued to sing along. She took her place next to her sister and placed her arm around her shoulder. They sang triumphantly, the original singer buoyed by the love and courage of her family member, until the song was finished.

There were other parts to the program, of course. A

young minister encouraged the graduates with the theme that "the sun will come up tomorrow, no matter what happens." The senior speakers were refreshing and challenged their young colleagues to seek significant tasks to the greater glory of mankind.

For me, however, the pinnacle of that program will forever be the performance by those two young women—especially the one who didn't stop to think of the possible embarrassment of walking down a long aisle from the back of the church to rescue her sister. Because at that one gleaming moment in their family history, the only thing that mattered was that her sister needed her, and she was prepared to answer the call and claim the victory of that moment.

Rita Billbe

5

THE POWER OF A WOMAN'S PRAYER

*Women, if the soul of the nation is to be
saved, I believe that you must become
its soul.*

Coretta Scott King

Divine Intervention

God, make me so uncomfortable that I will do the very thing I fear.

Ruby Dee

I've always considered Southern California my home—a place where you can visit the beach to soak up the sun and catch a wave, and swoosh down the snow-packed slopes of Snow Valley all in one weekend. Besides the places to go and things to do, it was a wonderful place to raise our son, Shawn. My husband and I were amazed that our union in marriage created such a tiny, beautiful baby. For the first time in my life, I felt whole. Our life was like a fairy tale that wouldn't end . . . "and they lived happily ever after."

Unfortunately, our fairy tale began to decay and so did our relationship and my life. Shawn and I left, under duress, and we returned to my roots in New Orleans where most of my family lived.

For the next few years, Shawn and I lived in an apartment we called home. It was small, but it was our castle. Shawn was close to the elementary school he loved and all the activities that came along with it for a ten-year-old. I worked in the admittance department at the local hospital, and two nights a week I attended the community college within walking distance, pursuing a license in radiology—a lifelong dream.

I was amazed at how circumstances that I had considered painful and embarrassing turned into God's plan of placing me, literally, in the path of a life that he preordained.

Just when the period of adjusting was over and we had accepted the fact that New Orleans was now our home, it seemed the path we had been set in was not exactly what we thought.

News came that Hurricane Katrina was threatening to hit land in thirty-five hours. New Orleans appeared to be directly in its path.

Most of us didn't think much of it at first, but as the news continued to urge us to evacuate, my family decided staying wasn't worth the risk. We packed up the car with our most immediate needs and each other and hit the road—along with almost everyone else.

"I can't believe we've been in gridlock for the past hour," Mama said abruptly.

We'd been mostly silent as we sat enduring the heat, inching forward a car-length at a time. I think we were all lost in our own thoughts and fears.

"We're only about twenty miles out of the city. Alexandra is usually three hours away without traffic. We probably won't get there 'til ten tonight," Dad interjected.

We nervously checked the clock and the drive time against the predicted arrival of the hurricane. None of us wanted to be stuck in the car on a crowded highway when the storm's fury hit.

Mama spoke sullenly, "I guess we weren't the only ones with leaving on our minds."

The sound of a blaring horn from the car in the rear

snapped me to attention. Traffic finally picked up a little. As we passed cars and they in turn passed us, I saw faces of fear, despair and numbness. Although they were young, old, black, white, brown and yellow, their faces indiscriminately showed the emotions of our shared plight. We all wondered what would become of our homes and our neighbors. If this storm was as big as they predicted, chances were strong that life as we knew it would never be the same. On the other hand, we wondered whether we were running from nothing. It wasn't as though we hadn't seen storms before. We couldn't help but wonder if the weather service was crying "wolf," and we were the silly ones who were running. Fear, questions, doubts and extreme temperatures all put bad moods on the rise.

As I looked closely, I saw children in the back seats of every make and model of vehicle imaginable, doing the things they do best—from playing with toys or watching cartoons on monitors, to laughing and irritating one another. They seemed oblivious to the seriousness of our predicament. I found myself envying their innocence.

My own son, Shawn, tried to change the conversation in a positive direction. "We can listen to CDs!" he said cheerfully.

He pulled a CD case from the side compartment on the door.

"Let's listen to this one." He opened it and slipped the CD into the player. Soothing music filled the air, creating a semi-tranquil atmosphere.

I smiled and responded, "Good choice, little man."

Maybe some of Shawn's optimistic vibe was rubbing off on me.

As I listened, I recognized a song I hadn't heard in a while, one from what seemed a lifetime ago. As the familiar chorus of "California Dreamin'" began, my mind drifted back, fondly, to my California days.

I must confess I'd never planned to stay in New Orleans. I'd thought about moving back to California. I missed the weather, gazing at sunsets over a watery horizon, watching pedestrians take their daily walks.

I missed my friends, my sister and her family. And Shawn had not ceased talking about California since our visit over Easter. Ah, but we were settled here now; I had a job; we were both in school; we had a home, our "castle." *No.* I turned my thoughts away from my dream and focused back on the road I was currently on. I knew in my heart that I didn't have the guts to make such a big move and take such a big risk right after getting settled. If that was God's will, a very clear sign would have to be delivered, otherwise I was staying put.

Once we finally arrived at our destination, we listened spellbound to the news as Hurricane Katrina battered our city—and beyond. We watched in horror at the devastation, with an odd numbness as if we were watching a sci-fi movie with amazing special effects. This couldn't be our city. These couldn't be our neighbors. We were left to our imaginations as we wondered if one of those homes under water could actually be ours. We just couldn't believe it. It was so surreal and painful and devastating and scary.

A week later, Shawn and I anxiously returned to our castle hoping to find that this really was just a bad dream and not reality at all, only to find that the few earthly belongings we took to Alexandra were the only things untouched by Katrina. Nothing was salvageable. The receding water left mud, mold and missing possessions that we assumed were carried away in the flood.

I couldn't stop the streaming tears. I felt so completely defeated. All we had worked for, all we had acquired, all we had built, washed away.

My little man matured a little that day when he grabbed

my hand and said, "It's all right, Mama. It is going to be all right."

It was then when my previous thoughts returned. Hadn't I declared just days ago that if God wanted us to move, he would have to give us a very clear sign? Now, we not only had to go, we could not stay.

I smiled slightly through my tears, grateful for his tender touch and optimism, and said to Shawn, "So, how do you feel about California?"

"Does California have hurricanes?" he asked.

"No," I answered.

That was all he needed to hear.

When my family voiced their objections, "Where will you go? What will you do?" I smiled and said, "I'll place my life in God's hands," knowing that the "master plan," no matter how difficult, is always perfect.

Now, less than a year later, I'm sitting on the Huntington Beach Pier in California overlooking the Pacific Ocean, counting my blessings, and watching the plan unfold.

Michelle Cummins

Holy Ghost Filled

Sister Baker stood in front of the church, ready to sing her solo. She was sharp! It was obvious she wore her Sunday best; the diamonds in her ears glimmered, and her white suit was flawless. She was the kind of churchwoman that I hoped to be: elegant, spirit-filled and beautiful.

"Good morning, Church. I'm going to sing a song that the Lord has put on my heart. Please, pray for me," she said in her gentle voice.

"Amen!" and "Sing that song, baby!" darted out from the congregation.

She started off slowly, holding on to each word, demonstrating the talent she had was truly a gift from God, "III looveee the Loooooooooooooordddd. . . ." She went on bringing the congregation to the edge of their seats as she played with the tune.

After Sister Baker finished her song, she lifted her hands and cried out, "Hallelujah! Hallelujah!"

Pastor Reems sat in his chair, nodding his head. "Yes! Yes! Well! I said, well!" he said in a deep, slow voice. "Jesus sho' is alive this mornin'!

The Church responded in unison, "Well!"

"Church, I said, Jesus sho' is alive this morning! I said I once was lost, ah. . . ."

"Come on, tell it!" a voice rang out.

"But Jesus, I said Jesssus!"

"You betta preach, boy!" Another voice encouraged.

His voice got higher and his words a little more emphasized. It was now time for the word, the sermon. My mom sat back in her seat along with the rest of the congregation. I sat back in my seat, too, held my baby doll and dozed off; it wouldn't be long before I'd be awakened.

The jazzy pitch of the organ ushered in the climax of Pastor Reem's sermon. His baritone voice suddenly skipped up to extremely high octaves, octaves that I never thought possible for a man.

He yelled, "And Jesssuuusss! I said Jeeeeeeeesus! . . ."

"Hallelujah!" was shouted back by the Church.

Pastor Reems stepped down from the pulpit and went back to his seat. Sister Baker walked back up to the microphone and began to sing.

"Yes!" The lady in front of me stood up from her seat and began to wave her fan toward Sister Baker. In response to this lady, Sister Baker waved her hand toward the ceiling, toward the Lord. As she waved her hand, her diamond studded fingers sparkled.

As Sister Baker came to the end of her song, she held the last note. It was a high one that seemed to be a stretch, even for her. She tilted her head to the side and stretched her arm out as if to say, "Jesus, help me hold this note!"

In the middle of this last note, the church went wild. It was like homecoming game, and Jesus just scored another touchdown. The congregation shot up from their seats like rockets; it was Holy Ghost time. The drummer's feet moved to a steady, fast rhythm as the organ followed along. Mother Jackson stood up and ran around the church, screaming. Two people beside me fell to their knees and cried, "Oh yes! Jesus!"

I turned to my mother, and she started up, but her shout was a little different from everyone else's. She just jumped straight up in the air; up and down, and then she started spinning in circles. Mother Jackson was still running around the church; I thought she might hurt herself because I'd never seen an old woman move so quickly. In fact, Mother Jackson had a cane.

The Holy Ghost must be real powerful! I thought to myself as I watched, truly impressed.

Sister Baker sang the people out of their seats, and I wanted to be just like her. Ushers surrounded my mother and the other ladies who had the Holy Ghost.

Sister Baker started moving to the beat, first bouncing her head, then adding a sway, and then her sweet voice belted, "Cain't nobody do me like Jesus!"

The Church replied, "Cain't nobody do me like Jesus!"

This song was different from the one she sang earlier; it was even more upbeat. Everyone hopped around, clapping and singing call and response. Our faces gleamed; Sister Baker's joy had been transmitted to all of us.

I looked around; everyone was jumping, running and yelling. Sister Baker was now clapping her hands as she joined in praise with the rest of the church. Since she joined, I thought I'd join in as well. I stood up, placing my baby doll on the chair. The drums started playing, and the organ came in; this was the prime time for demonstrating your Holy Ghost–ignited praise.

I lifted my hand up first, and then I began shaking it, "Yes, Lord!" I whispered, a little embarrassed. But as the drums continued, I felt more comfortable, and my feet started moving.

"Yeesss, Lord!" I shouted this time, "Thank you, Jesus!"

I jumped back and forth to the beat of the drums and enjoyed praising the Lord with all the other adults; I felt the Holy Ghost, and it was great! I danced up toward the front of the church in order to get a closer look at the amazing Sister Baker. She smiled at me; she was gorgeous! She waved her soft hand in the air and rocked back and forth as if the music controlled her. I moved even closer; I wanted to touch her. She glanced at me and motioned me toward her. She grabbed me and gave me a hug; I couldn't believe that I was standing in front of the church next to Sister Baker. Her sweet scent encompassed me; it was like heaven. I danced and clapped, filled both with the Holy Ghost and with Sister Baker!

Then I looked up.

I saw my mother walking toward me; her face had quickly turned from a sanctified Holy Ghost–filled sister to an angry mother. I looked up at Sister Baker for some type of help. Fortunately, Sister Baker saw the fear in my eyes; she stopped my mother in the midst of her angry walk, grabbed her by the hand and said, "Come on and help yo' baby praise the Lord!"

My mother gave in, but I could still see the discomfort in her eyes. We stood in front of the church rocking, clapping and dancing. Sister Baker started singing again, "Cain't nobody do me like Jesus!"

Then she handed me the microphone, and without even thinking about it, I belted, "Cain't nobody do me like the Lord!"

I sang, and the congregation continued praising. My mom looked at me and her whole face changed. Her discomfort from before was suddenly replaced with a look of astonishment, and then a glowing smile.

She lifted her hands up and exclaimed, "Thank you, Jesus!"

As the song winded down, Sister Baker pulled me close and whispered, "The Lord has blessed you with the gift of song. Baby, you betta sing it!"

Kiana Green

God's Will

My relationship with God has always been quite simple: He's the Father and I am a little girl always working to please him and be the dutiful child. For the longest time, though, that also meant that I didn't bother him with praying for trivial things. I didn't pray for my teams to win when I used to play in sports. I didn't pray for boys to like me. I certainly didn't pray for money. To me prayer was meant for life or death situations and that I was just supposed to follow my intuition and common sense (which are God-given gifts) and make my way with everything else, but that all changed for me recently.

When I lived in New York City I used to live down the street from a store that sold candles, towels, bedding, accessories and the like. One day I saw that the store was going out of business so I went inside to shop for bargains. I noticed a sign: "More Downstairs—Furniture 50-60 Percent Off!" I never knew this place had a downstairs or that it had furniture so I went to check it out. There wasn't much left. The walls had been stripped of all decoration and the room looked like a plain old basement under the blue fluorescent light. I wanted to leave, but one piece caught my eye: a chaise lounge. It was big (wide enough for two) and overstuffed, with fat arms all covered in a brown tweed upholstery. Now I had known of chaises as beach chairs and lawn furniture. I'd never seen one as indoor furniture.

Well, I plopped down into that chaise and fell in love. I thought, *This is the most amazing piece of furniture ever!* It was functional, but entirely frivolous. I loved that there was absolutely no reason to have such a thing in a home other than for pure luxury. I started seeing myself sitting in the chaise in a home office and reading and editing pages with my feet up and a cup of tea by my side. The chaise felt great—my whole vision felt great—and I knew I wanted it. Unfortunately I found the price, about $1500, (and that was with the going-out-of-business discount) too steep. Also, while our apartment was larger than the average Manhattan apartment, I knew there was no space for it. It was silly for me to want such a thing and I reluctantly told myself as much and left the store.

A few weeks later my husband and I were in the neighborhood thrift store shopping for shirts. While he trolled the racks, I looked for a place to sit down. There, near the front of the store with other secondhand furniture for sale was a chaise. It was narrower than the one I had seen at the other store. The white twill cover was dingy and the cushions thin. I sat down and ran my hand over its raised piping and checked out the price tag: $225. I could afford that! I started to think about where I could put it, but in my head I wasn't seeing my apartment. I kept thinking about my vision and the only thing that made sense to me was that one day I would have a house with my own office and enough room for such a piece of furniture. Maybe I should just keep working toward that. Then another thought came to me, clear and undeniable: *This is not my chaise.*

I held the thought in my mind and told no one about it.

Not my husband, not my friends. It all seemed so silly. I had work that I loved, a wonderful husband and a great place to live. It made no sense to ask for more, especially something I didn't need. I put the chaise down as something I'd buy for myself one day when I hit it big.

Not long after this I got a phone call from my beloved friend Jenny. We used to do yoga together twice a week at her place, but I hadn't seen her in awhile. There was a lot of work going on in her apartment because her great room was being redone by *O at Home*, Oprah Winfrey's decorating magazine. That day on the phone she said, "Come over, I have something for you."

"Okay," I said, thinking that she had found a gorgeous designer bag or a beautiful new dress for me. We shop together often so she knows my taste for the colorful and the sequined. She will pick up pieces she knows I will love so I was eager to see what her latest adventure had uncovered. When she opened the door I could tell she was excited, too.

"Look, you don't have to take it if you don't want it," she said quickly. "But this just has Fronie written all over it and I think you're supposed to have it." She took me into the room she used as an office, but we almost couldn't get in. It was full of boxes and pieces of furniture. The blinds were down so Jenny had to turn on a light. She said, "This is for you."

There, practically glowing in the center of the room, was a chaise: yellow, slim, with a curved back, tufted fabric and mahogany legs. It was sleek, smart and fabulous. I was stunned.

The designer had brought it in for her living room, but Jenny felt the chaise wouldn't survive being subjected daily to her two dogs and eight-year-old son. She told me she had been at a loss what to do with it so she sat down with her housekeeper to do some brainstorming over the situation. Together they looked at the chaise for a long time. "Then," Jenny said, "we both looked at each other and said, at the same time, 'This is Sophfronia's chaise.'"

I stood there and fought back tears because I just couldn't explain to Jenny how humbled and loved I felt in that moment. I felt as though God were saying to me, "Anything you want, little girl. *Anything*." And price was definitely no object. That first chaise I had seen cost $1,500. The second, $225. This one, which so perfectly suited me and my home in terms of size, color and style, carried a retail price of over $8,000. I got it for free. From then on I knew it was okay to share all of my dreams with God, and that it was all right—in fact, his wish for me to want big and dream big. I would never hold back again.

Today I do live in a beautiful 3,000 square-foot house where I have my own office and library with inspiring views of Connecticut's woodlands. And my chaise? It's in my bedroom where it sits with a tall Arts and Crafts style reading lamp and stacks of books on the floor. I love watching my toddler son climb onto the chaise and that is where we read together. Is this what I asked for? Well, no, not quite. This is even better.

Sophfronia Scott

The Bus Vouchers

No matter what accomplishments you make, somebody helps you.

Wilma Rudolph

Leaving home for work late one day near the end of December, I missed my normal bus and had to catch the later one. I checked my watch and knew I could still make it on time, but I was cutting it close—a stressful start to the morning.

As I sat waiting for the bus, I realized that the end of the month meant the beginning of a new one, which meant it was time to buy my bus pass for January, a cost of $100. Mind you, that was $100 that I didn't have. The holidays had just passed, my husband was unemployed at the time and things were very tight for our family. I sighed audibly. If I couldn't get to work, things would only get worse.

Seeing no other viable options, I began to pray and ask God to help me solve this problem, to send me the money to meet this need, as I had done in the past for other things. I offered my problem to God, which if nothing else, made me feel better and more prepared to face my day.

Continuing to pray, I rode past one bus stop. At the second stop, a lady got on the bus whom I had met several weeks prior. She and I often took the same evening bus home and had shared scriptures together and conversations about ways to share God with co-workers. Happy to see her, I smiled.

As she reached my seat, she said, "Good morning, I have something for you." I thought perhaps she had a passage she wanted to read to me or a book she wanted to share.

She sat down and, whispering across the person between us, asked if the company I worked for paid for my transportation. An odd question, I thought, especially in light of my recent concerns, but I let her know that they did not.

She had the person sitting between us pass me an envelope. I opened the envelope and there were bus vouchers for the months of January, February and part of March—worth $226! I can only imagine how surprised I must have looked! God had certainly answered my prayers before, and I trusted that he would again, but I didn't expect it to happen so quickly and efficiently, immediately after uttering the prayer!

I looked up at her speechless and she explained, "I accepted a position in Texas and will be moving there within a few days. I prepurchased these bus vouchers and they are nonrefundable. I didn't want them to go to waste, so when I prayed over what the best thing to do with them was, spirit told me to give the bus vouchers to you. I took an earlier bus than I normally do, hoping to see you this morning."

Obviously, God had been working on the solution even before I recognized the problem. We cried together, all the way to work, when we recognized how clearly we were both a part of God's plan.

This turned out to be the perfect way for me to share God with my co-workers as, needless to say, I shared the testimony with whomever I could find that would listen.

Ruthell Cook Price

You'll Do It for Me

Faith is the first factor in a life devoted to service. Without it, nothing is possible. With it, nothing is impossible.

Mary McLeod Bethune

I couldn't believe I was in a place like this. As I walked down the hall, I found myself silently pleading with God for an answer to the question, *Why is this happening to me?*

Safely in the cell, a hollow sigh escaped my lips as I checked out my new surroundings. The furnishings were simple . . . an iron bed frame with no mattress and a toilet— on top of which sat a carton of ice tea.

There were two other girls in my new temporary home, and we spent the next few minutes getting acquainted. One had shoplifted a pair of socks from the dollar store; the other was too incoherent to share what she had done; I had spanked my son.

The series of events that led me to this moment constitutes another entire story, but let it suffice to say that I was not the kind of girl who generally ended up in a place like this, nor the kind of mother who would be accused of abuse. As the mother of six, one only a few weeks old, it was not only remarkable but unfathomable to my family and to me that I was in jail, with Christmas only a few days away.

Before long an officer fetched me from the cell and escorted me to have my fingerprints taken. The process lasted about five minutes, and when I returned, my room-mates were gone and so was the tea.

Within seconds, a woman who put fear in my heart was being led to the cell, and she was not happy. Neither was I. We stood face to face . . . okay, head to chest . . . okay, how about toe to toe. She towered over me. Her eyes darted toward the toilet and then rested firmly on mine. It felt like staring into two torches. Her chest heaved, and from her mouth the words spewed like lava from an erupt-ing volcano. "Who took my tea?"

I returned the stare while craning my neck and attempted to respond with an equal amount of bass in my voice, "Not me." I seized the opportunity to walk away tri-umphantly and plopped myself onto the bed. I had forgot-ten there was no mattress. Ouch. I sat on the cold iron contemplating the possibility of being killed for some-thing I didn't even do.

She stood momentarily looking at me and then pro-ceeded to climb atop the toilet. It turns out her boyfriend was in the cell adjacent to ours. They had both been arrested and conveniently, there was a little cut-out window above the toilet through which they could communicate.

As I watched her, contemplating my impending doom, an inner voice whispered gently, *Ask her if she is okay*. I almost choked. I thought to myself, *You have got to be crazy. I'm not talking to her*. But the voice was insistent. Despite my inner grumbling, I had to obey.

She climbed down from the toilet and took a seat next to me, obviously annoyed. I swallowed hard, looked her in the eyes and asked quietly and respectfully, "Are you okay?"

Immediately, her countenance was transformed. Her face became soft. I could see that she was vulnerable, confused and afraid just like me.

She began to tell me about how her boyfriend had violated a restraining order, and when the cops came to arrest him, he squealed on her for having numerous outstanding warrants. Now, they were both in jail.

She explained how the officers refused to take her to her house to get her heart medicine. Her anger was fueled by their refusal to fulfill a basic need.

"Baby, you gotta keep your faith," I said in an attempt to encourage her. I was probably speaking as much to myself as to her, but I felt her frustration.

"Yeah, yeah, I know. Jesus gonna work it out," she responded sarcastically. "I tried that stuff, and look what it has gotten me. I was trying to live right, and now I'm gonna be sent back to prison."

"Listen, your faith is all you have," I told her while trying to convince myself. "I don't understand why God is allowing me to go through what I'm going through, either, but I have to hold on to my faith. Faith is all we have. We have to hold on."

In between toilet-top dialogues with her boyfriend, we spent the next hour sharing as only sisters can. We talked about faith. We talked about our kids. We talked about forgiving and being forgiven. She told me what her future held, being sent back to prison for the next three years. She shared what it was like to be an inmate there, and it brought tears to my eyes.

Toward the end of our time together, she climbed atop the toilet one last time and made a bold declaration to her boyfriend. "Baby, I've decided what I'm going to do when I get back to prison. I'm going to stay to myself, and I am staying with the Lord." I was engulfed by joy and a sense of purpose as an inner voice answered my earlier question, *This is the reason why you had to pass through here.*

Within minutes, the officers arrived to transport me to my next destination. Before leaving, we embraced like true sisters and newly made best friends.

She looked at me teary eyed and said assuredly, "I am going to see you again." With that, I was led away. I hoped that we would meet again—on the outside, not the inside of this system. I was sent home on my own recognizance, with an impending court hearing ahead of me. I had no idea what the future held for me or my family.

Yet, in spite of my personal anguish, I could not get her off my mind. For the whole next month, I prayed for her every day. The urgency was something I could not get away from. Though a blanket of depression attempted to smother me as I faced the possibility of a prison sentence, I prayed for her. Then quite suddenly, at the end of January, the urgency was gone.

On a brisk February day, my girlfriend called to let me know she had free tickets to the circus for my children and me. Initially, I was elated, but soon depression engulfed my entire being, and I tried to find excuses not to go. Not able to find one that she would accept, I got the kids ready and went.

We got to the front gate and presented our tickets. I walked through the gate first and briefly glanced at a vaguely familiar face. I continued to walk, but that inner voice commanded me to turn around and look again. Our eyes met and our mouths dropped open. It was her. Barely able to speak, we cried and held each other for what felt like forever. She told me that, for reasons she could not explain, she was released and exonerated at the end of January.

Inside the circus, her seat was a few rows behind mine.

Every now and then, I would turn around to watch her. She was beautiful, happy and free. Now, rather than me helping her to find her faith, unknowingly she was helping me to reclaim mine. I watched, and the inner voice spoke. *This is the reason you had to come here today. I wanted you to see the fruit of your labor and to know that if I did it for her, I will surely do it for you.*

So right there, in the midst of the gaiety and in the presence of my friend, I lifted my eyes to heaven and boldly reaffirmed my faith.

And just in case you're wondering, God did do it for me! Now, my family and my faith are stronger than ever.

Nancy Gilliam

Solid Ground

A violinist has a violin, a painter his palette. All I had was myself. I was the instrument that I must care for.

Josephine Baker

I have worn many shoes in my lifetime. . . .
The worn, dusty sandals of a child, sitting quietly on my
   grandma's porch as I watched her plant a peach tree
   and sing church songs in the front yard of her small
   flat.
A frayed pair of black-and-white tennis shoes, as I
   anxiously waited to be picked for a game of baseball
   in the housing projects where I grew up.
My shoes were my own, sometimes purchased, but most
   times, hand-me-downs.
But my feet were on solid ground.

I have worn many shoes in my lifetime. . . .
My first pair of jellies, I can remember them so clearly,
   powder blue, with glitter sparkles. A preteen now,
   feeling more like a young lady and less like a child,

I loved those shoes. They were so uncomfortable, and
yet they were my favorites.
I can still picture my first pair of pink high heel shoes,
worn to my first dance. I broke the right heel trying to
do the hustle and ended up sitting on the sidelines,
while the boy I liked danced with another girl with
two good shoes.
My shoe—beyond repair; my spirit—intact.
And as I look back on that day,
My feet were on solid ground.

I have worn many shoes in my lifetime....
I recall so clearly the green open toes I wore when I
met the boy, my first love ... who stood so tall, and
seemed so sure of himself that I wanted to be in his
presence, even if my presence didn't have the same
impact on him.
The borrowed maroon shoes of a future sister-in-law,
while I took vows I didn't understand, because the
boy, my first love, and I conceived a son at a time
when common sense and wisdom had not yet entered
our teenage minds.... Afraid, because I had to grow
up fast; confused, because the boy, my first love,
refused to do the same—and yet
My feet were on solid ground.

I have worn many shoes in my lifetime....
The black flats with the tiny scuff on the left toe, I wore
to bury my twenty-two-year-old baby brother....
The snow-white tennis shoes with the purple lining
that were on my feet the day I found out the State
Department of Corrections would not allow my
mother to say good-bye to her son, one last time,
before I buried him.

The tattered yellow flip-flops that were on my feet the
   day I saw the boy, my first love, now a man, on
   television, being sentenced to the death penalty.
And in spite of it all, or maybe *because* of it all . . .
My feet are on solid ground.

I have worn many shoes in my lifetime. . . .
The dust-covered construction boots I wore as I
   proudly contributed to the building of my very
   own Habitat for Humanity home.
The white hospital scuffs I wore, after giving birth to
   my second man-child miracle.
The patent leather sandals that adorned my feet when
   I proudly escorted my eldest son to the airport to visit
   the college he would attend in the fall.
And the fuzzy pink house slippers I wear now, as I lift
   my hands, my heart and soul to give praise to a higher
   being, who has made it possible for me to live my
   moments as a strong African American woman, one
   moment at a time, one step at a time.
Sometimes in shoes, sometimes on bare feet, sometimes
   on my knees, but . . .
Thank God, always,
On solid ground.

Yvonda Johnson

Lord, Please Make One for Me!

People see God every day. They just don't recognize him.

Pearl Bailey

Lord, I know that you made Adam in your image and
    he proved how imperfect he could be
But if you should decide to make another, this time God,
    could you make a man for me?

It would be nice if he could be a good listener, 'tho when
    I'm nervous, I do ramble on and on
And could you please give him some strong shoulders so
    when I'm stressed, I'll have someone to lean on.

When it comes to patience, he will need a double portion
    'cause sometimes I can really stretch one's nerves.
Make him just a little shy; let him be pleasing to the eye,
    but from 1 to 10, I'll grade him on a curve!

Give him plenty of compassion, make him stern but
    understanding.

Give him the deep-set eyes I'd fall for but make it a
   happy landing.

Oh, and Lord, please make sure that his self-esteem's
   secure, and if he's just a little stubborn, that's okay.
Give him a good job and a future. Help him to reach his
   goals, but I don't want him if he's all work and no play.

A little sensitive and unashamed if he should shed a tear
   and not afraid to say just how he feels.
I guess what I want to say more than anything, today,
   is God, I need a man that's real!

Give him a tender heart, and I'd love it if he's smart. It
   would be a blessing just to hold good conversation.
Give him height but not too much; add a slow hand and
   gentle touch and a voice that sends my heart to
   palpitations.

Lord, please add a sense of humor and a very sexy laugh,
   and let him blush if I should whisper my intentions.
Give him passion, lots of passion, P-A-S-S-I-O-N, and oh
   God, please, bless his imagination!

He has to love you first, then I won't worry about us;
   above all else, he must become my friend.
Oh, and before you send him down, dip him well in
   chocolate brown and give him (sigh) an adorable
   rear end!

Lord, I know that you made Adam, Solomon, Abraham
   and more. Hey, even David strayed a little from your
   plan.
But you loved all your creations 'tho they fell into temp-
   tations 'cause you've always hated sin but not the man.

So, I bring this task to you because you know me. You
    alone know who my soul-mate ought to be.
So, if you're ever in that creative mood again, Lord,
    please—could you make a man for me?!

RuNett Nia Ebo

6

LOVING BLACK MEN

It is one of the facts of life that there are two sexes, which fact has given the world most of its beauty, cost it not a little of its anguish, and contains the hope and glory of the world.

James Baldwin

My Divas

When we love black women, we love ourselves,
and the God who made us.

Michael Eric Dyson

To all my Divas who are working long hours to make
ends meet. My Urban Queens holding down the home
front while my strong black brothers labor in the work-
force to earn their keep. When God created you, the black
woman, he took the strength of mountains, the sweet fra-
grance of a rose, the passion of a lioness, the power of a
mighty storm, placed them all in a blender and pressed
the button, Mix—Her.

You are all and everything a black man will ever need
and nothing less. You are the shining one, giving life to my
universe. When I'm in your presence, mmmmm. I thirst.

Your tears represent the water that flows down an
island fall. Every tear that you shed for me, because of me
. . . God catches them all. You are the lily in my valley
planted just for me. You're a descendent of kings and
queens . . . Akhenaton and Nefertiti.

When God created you, he made your lips round and sweet. When I sample your nectar, baby, it tastes like a seasoned Georgia peach. Your hips are round like the mound of an African gazelle, and when you walk through my space, your grace shakes, casting a spell on me, so I stare. Oh my God! I'm in awe, hurry, look over there. Your skin is dark and creamy for a reason. You have the ability to endure the elements of all four seasons. No other women or race is created like you. Your high cheekbones, the power of your hair, the muscles in your calves, all made to help me through the trials of life. When I come home after a long day's work, at night; one touch, one kiss from you makes everything alright. From one Black African Warrior to a Mighty Sister, there's one thing I want you to take with you wherever you go.

You are my Diva:

> **D**ivine, dark, delightful and delicious
> **I**ntelligent, intellectual and independent
> **V**ictorious and virtuous—The woman whom I will always
> **A**dore.

You were made just for me, a black man; please come soothe my soul.

Antonio Crawford

218 LOVING BLACK MEN

Love, Laugh and Live Today

I am at a ripe age of thirty-five years. There are many roads in life and often turns leading one to the true test of self. Regardless of the thoughts of the masculine ego, there is much to learn from our wives, mothers and sisters. The strength of a man is a physical novelty, but true strength lies in our partners. Who among us can fathom the pain a black woman can endure? I am not qualified to pretend to understand a day as one of my sisters, let alone my wife, Valerie.

In our four years together, Valerie and I have overcome many of life's trials. When we started out we had no worries, and with only the wind at our backs, victory was ours. Our souls soared without fear as we planned our future. Some say the greatest of gifts is one's self. We chose to present our gifts in matrimony.

A quick trip to the doctor for a check-up is a normal part of wedding planning. I saw the one-hour trip as a small sacrifice in the name of love, or so I thought. Like any other day, I called home to chitchat with my wife-to-be and heard a strange sound in her voice. I heard fear, longing for yesterdays, and a soft hint of the pains of tomorrow that would shortly come crashing in.

Subtlety does not cushion the blow of bad news, and Valerie has always shot straight from the hip. "I have cancer," she said. "I have cancer."

Always worried about my well-being more than her own, Val asks me, "Are you okay?"

My ego rose to the occasion. "Of course, I am," in response to her question. Under the circumstances, I can prove my love and support for my wife!

My arrogance surpassed my ability to maintain composure, as a day turned into weeks, and weeks into months. I question my resilience after three surgeries and her loss of hair. My stamina buckled when my love's beautiful skin and nails changed to a murky brown. I cannot sleep because she is always in pain. Chemotherapy not only attacks the disease; it also attacks the whole body. In order to remove the beast, I guess we must call upon the help of the monster.

I witnessed my strong black woman slowed to a crawl. Am I now to become her parent because she depends on me more? No! Valerie continues to fight. Val still walks three miles around Lake Merritt, she maintains regular trips to the gym and continues with her tai chi classes. It is truly amazing to witness that level of drive firsthand. I have forgotten much since my childhood. The times I cherished watching my mother be the strong black woman in my life almost slipped my mind. Valerie is that breath of fresh air, a constant reminder of those days.

I have watched my wife ride the waves of life, as I tossed and turned. I have seen her turmoil disrupted with a smile. I am renewed daily with her loving touch. After searching high and low, I found my heroine in my arms.

They say the black woman is strong. I say the depth and scope of her strength is incomprehensible. Women do not try to be strong; it is just in them to be that way.

Charles Stanley McNeal

King Kong

I ain't tryin' to go with no gorilla.

Patti LaBelle

I was sitting behind my dad looking at the back of his big rust-colored corduroy easy chair. There was nothing different about this visit. I would make a comment about something on the news, and he would respond. I struggled to keep words passing between the two of us. My dad was a quiet man. He spoke mostly when he had something to say.

He swiveled toward me in his chair, peering from a side view over its top.

"Susan," he started.

I knew the conversation was going to be serious; usually he just called me "Baby," a nickname he gave me because I was the youngest of his three children. My mom often told me he had a connection with me from the very beginning that was different. He sent her a dozen gladiolas when I was born. When I came home he laid down beside me in the bed and examined my toes and fingers. It was a first.

"I don't know if you ever think about getting married, or even living with someone for that matter," he continued.

Then he paused, which was his custom—talking slowly and deliberately with skillfully timed pauses, timed so that they had the same effect on me as suspense movies. The music picks up. The screen darkens. There is a corner draped in shadows. The camera pans the shadows slowly and you see a half-opened door. You know someone is hiding there, someone with murderous intentions.

"But if you do," he went on, "and you and your old man get into a fight. Don't call me. . . . I won't come."

As he makes his point, I am looking at the top of his fuzzy, white head. His head is tilted to one side, a way of holding it that I inherited. He is looking straight into my eyes.

"I won't come even if you are screaming and hollering."

Pause.

I couldn't believe my ears. My heart and stomach seemed to share the same space. Had I heard him correctly? How could my father forsake me like that? How could he be so mean? Barely breathing, I looked at him with the same tilted head, searching for understanding.

He continued, "But if you can just make it across this threshold," nodding in the direction of his own front door, "King Kong ain't coming in here to get you."

Most girls fall in love with their fathers when they are little. However, it was in this moment, knowing that my father would fight King Kong for me, that I fell in love with my dad.

Susan Madison

It Was Magic

Where are we going? Are we there yet? Why did Mommy do my hair in Shirley Temple curls? Shifting and squirming in the back seat of Daddy's Chevrolet, my little body kept rhythm with the thoughts that raced through my mind. I didn't know what was going on, I only knew that it was going to be magic.

How did I know this? I was with my daddy, and everything he did was magic. His was the kind of magic that caused little girls to dream and believe that dreams do come true. Once, he brought home this big old piece of wood. After a few nights, that same wood sat on our roof in the form of Santa and his reindeer. Another time, he bought all this sand and had it dumped in our front yard so that his little girl wouldn't have to wait to go to the beach to build a sandcastle. Magic!

Where are we going? Are we there yet? Why did Mommy do my hair in Shirley Temple curls? After riding for what seemed to be forever, the motion of the car and the incessant thoughts proved to be too much for me. Against my will, I drifted off to sleep.

"Beep! Beep-beep!" The blare of horns honking jolted me from my unwanted nap, and then the brilliant lights overtook me. I pressed my face against the back seat window. Beneath the lights, people paraded in every direction.

"What is this place, Daddy?"

"This is Broadway."

"What are we gonna do in Broadway?"

"We're going to see *Hello, Dolly*.

I struggled to figure out how do you "see" hello. I wanted to ask, but I was more concerned that the people on Broadway were moving faster than the Chevy. I started fidgeting, anxious to leap from the car and move with the crowd. I longed to strut like the ladies in their high heels and make my hair bounce just like theirs.

Finally, Daddy found a place to park. We got out of the car and walked hand in hand . . . forever, and very quickly, too. It was as if my feet were flying over the ground. Lost in a sea of legs, I held Daddy's hand tightly. The view from the Chevy was better, but this feeling was nothing short of magic.

Eventually, we stopped in front of the biggest movie theater I'd ever seen. *Wow! This must be some special movie. Everybody's dressed up, just like me. Ooh, that lady's wearing curls just like me!*

When we got inside the theater, it was like being in the land of the giants. Everything was bigger than life, or at least bigger than I was. The ceiling seemed as far away as the sky, and the chandeliers twinkled like stars. Daddy handed the usher our tickets, and we were escorted all the way up to the second row on the left-hand side. Before me was a huge stage draped with thick, velvet curtains. Below, men in black tuxedoes sat in a hole in the floor with all kinds of musical instruments. Up above my head was heaven. I settled into my plush, velvet seat feeling like a princess.

In the midst of enjoying the ambience of this magic "kingdom," I noticed the lights beginning to dim. The instruments started making strange noises. All of a sudden, everything became eerily quiet. Then one of the men in the hole lifted his "magic wand," and the whole theater pulsated with music I had never heard. Oboes and piccolos, violins and cellos, flutes, kettledrums and chimes created the richest, fullest sound I had ever heard. My heart raced as the curtain began to part. Momentarily dismayed because there was no movie screen, my emotions rebounded quickly as the stage was taken over by real live people who all looked like me. Real live people leaping and spinning, singing and swirling, smiling, shining! My head snapped back and forth as if attached to a rubber band. There was so much magic to see, and I wanted to make sure I didn't miss a thing.

I noticed a man with a smile as bright as the sun. And then, there was this beautiful, sophisticated and sassy lady. They were doing a lot of the talking and singing, and I remembered seeing both of them before. Maybe on "The Ed Sullivan Show"? Or was it on Daddy's album covers? Sensing my recognition, Daddy leaned over and whispered, "That's Cab Calloway, and that is Pearl Bailey." My mouth dropped, and I don't think I ever bothered to close it. I spent the rest of the evening totally engulfed in my first Broadway experience.

At the end of the finale, I could sense my magical evening was about to end, or so I thought. The cast came out to take their bows, and the crowd cheered. Pearl Bailey came out to take her bow, and everyone stood to give her an ovation. I stood up too, and clapped my little hands as loudly as I could. That's when Daddy bent over and whispered in my ear.

"Go say hello to her."

My eyes widened in disbelief as he lifted me in the air, walked to the edge of the stage and placed me on it. My eyes bugged, my knees locked and my heart stopped. I was frozen with no hope of ever moving again until I recognized the possibility. This might be my chance to create some magic for the one who had created so much magic for me. So for that very reason, I narrowed my eyes, focused on Ms. Bailey's dress and began my journey across the stage.

With every step, I could hear people gasping, whispering and sighing. The sound from their reactions echoed fiercely in my ears, making my feet feel like I had on cinderblock shoes, but I refused to stop. I finally reached the center of the stage, swallowed the lump in my throat, grabbed her dress and tugged. She looked down in utter amazement.

"Where did you come from?"

Innocently, I pointed in the direction of my daddy and replied, "Over there."

Oohs and aahs filled the auditorium. Ms. Bailey lifted me into her arms, hugged and kissed me leaving a crimson lip print in the center of my forehead. She set me back on the ground and held my tiny hand in hers. At that moment, she stole my heart, and I knew that one day, I wanted to act and sing on the stage just like her.

About four years later, I made my professional stage debut. But Daddy didn't live to see it. He died six months after he took me to see *Hello, Dolly*, but he did get to see his baby girl on a Broadway stage with Cab Calloway and Pearl Bailey. In the short time we had together, he created enough magic to last my whole life. He created moments that cause little girls to dream and believe that dreams do come true. And that night, I got to create a moment just for him, and undeniably, it was magic.

Nancy Gilliam

Forgiving Daddy

The telephone's shrill ring startled me from a deep sleep. It was two o'clock in the morning—who could be calling at this hour? I tried to quiet my pounding heart as I picked up the phone. "Hello?"

My mother's familiar voice answered on the other end of the line. It sounded drawn and tense, and before she could finish a sentence, she started to cry. My husband stirred slightly, and I answered in a hushed tone, "Mama, what's wrong?"

"It's your daddy. The doctor says he won't make it through the night. I need you to come." I sucked in my breath.

"I'm on my way."

I awakened my sleeping husband and began packing a bag. I wanted to catch the first flight out—I had to make it in time! I just *had* to see Daddy alive one more time.

Although outwardly I was calm and methodical as I concentrated on the things that had to be done, a fire was raging in my brain as childhood memories of Daddy burned through it. I crunched my belongings into one little suitcase. My husband took me to the airport and said a

loving prayer before I hurried off to the gate. As I boarded
the plane, other passengers were already seated. I began
to pray under my breath as the plane taxied down the
runway heading for my hometown. It was ironic that my
first trip back to my birthplace—to the hospital where I
was born—was because my father had returned to that
very same place to die.

The plane arrived a few hours later and I went directly
to the hospital. From the hallway I could see my mother
sitting at the side of my father's bed, her head drooped in
a fitful, upright sleep. My heart broke at the sight—both
from Daddy's condition and seeing them together again
after all these years. She probably sat up all night and was
exhausted.

"Mama?" I threw my bag to the floor and ran to her; we
dissolved in tears for a moment before I managed to ask,
"Any change?"

"No. No change." I turned to face the hospital bed, my
heart leaped into my throat. *Who* was this man? This was
not my father—not *my* handsome daddy with the stunning smile! This was not the sophisticated military man in
uniform that I remembered. This was a *stranger*, an *old*
man—all skin and bones with sunken eyes—and where
was the full head of silver streaked hair? A silent scream
rose from deep in my belly. *Who are you? Where's my daddy?*
But I knew the answer. The daddy I remembered was the
daddy of an eleven-year-old girl, because that was the last
time I had actually seen him. My memory of Daddy was
frozen in time from nearly thirty years before!

As a child, I explained it away. Because he was in the Air
Force Daddy was gone a lot, but I was sure that one day
he would come home to stay. As I grew older, I called it
something different—abandonment. Why he did it didn't
matter to me as a little girl. I didn't care about how discrimination or some other social injustice made it hard for

black men to keep their families intact. I didn't ever care whether my mother wanted him there or not. *I* wanted my daddy at home, so I grieved the loss of that relationship for a very long time.

The turning point in how I felt about Daddy came after living without him for several years. My sister and I were going with our church to the nearby town where he lived. Somebody told us that Daddy lived right next door to the church, and they would let him know we were coming. I was terribly excited as I imagined our meeting. *I'll run to Daddy and give him a big hug! Then I'll tell him about school and how smart I am and maybe invite him to come hear me lead a song with the choir. He'll be so glad to see us! He'll explain why he has been gone for so long and tell us how things will be different from now on. Maybe he will even come home with us!*

I counted the days leading up to our visit. I was giddy and giggly when we arrived and knocked on Daddy's front door.

"Hellooo! Daddy, we're here! Daddy? . . . Hello? Anybody home?" But Daddy was not there. A fury rose in me that I had never known before. He *knew* we were coming! He was not there to tell us how much he missed us, or how pretty we were, or even how sorry he was for being gone all those years. He was just, once again, *not there!* That day I decided that I would never forgive Daddy. From that day on, I hated him, and I didn't care if I ever saw him again.

In spite of my feelings, I thought of Daddy often. Every Father's Day, I thought of him. When I graduated from high school and then college, I thought of him. When I got married and my mother walked me down the aisle, I thought of him. When I had my first child, I thought of him. But I never made any attempt to call him or write to him. As far as I was concerned, Daddy was already dead.

As an adult, I renewed my relationship with God and

was reminded that, as a Christian, forgiveness was required of me. In fact, the Bible says that God cannot forgive me if I don't forgive others! I also knew that if I let the bitterness grow in me unchecked, it would ultimately do the most damage to *me*. I realized then that no matter how hard it was, forgiving Daddy was something that I *had* to do. I was determined to let go of the pain in my heart—to give it to God and let him handle it. Only then did I find the strength I needed to forgive Daddy—once and for all! I truly forgave him, and I prayed that someday I would have an opportunity to tell him so face to face.

Daddy's raspy breathing brought me back to the reality of the hospital room. I prayed the heavens down that day.

"God, please! We need a miracle! Now that I'm with Daddy after all these years, please don't let him die!" I took Daddy's hand in mine.

"Daddy . . . can you hear me?" Labored breathing was the only reply. I bit my lip and tightened my grip on his hand. "Daddy? . . . It's Carol."

After what seemed like forever, Daddy's eyes fluttered open, and he looked at me with a clear and final recognition.

"Cal?" he whispered hoarsely with the Southern twang that I remembered only in that instant.

"I'm here, Daddy." Daddy gazed at me only for a moment, but with such love—and such regret—that my heart felt like it would burst. Nothing else could have had a more powerful impact on me. Just as quickly, his eyes closed and he never uttered another word before he slipped into eternity.

That day, in my heart, I knew Daddy had asked me to forgive him. And that day, I was so thankful that I already had.

Carol Ross-Burnett

A Twenty-Dollar Education

When you educate a man, you educate an individual, but when you educate a woman, you educate a nation.

Johnetta B. Cole

"Dad," I said, addressing the man who had given me life, divorced my mother when I was only six months old, and yet remained my father in every sense of the word for the rest of his life, "with the cost of tuition, I don't know how Al (my husband) and I can afford to send our daughter to college."

Dad simply said, "Give her twenty dollars, and if she really wants to go, she'll go."

I smiled, remembering my own twenty-dollar college education.

I admit it sounds a little unbelievable—a college education for twenty dollars. But I knew of what he spoke. As an eighteen-year-old graduate of Canton McKinley High School, my grades got me scholarships, which I could access only upon acceptance and admittance into a college. At first, I had dreams of Fisk, Tennessee State or Howard. Totally out of the question, but I did dream. Although I seldom asked my father for much, beyond the emotional support, wisdom and love he freely gave, this one time I needed money, and my father was my last hope.

"Dad," I said over the telephone, "can you help me? I need money for college."

"Sure," he said, "I can give you some money."

Not sure he understood, I said, "I mean now. I need it right away, by Monday, or I will lose my scholarships. I can get a ride to your house if you can give me some money."

"All right," he said, "come on up."

"Up" was Akron, Ohio, a neighboring city and a thirty-minute drive north. Traveling the highway in a boyfriend's car, I figured out my whole life. I would take my father's money and combine it with the scholarships to pay for my first semester at Malone College. With my father's help I could get a college education and graduate. In four years I would be a schoolteacher, something I had wanted since the eighth grade. I contentedly daydreamed throughout the entire ride.

We arrived at his home and he immediately began talking politics. After an hour of whether or not Kennedy was doing a good job, and what would happen to the country if Richard Nixon became president, it was time to leave.

"Here," he said, opening his wallet and removing a twenty-dollar bill that he handed to me, "This is all I have."

I took the money, thanked him, kissed him and we left.

I cried all the way home. My dream was shattered.

That was Sunday.

On Monday, I took the twenty dollars and paid the application fee to Malone College—exactly twenty dollars. Eight years later, after much hard work, my dad was there—watching his baby girl graduate.

I'm not quite sure how I did it—a few scholarships, a few jobs, a few loans, some family support and a lot of determination. That simple twenty-dollar bill made me look deep within to decide how badly I wanted my dream. I had to look past what seemed possible and believe in what seemed impossible in order to achieve it. While my dad had only given me twenty dollars on this occasion, he had given me far more of value over the years.

Some might call him an absentee father because I never lived under the same roof with him. But his presence in my life was anything but absent. I learned so much from this proud African American man. He taught me how to use my hands, so I do not have to call plumbers or electricians to make minor repairs. He taught me how to use my mind, so I could earn a bachelor's and two master's degrees. And he taught me how to use my inner strength to persevere when all I had was twenty dollars. My father's guidance was an account I could withdraw from, even when there was no money.

The day my daughter graduated from law school, I sat between my husband and my father as we watched her walk by in her cap and gown.

I squeezed Dad's hand and said, "Look what you can get for twenty dollars!" We both chuckled as we shared that moment and that memory, knowing that the tenacity and perseverance that he had passed to me had been passed on to her. I couldn't help but reflect on how this strong African American man had contributed to this amazing African American young woman before me. Here we were watching the fruition of our combined efforts as my daughter accepted her law degree.

Later that day, when I told my daughter how proud I was of her accomplishment, I shared the twenty-dollar story with her.

When I finished, she said thoughtfully, "Granddad gave you more than twenty dollars; he gave you all he had." Amen. That he did.

Nadine McIlwain

No More Drama

*It is better to continue to try to teach or live
equality and love than it would be to have hatred
and prejudice.*

Rosa Parks

Rashaad's eighth-grade graduation! I looked forward to
this day for a long, long time.

Everything leading up to this day had been really
stressful. Due to the large number of graduates that year,
students were only allowed two invites per graduate.
After some coercion I was able to get another ticket, but it
still wasn't enough to accommodate our immediate family. When black folk have a graduation, everyone and their
grandmama have to be there, so the question became,
who would be able to go, and who wouldn't?

Graduations have always been important in our family.
Although my mom graduated from high school, my dad
did not. As the eldest of five children, he had to drop out
of school at age ten to help support his brothers and sisters when their father died. He eventually obtained his
GED as an adult and always emphasized education as a

path to success in life. Nothing was going to stop my mother from attending this ceremony! She was diagnosed with a malignant brain tumor and believed this would be her last opportunity to see either of her grandsons graduate. My eldest son, Gerald, wanted to be there for his brother but, due to the scarcity of available tickets, he wouldn't be able to go. Clearly, I could not deny my parents the opportunity to see their grandson graduate.

The relationship between my estranged husband and me was stressful during our marriage and continued to be so after it ended. I wasn't looking forward to seeing him again, but I knew he had a right to be there. It's hard to be objective when you are a single mother raising sons, and it is hard for the absentee father to form a relationship with the children when he knows he has to go through the mother to have one. I would just have to grin and bear it.

Graduation day was beautiful! The temperature was warm and pleasant. I could swear that the sun shone extra bright because my son was graduating. The skies were bluer than the bluest eye, and the clouds looked like cotton balls fluffed especially for this day. I was so proud of Rashaad, having completed his intermediate education at one of the top public schools in the city. As a result, I believed he would have a bright future.

Ultimately, the drama I anticipated began. Grandma was supposed to wait at home for me to pick her up. She changed her mind, so we picked her up from the local bus stop. Gerald was feeling left out because he was unable to attend the ceremony. Grandpa was getting on Gerald's case for not appearing to be supportive enough to his brother. Rashaad was quietly yet excitedly getting ready, trying on his cap and gown. I nervously tried to calm my fears because, without a ticket, I realized I may not be attending the ceremony.

Finally, we arrived. The schoolyard was resplendent with blue and gold decorations. There were so many people. Many parents took pictures with graduates before they went inside to line up for the assembly. We all smiled at each other, celebrating the collective and individual achievements of our children. I was truly filled with joy.

While waiting for the announcement to enter the auditorium, I saw my mom speaking to a thin, gaunt man with gray hair, dressed in a wrinkled tropical shirt, olive green khaki shorts, ankle socks and worn-out moccasins. When mom embraced him, I began to look a little closer. Surely this could not have been the father of my children! I felt embarrassed as he looked toward me with an uncomfortable smile, not sure of how I was going to receive him. In my mind, I immediately began to judge him. *He looks old enough to be my father! Surely he did not come to his son's graduation dressed like he jumped out a window. I wonder what he must have been thinking when he left his house. Was he aware that he was going to his son's graduation ceremony? Was he cognizant of the need to be more appropriately dressed?* I coldly returned his greeting, deciding not to address the attire issue for Rashaad's sake.

Then something happened. I noticed that Rashaad did not appear to share my vision and my disgust. He was overjoyed just to see his father! I was so busy focusing on his father's outward appearance that I neglected to see what was really important about that day: a father making a humble effort to share an important day with his son.

As guests began entering the auditorium, I watched my parents go inside and told them to enjoy the ceremony and not to worry about me. I gave my son's father my ticket, deciding he really did deserve to be at his son's graduation, no matter what. Life had obviously dealt him a bad hand, and I decided not to make it worse. He took the ticket and went inside. At that moment, I recognized one of the school aides, who was collecting invitations and guarding the auditorium entrance. I asked if I'd be able to enter the school and watch the ceremony from the hall.

She replied, "No, but you can sit inside with your family."

"But I don't have a ticket," I told her.

She nudged me gently and said, "Just go inside." I thanked her quietly and went in. No questions asked, just feeling like I was being blessed. I was filled with pride as I watched my baby, looking all grown up, passing through this accomplishment.

After the ceremony, we went into the schoolyard for refreshments and awaited the graduates' arrival. We had planned to dine out, and I was anxious to get to the restaurant. I reluctantly invited Rashaad's father to join us, but he declined, saying he had made other plans.

Without warning, he turned to me, leaned over and kissed my cheek, whispering "thank you" in my ear. Although he just said "thank you," what I saw in his facial expression was "Thank you for doing such a good job in raising the kids without me. Thank you for not making this difficult for me today no matter how I was dressed or what you were thinking. Thank you for allowing me to be a part of this day."

I said, "You're welcome," and waved good-bye.

The stress had dissipated, and I felt as light as a feather. That moment filled me with a lot of hope that that one act of kindness could make such difference in our lives. On that day I had prepared to totally focus on Rashaad's needs and not my own. I decided to embrace the spirit of forgiveness by letting go of my judgment of his father and just celebrating the day. Apparently, he had come with the same intention. Rashaad was able to look off the auditorium stage and see his parents and grandparents there, together, loving him—regardless of what either of us were wearing or how we felt about each other.

Suddenly this day was not just about a graduation for my son, it was a graduation for all of us into a new era of healing. A celebration took place within my heart; knowing that peace between our families would ultimately come, and the cycle of pain would not be repeated. Although he had already left, I sent a silent thank-you to him, too. Thanking him for joining me in taking steps to break down the wall so that there would soon be no more drama in our lives.

Patricia L. Watler Johnson

A Daughter's Forgiveness

Years ago Papa (my grandfather) lived by himself across town. During wintertime he would come stay with us, and when spring came he would go home. Well, one year he just stayed and made our home his home.

Over the years Papa remained feisty, going 'round and 'round with his grandchildren and sometimes with his daughter—my mom. He was still feisty long after his health began to decline, his body betrayed him and his mind began to forget the people who were closest and dearest to him.

One afternoon last December, I was visiting Papa and Mom. My son, Lil' Kevin, was outside playing despite the frigid winter air when I went into the house to get his football. Papa was lying in his bed where he had been for several weeks.

As I walked past the dining room table, I looked through the French doors leading into Papa's room and saw Mom standing at his bedside shaving his beard. For some reason, I stopped and watched for a few minutes unbeknownst to her. There was a gentleness in the way she looked at him and shaved the hair from his face that captivated me.

At first, I thought, *What a wonderful act of a daughter's love!* Then, stories and memories of the many trials and tribulations surrounding their father–daughter relationship flashed through my mind. My mom being so angry at Papa she couldn't see straight, eat or even mutter a word, or the times when she may have hurt his feelings and he definitely hurt hers. And as I continued to watch her gently shave him, I realized that what I was witnessing was a loving gesture of a daughter's forgiveness, a willingness to put right or wrong to rest for the sake of peace, love and sweeter memories made in the current moments.

It was Mom's love for Papa that invited him to visit, but it was her forgiveness that allowed him to stay. She didn't see him for the words he had said or the things he had done throughout the years. She only saw a soul who needed a home. Shortly thereafter, on a cold winter's day during a horrific snowstorm, Papa died with Mom by his side, having forgiven him and now forgiving herself for anything she may have ever said or done to hurt or disrespect him throughout the years. Now, the only thing that remained was love.

With a daughter's forgiveness, Papa didn't have to live alone. With a daughter's forgiveness, Papa didn't have to die alone.

With an amazing example of love, devotion and compassion, I have been shown how to live—and now, how to forgive.

Dawn Nicole Patterson

A Gift from Above

Dipped in chocolate, bronzed with elegance, enameled with grace, toasted with beauty. My Lord, she is a black woman!

Yosef Ben-Jochannan

Black Woman

Your Presence:

At first glance in the morning, is the way I like my coffee—black and sweet. Up before me floating from room to room causing a reaction in me that only can be described as earth shattering. When I see you, I feel as if I am experiencing an earthquake when it's simply you making my liver quiver and my heart palpitate.

Your Smile, Your Eyes:

When you give me your smile it is so bright, it can light a room the size of a basketball court. At night, no lights are needed because your smile shines so brightly. When in the presence of others, your eyes let me know that I am your man.

Your Lips:

So sweet that all the chocolate on the planet could not match them, identifying you as a black woman, full, safe, and chocolaty. Your lips are sweeter than all the sugar canes in the fields of Lebanon. When my lips touch yours all sound around me dissipates and I float into a state of trance. The two of us are floating as if we are bouncing into galaxies way beyond our galaxy, looking for one to name after you, the black woman.

Your Arms:

The journey to your womanhood has developed arms that are often stronger than mine. When life is daunting for me as your man, you hold me with your tender yet stern loving arms. Your arms give to those in need a sense of hope like no other arms can. Your arms are the arms ready to hold the tiniest of God's creations in love. Your arms are the arms that this 6-foot, 2-inch man is looking, wanting, hoping soon to be held by.

Your Voice:

Your voice identifies you as a black woman and if listened to closely, it can move and give insight to the lowliest of spirits and heart of man. A voice that makes me—and others—feel wanted and needed. When words of wisdom are spoken to the world, people that come to know you look for the opportunity to be in your presence. It is a voice of comfort that makes the weakest of them all feel safe.

Your Mind:

You are so valuable to black men that many cannot and will not accept your God-given outlook. But for those of us who have understanding and are able to accept your beautiful mind, we sit on top of the world. With your mind you are a great complement to man, you help us move mountains and stand when we think we can't. Though we as men often forget, we must remember that God put you here to complete our minds through the power of you, the black woman.

Your Energy:

We understand that energy is the make-up of Almighty God, and we exist off that power, that energy. My black woman, you have that energy and took all of life's vicissitudes and turned into an expression of beauty just as God has intended. And with that energy you have transformed the lives of many.

My Request:

Thank you, God, for giving me this gift from above. I only ask that you give me as a black man the understanding, the wisdom and the strength so that I can love and accept all of the beauty that has been stored up just for me in the black woman.

Leslie Ford

Where Have All the Old Men Gone?

We must cherish our old men. We must revere their wisdom, appreciate their insight, love the humanity of their words.

Alice Walker

I don't know how it was in your neighborhood, but in the 1940s in Detroit the black neighborhoods were host to some of the most unique citizens in United States history—The Old Men.

It should be noted that not every old man was an Old Man. The rules for inclusion in the club were strict and rigidly adhered to. The gentleman had to be at least sixty-five years of age. In truth, this was one club where older was definitely better. He must have lived a fast lifestyle—a lifestyle designed to lead to an early grave and a beautiful corpse. It was also extremely important that he hold the reputation of having played fast and loose with women's affection all of his born days. Last but not least, it should be common knowledge that only the vicissitudes of old age had caused him to forsake his reprobate ways. I am pleased to report that in 1943, the west side of Detroit had a lively assortment of Old Men within its boundaries.

Mr. Larry Wilson, better known as Gray Cap because he always wore a gray knit cap, was the leader of the group and set the style for the others. John Henry Lewis ran him a close second, and on that rare occasion when Gray Cap was absent from the fray, Lewis took command. All summer long Gray Cap and his cohorts would stake out a corner or storefront and open up shop for the day. Both residents and shop owners welcomed them, for they served as entertainment for the residents and security officers for the stores. Who would think of robbing a store where a gaggle of old men sat at rusty card tables and played checkers for hours on end blocking entry to all but the most determined customers?

When fall came, and the north wind began to nip at their heels, they would move their table and chairs inside one of the local markets, setting up business near the front door—the better to thwart the escape of any would-be robber.

Gray Cap was a stellar example of all that an Old Man should be. At last count, he had fathered at least twenty-seven children, only seven of them by legal wives. The mothers of the balance were an eclectic mix of old maids, young girls, love-struck matrons, ladies of the evening, and the confused wife of the pastor of the Gleaning Light Baptist Church.

While John Henry Lewis could in no way match Gray Cap's statistics, he did have one unique credential of his own. He was the only man in the group who had fathered children by two sisters who delivered their babies on the same day. All of the area pastors preached hellfire and damnation sermons on the subject, vowing that the church would live to see John Henry destroyed in a hailstorm of God's rage.

The men of the neighborhood, both single and married, held a grudging admiration for The Old Men. Although most of them had sowed their wild oats as youths, the pressure of marriage and parenting had caused them to mend their ways. While they publicly censored The Old Men for their nefarious ways, in their hearts they had to respect men who did everything the church preached against and still lived to tell the tale.

As for the ladies of the neighborhood, the very mention of The Old Men would bring snorts of derision from every female on the west side. From grade school girls to the matriarchs of the neighborhood, the reaction was the same. To quote our neighbor Mrs. Eubanks, "There will be a special place in hell for each and every one of them."

As a fifteen-year-old female observer of the vagaries of life, I held a different viewpoint. If all the ladies in the area loathed and despised The Old Men, why didn't their actions support their positions? Curious to a fault, I set out to resolve the puzzle for myself.

It was Mrs. Eubanks who first noticed the change in my daily pattern. Instead of joining my friends on the corner for a daily dose of camaraderie, I took to following The Old Men wherever they set up shop. Quiet as a mouse, I watched and studied the actions, and interactions, between The Old Men and the neighborhood ladies they encountered. It was a revelation.

When my mother, prompted by Mrs. Eubanks, asked why I was following The Old Men around, I answered, "Because they're so funny; they make me laugh."

My mother smiled and replied, "Those old coots are funny, but don't spend all your time following them around. I don't want your head filled with their nonsense."

Having removed the major roadblock to my investigation, I forged ahead. My big break came when I heard an exchange between Mrs. Morton and Gray Cap. One Saturday afternoon, as Mrs. Morton threaded her way through The Old Men into Ryan's Food & Vegetable

Market, Gray Cap mumbled out loud, "My, my, I don't think my heart can stand it."

I held my breath as I waited for Mrs. Morton to lower the boom on Gray Cap. It is true that she gave a derisive snort, while simultaneously struggling to hold back a giggle. Suddenly I knew the answer to the puzzle—she liked it! Somewhere in her subconscious it registered as the compliment it was intended to be. It pleased her feminine side. It demonstrated that she still had it!

In only a day of concentrated study, I proved the truth of my hypothesis. I witnessed women crossing streets, going out of their way to pass by The Old Men to receive their racy, but comforting, comments as they passed their way. Women who had not received a flirtatious word from their husbands since their courtship days could return again, if only for a few minutes, to a younger, sweeter time. Although I was only fifteen years old, I knew in the core of my being that no matter what the church said, these were holy words.

There are things that you believe because they are true, and there are things that you believe because you want them to be true. I hold fast to the belief that I received the last compliment paid by the last of The Old Men, Stanley Clay.

One day in August 1955, no longer a teenager, I walked past Mr. Clay leaning against a railing in front of Cole's Funeral Home. Over the years, one by one, The Old Men had left this vale of tears until only Mr. Clay was left. All day, he wandered from store to store. While a gaggle of Old Men was welcomed, a solitary Old Man soon became a nuisance. His children and grandchildren housed him only to receive his pension check. As I passed Mr. Clay, he looked up and gave me a weak grin. Then with great effort, he pulled himself up and said, "Hey, Miss Looking Good, if there's anything dead in there, it'll sure wake up when you walk in."

Instinctively, I straightened my shoulders and sucked in my stomach. My walk took on the slightly seductive sway it had held in younger days. Chin up, and legs set at a slight angle, I walked—nay strutted—into Cole's Funeral Home.

Less than three months later, I again entered Cole's Funeral Home. This time it was to pay final respects to Mr. Stanley Clay. As I looked down on his body, I wanted to believe that the words he spoke only three months before would come true; that somehow he would wake up and give me that devilish grin and sly wink that was his claim to fame.

Now that I am a grandmother, I sometimes wonder, *Where have all The Old Men gone?*—The Old Men who served a special purpose in the lives of the men and women in my neighborhood so long ago. Did they realize how important their services were to the people around them? Somehow I think they did. Have they been swallowed up in the pervasive youth culture rampant throughout our country? I don't know. I do know that I miss them.

Marvin V. Arnett

7

BREAKING THROUGH MY BARRIERS

If the first woman God ever made was strong enough to turn the world upside down all alone, these women together ought to be able to turn it back, and get it right-side up again!

Sojourner Truth

Music in the Rooms

Blacks and whites were making efforts to change things, and music helped bridge the gaps.

Mary Wilson

In the early fifties my grandmother Hattie Taylor-West came up with a plan to bring money into the house by renting rooms out. Fortunately, there was a large theater located around the corner from our house, and it just happened to be a vital part of the "chitlin circuit" in the North. Musicians, singers, comedians and anybody who was somebody found a way to grace the stage at the Fans Theater on their way to New York and the bigger, brighter lights of Broadway. Whenever the shows came to town, they would sell out and our house became the focal point for extraordinary entertainers who needed a place to stay. As a young, impressionable little girl, I often wondered why these larger-than-life people came into my space and then left so quickly. I didn't quite know or understand exactly what it was, but there was always a heightened sense of excitement in the air when they came. I knew there was something "special" about them, and I loved being in the middle of it all.

Most of all I loved listening to the music in the rooms. There was just one problem: the guest quarters were supposed to be off-limits to inquisitive little girls.

"Chile, don't let me catch you buggin' the guests!" Granny would say before she launched into reminding me that these were busy people with jobs to do, and they didn't have time for curious, admiring, wide-eyed little girls. But I simply couldn't resist. The sounds were too compelling, too inviting, too enchanting for me to avoid.

Thumpa, thumpa, thump! I heard the beat as I tiptoed down the hallway, half-hidden by the huge gray shadows. I pictured a large, shiny, brand-new shoe tapping against the hardwood floor inside the room, behind one of the closed doors that held the secret to the music in the rooms. The sweet, hypnotizing rhythm made me move down the long hall with quickness in time to the beat. I moved closer and closer, and finally I was able to press my tiny ear to the door. The rhythmic thumps were so loud, my head was bobbing, my feet were tapping out the beats, and then I heard the horn. Tat ta ta ta! *Oh boy*, I thought to myself, *it's warm-up time, and Mr. Louie is playing my song.* Of course, I thought *every* song was mine; after all, no one else was there to hear them. As the music swelled into a loud crescendo I knew that Mr. Louis Armstrong was definitely in the house!"

"La, la, la, la, la, la, la, la, la." What a sweet, heavenly, melodic sound, and it went higher and higher each time around. Another day and my ear was pressed up against another door. My heart was pounding like it was going to jump right out of my body as I simultaneously kept watch over my shoulder to avoid getting caught. This weekend, Mr. Duke and his lady singers were staying with us. Sometimes the ladies let me come in the room to listen— of course, Granny didn't know I went. As I made my way down the hall I silently hoped, *Maybe today . . . I sure hope so!* My insides were quivering like a bowl of jelly. The singers were practicing a voice exercise that they called scales, and they did it every day before they started singing the real songs, just like clockwork.

I can do that, I told myself as I started to daydream, my lofty thoughts taking me away from reality. I envisioned myself all dressed up in fancy clothes standing in front of an audience. *I am going to be just like the beautiful, elegant, dark chocolate, creamy caramel ladies who sing with Mr. Duke Ellington. I'll be his favorite lead singer... do re mi fa so la ti do...* My daydreaming interfered with my ability to keep watch in the hallway.

"Bunny, what are you doing?" My sister Irene caught me again. "You know you're not supposed to be down here. I'm going to tell Granny."

"I'll give you some of my chicken and dessert tonight. Don't tell, *please*???" I could never understand why she didn't just join me in the halls, but Granny's "finger-licking good" food was the key to keeping my sister from telling on me. Crispy, hot fried chicken fresh out of the frying pan, dumplings (rolled out just right and not too thick, of course), collard greens with ham hocks, string beans with a few potatoes thrown in, baked macaroni and cheese, mashed potatoes and homemade gravy, melt-in-your-mouth biscuits, pound cake from scratch with cream cheese icing, a bumping banana pudding—no one could pass up extra helpings of my grandma's delicious food. I'm sure that was part of the reason she was so successful—and I seldom got in trouble.

The next day was much like the last. I would try to stay in our part of the house playing and helping Granny with chores, but each day new and different sounds would be coming from downstairs. *I will be quiet as a church mouse and just tiptoe past the room,* but I knew I wouldn't be able to stop myself from snooping. I was being drawn by the sounds on the first floor. From a brightly decorated room with a large bay window, I could hear Mr. Bill playing the old piano Granny always kept tuned up and polished. I inched closer to see if I could look through the curtains. My heart leapt when I recognized the tune, and I started humming the sweet melody of "April in Paris" floating through the air. I could not have been happier.

I absolutely loved the days when Mr. Bill would stay with us. He was a bandleader and always brought a lot of funny, crazy musicians with him. During his stay there was music in *every room*, and I was in heaven running from door to door. Everyone else called him Count Basie, but we called him Mr. Bill. I loved the room with all the windowpanes where Mr. Bill created, played, rehearsed and then ebbed and flowed with his music. The incredible sounds coming from this room were upbeat, and I got lots of exercise dancing to the tunes of Mr. Bill. I will always remember the time he walked out in the hall while I was dancing to the sounds coming from all those closed doors. He simply smiled at me like he understood—I was a music lover in the making. I think the musicians kind of liked knowing they had an admiring audience on the other side of the door.

Sometimes I long for those good old days, but when I find myself missing my Granny and those special days in her house, I simply sit in my big comfortable chair, put on some music, close my eyes and move door to door in my mind, pressing my ears close. I dance with those poignant, vibrant and lasting memories of the elegant yet kind entertainers, the fabulously talented musicians and the "sure nuff could sang" singers who took time out to encourage the little girl who was drawn to the music in the rooms.

What happened to that curious little girl who danced outside those doors? My whole life has been full of the most beautiful music—from gospel to blues, from big band to R&B, from jazz to hip-hop, and to this day, I love it all. And now I'm the one making music "inside the room" as a professional gospel singer. When I lead praise and worship or when I am in the studio doing background vocals, I am ever mindful of who may be listening in the church or at the studio door—because it may just be another little girl loving the music and dreaming big dreams.

Carolyn West

Turning My Mess into My Message

I was an ambitious and talkative teen who loved to "be in the spotlight." When I was fifteen I remember writing in my journal, *I can't wait to get away from here. It's so boring. I want to live in New York where the action is.*

In 1991, I entered Norfolk State University as a mass communications major. I'd always enjoyed school, but for me college was simply a necessary detour along the way. From the moment I walked on campus my goal was to graduate as quickly as possible so I could move to New York and live my dream of becoming a journalist.

I took my course request form to my advisor, who having seen her share of overzealous freshmen, sweetly said to me, "Baby, most students are lucky to graduate in five years. You'll make your mama proud to finish in four."

I pretended to listen, but honestly I wasn't concerned about what anyone else thought. All I wanted was to make my dream come true as fast as possible.

Seeing that I wouldn't be dissuaded, my advisor reluctantly agreed and signed the form. And so began my race for the finish line—New York was almost within my grasp.

If moving to New York was the engine, then it was fueled by my desire to have a lifestyle that I'd only imagined. My dream inspired me to press forward through a full course load, endless term papers, and seemingly more chapters than anyone could ever read in a lifetime, let alone a semester.

But despite my determination and book smarts, I was naive about the way the world worked. My sophomore year, I got my first credit card, which was to be strictly for emergencies.

The first "emergency" turned out to be the sale at Nine West. And what started as a fashion emergency became an obsession. It was intoxicating, and I felt invincible. Quickly my cafeteria meal plan was replaced with restaurant dinners where I happily paid for my "friends" to order to their hungry hearts' delight. When I wasn't at the mall or eating out, I was hitting the books, juggling an insane course load and holding fast to my dream of moving to New York one day soon.

I got good grades and was even awarded two internships—at a radio station and a newspaper. My professors were impressed with my determination and hard work. In the fall of 1994, just three and a half years after coming to N.S.U., I got what I'd been waiting for; word that I was approved to graduate.

So, less than a month before my twenty-second birthday, I boarded an airplane to New York with a one-way ticket, a high GPA and a very low credit score.

I walked into the human resources office ten minutes early for my face-to-face meeting after having been invited by the account manager, whom I'd impressed during a phone interview just two weeks before.

I was interviewed by several people before being shown around the office and even introduced to someone as the "bright young lady we're looking to add to our team." The day was going incredibly well, and I was confident that this was my date with destiny.

I waited in the reception area in anxious anticipation for the job offer I assumed was coming next. When my name was called, I quickly jumped to attention and walked into the office of the human resources director.

I tried to remain calm as she looked over the papers on her desk for what seemed like an eternity. Finally, she looked at me and said, "Sanyika, everyone here has been really impressed with you." I nodded, trying to seem more confident than arrogant. In a calm tone she continued, "You're the best candidate for this position. . . ."

I know, I thought to myself.

"We want to hire you for this position. . . ." The anticipation was killing me. *Get on with it then*, I thought, a little annoyed at the delayed delivery.

Again she spoke, "In considering you as the final candidate for this position. . . ." My insides were screaming. I was hanging on her every word. "We had to review your credit report. In doing so we realized that you haven't been responsible with your personal finances, therefore we cannot assume that you will be responsible on our behalf either. I'm very sorry."

If she said anything after "I'm very sorry," I couldn't tell you what it was. My senses were short-circuiting all at once. I fought a fierce battle within, as every emotion I had threatened to overtake me. I bit my lip to choke back the tears that were threatening to come pouring down my face as I swallowed back the biggest lump my throat had ever produced.

I watched her slowly rise from her chair and extend her hand toward me, which I took more to stop the room from spinning than anything else. I managed to say, "Thank you for your time." But the battle over my emotions left me numb and incoherent.

The life lesson I learned that day was more valuable than all the book smarts I'd worked so hard to acquire. Actually the lyrics from India Arie's song, "Slow Down" summed it up best. I was moving too fast and ignoring all the warnings along the way.

I was certain that I was the only one in the world to mess things up so bad. I was embarrassed, frustrated and honestly didn't know what I didn't know. All I knew was that I needed more education, and I became passionate about finding solutions for my credit problems.

Soon it became apparent that there was no one book, program, pill or potion that would magically make my troubles disappear. I couldn't rush this process, like I had before; it would require a lifetime commitment to learning and applying the money lessons that I was never taught in school to repay my debt and reclaim my life.

I was determined to stay in New York, and while I pursued my original dream a new one began to form. By talking to others about their money challenges I learned that whenever you think you're "the only one" who's made a big mistake; there are thousands more people thinking the same thing.

I realized that the absence of financial literacy lessons in school wasn't something to be *angry about,* but rather an oversight to *do something about.* What seemed like a cruel twist of fate became an awesome opportunity. Now I put my gift for gab to full use by teaching and writing about money management, debt prevention and savvy saving tips to teens, college students and even parents so that they won't make the same mistakes I did and can successfully land their dream jobs.

My mess has become my message. How's that for a dream come true?!

Sanyika Calloway Boyce

The Graduation

Education is the jewel casting brilliance into the future.

Mari Evans

The year was 1945, and Ruth Alston was about to embark on a journey that would forever change her life and affect the lives of her descendants, just as the plight of Sojourner Truth and Harriet Tubman had affected the next generation of young black women born into freedom because of their determination. Ruth had waged a battle despite having to walk three miles alone in the early morning hours through dirt roads full of haunts. She would then stand and wait for the bus to come and transport her the remaining ten miles to the only colored high school in the area.

It was during Ruth's sophomore year that Elsie Louise Smith had moved a mile from her on the old Jordan farm. Elsie shared her desire to obtain her high school diploma. Each morning Ruth would strike out on that one-mile journey and Elsie would watch for her from the window to round the bend, then she would head out to meet her.

Together they had endured the scorn and laughter of their peers, those who had dropped out, stating that it was "too difficult."

Too difficult! Ruth would often repeat to herself. Her generation had no real idea of what difficult was. Difficult was what her ancestors had to endure: not being allowed to attend school, or learn how to read and write, and seeing one's family ripped apart at the whim of someone else. No, she did not see the task before her as difficult, more like a torch of hope that she was more than willing to carry.

It was an extremely warm Carolina morning as Ruth pushed the burlap curtain back so that she could look out the window. Today was the culmination of all her dreams, and despite her best efforts it looked like the moment might pass her by.

"Come on away from that window. I told you to go ahead and get yourself dressed. Your papa wouldn't let you down on your special day. He'll be here any moment."

Ruth knew there was no need to argue with her mama. Hattie thought that the sun rose and set on Papa's head. In truth, Papa was no saint. He swore a little too much and liked to have himself a shot of corn whisky too often for anyone to mistake him for a saint.

"Yes, Mama," she reluctantly replied as she turned away from the window and walked down the dimly lit hallway to her small bedroom. There she looked at the lovely yellow and white dress that Mama had spent the last two weeks making. It was the prettiest thing that she had ever seen. The collar and sleeves were trimmed in a yellow silklike material, and the dress had little white flowers interwoven into the fabric. Slowly Ruth began to unbutton her old work dress as a thousand memories came rushing back to her.

There had never been a doubt in her mind that she would graduate from high school. She remembered when her older sister, who had gotten pregnant and married instead of going to school, yelled at her, "What you wasting your time on trying to get an education? In the end it won't matter. I need your help with Junior. Your homework can wait!"

Ruth looked at her sister, and for the first time she realized that they were nothing alike. "You know, Retta, I am going to graduate because that's my dream. You're going to have to take care of your own child." Ruth walked out as her sister screamed names at her departing back.

Later that evening as expected, Loretta and her husband, Bobby, had brought Bobby Jr. over to visit his grandparents. Papa and Mama had listened to them explain why Loretta needed her sister's help. Papa stood, lit his pipe and walked over to the window.

"I reckon that helping or not helping the two of you is Ruth's decision. Bobby, you married one of my daughters, not both. Getting married and starting a family is a big responsibility. One that the two of you said you were ready for."

"But, Mama . . ." Loretta began in her typical whining voice.

Hattie looked at her husband and the set of his mouth did not lend itself to any further discussion. "Papa has spoken."

The noise of the old Model T coming down the road brought Ruth out of her reverie and back to the present. She raced down the hallway yelling, "Mama, he's here!"

Hattie wiped her hands on her apron before pulling it over her head. "I reckon you better run and slip your shoes on." Before Ruth could move, the door swung open.

There stood Papa. He stepped into the hallway and with that gravelly voice of his stated, "I didn't forget, Babyray." He walked hurriedly down the hallway and stepped into the room that he shared with Mama. After splashing some water from the wash basin on his face and changing out of his blue overalls, he dressed in his Sunday-go-to-meeting clothes that consisted of a white cotton shirt that had seen too many washings and a pair of black pants. Papa combed his long gray hair back and picked up his keys.

Papa had driven that old Model T as fast as it would go, not slowing down until he needed to make the turn into the dirt field by the school. Ruth saw her class marching from the schoolhouse to the building that served as the gym. She hurriedly climbed out of the vehicle before it came to a complete stop, nearly tripping in the process.

Elsie turned her head at the sound of the commotion and yelled, "There's Ruth!" As she approached her friend, Elsie stated softly, "It just wouldn't have been the same without you." The two friends embraced as Mrs. Davis instructed the class to halt their progression. With the help of Ms. Davis and Elsie, Ruth quickly donned her cap and gown and took her place in line.

The sound of the organist at her daughter's college graduation brought Ruth out of that memorable passage she had journeyed some thirty years ago. It was the adversity of those times, and all she had endured, that brought her to this moment in her life. Ruth stood and applauded loudly as her daughter, Elizabeth Hattie Jacobs, walked across the stage to receive her baccalaureate degree in English. Turning, Ruth looked at her husband, then she embraced her mother.

"We made it, Mama. We changed the rules." Ruth held on to her mother as tears rolled freely down her cheeks. Her only wish was that her father had lived long enough to see this moment. He had drifted off to sleep when Elizabeth was five years old and had not awakened, the result of a heart attack. As Ruth looked around the large stadium full of the hope for the future, she felt Papa's presence in the form of a warm caress against her cheek. Smiling she turned back to her mother, "Papa knows."

"My child, your Papa always knew that this is where your dreams would lead you. And Elizabeth's dreams will lead her even further."

Under the bright sunlight of a beautiful May afternoon and miles away from the hardships of a sharecropper's life, Ruth reflected on her journey. Each generation had a responsibility to open doors and remove obstacles for the next generation. Ruth, through her determination to graduate from high school, had begun to build a foundation for the future.

Bernetta Thorne-Williams

Reprinted by permission of Jerry Craft. ©2006.

More Than a Dream

There is a spirit and a need and a man at the beginning of every great human advance. Every one of these must be right for that particular moment of history, or nothing happens.

Coretta Scott King

I was only ten years old when Martin Luther King, Jr., was assassinated and do not remember experiencing overt discrimination. I did not drink from colored water fountains or sit in the balcony at movies. I have heard horrendous stories from relatives, seen movies and read books about the civil rights struggle, but I grew up in a Northern city, attended integrated schools and counted my white classmates as friends. I recognize that I have benefited from the civil rights movement, but outside of paying NAACP dues, making a conscious effort to be aware of black history and instilling a sense of pride in my children, I did not feel there was much I could do to advance Dr. King's dream. I am not an attorney, politician or religious leader, and while I have run into an occasional bigot, the overwhelming majority of my interactions with whites has been positive. What impact could I, a "regular person," have? That question was answered when I visited the museum.

I must admit I lived in Memphis almost two years before I visited the National Civil Rights Museum. We have a tendency to undervalue things in our own back-yard. As a newcomer to Memphis, the Beale Street clubs were first on my list of things to see and do. I saw Graceland and Elvis's plane, the *Lisa Marie*. I went to one of the biggest events in the city, the annual Southern Heritage Classic between Jackson State University and Tennessee State University. The football game and concerts give the city a festive spirit all weekend. I had even found flea markets I liked to scour for hidden treasures. And, I'll confess, I visited the nearby casinos in Tunica more than once. I did all of these things before I visited the National Civil Rights Museum. But once I went, I couldn't believe it had taken me so long to tour this important landmark.

Images of Dr. Martin Luther King, Jr., permeate our society. More Americans can recite his "I Have a Dream" speech than the Constitution. We commemorate his life on the third Monday in January. But in all of this celebration, Dr. King has been placed on a pedestal, and we tend to forget he was a real person. He was a great, anointed man. Yet still a man. A visit to the National Civil Rights Museum reminds me of his humanity and reveals how important the actions of "regular people" can be.

The first thing that strikes me about the museum is the neighborhood. When I first turned onto the street the museum is on, I thought, *This is it?* The National Civil Rights Museum is not housed in a fancy edifice with columns and marbled halls. The museum is located at the Lorraine Motel, the site of Dr. King's assassination. It is not on a major street and is not in the best part of town. The neighborhood is now being revitalized, but even in 1968, I am sure more prestigious accommodations were available. Segregation downtown had ended, and there are hotels with scenic views of the mighty Mississippi River that would have been more worthy. This man had dined with kings and presidents. He had won a Nobel Peace Prize and was revered by millions. Yet he stayed in a two-story motel in a working–class area of town. It is reported that he stayed in this motel to be closer to the working people—the "regular people" he had come to help. This neighborhood is tangible evidence of his humility.

The next thing I notice is the vehicle parked in front of the museum. It is a white 1967 Cadillac Coupe de Ville. This is the vehicle he was driven in when he came to Memphis. We often think of him as the "dreamer." We see him marching in Selma, giving a speech in the nation's capital and being heckled in Chicago. His image is associated with pivotal moments in history, and it's as if he floated from place to place. He did not float. He needed transportation to get to all these places. That Cadillac reminds me of his humanity.

Inside the museum, we climb a flight of stairs and walk single file into 1968. We speak in hushed tones, as if we have entered a church sanctuary. Mahalia Jackson's stirring contralto is in the background and seems to waft down from heaven. We are on hallowed ground. Even children, who have been antsy in other parts of the tour, quiet down.

The tour guide has ushered us just steps away from where Dr. King had his last meal. The bed is unmade. A coffee cup and ashtray sit next to his room service tray. The room looks as though its resident has just stepped out for a moment. But this is Room 306 of the Lorraine Motel, in Memphis, Tennessee, the last place Dr. King slept.

Room 306 is a sparse room with modest furniture. After

the speeches, interviews and crowds, he returned to a room like this, rather than to his home and family. He not only sacrificed his life, he sacrificed precious time with his wife and children. I often travel for my job. That travel is a way to provide for my family, and the objective is a paycheck. Would I endure the road if the reward were not going to be financial? Would I leave my comfortable home and family to face violence and hostility? I am grateful I don't have to answer those questions because Dr. King and others made the sacrifice for me.

Room 306 is also evidence of his honesty and commitment to his calling. Dr. King and Reverend Ralph Abernathy shared a room. In these days when so many religious leaders are viewed with suspicion regarding their financial motives, and scandals plague so many charitable organizations, it is refreshing to know that Dr. King's motives were genuine. He stayed in a modest motel and shared a room to save money. He had an honorable calling and did not try to profit from it.

This hotel also demonstrates to me that Dr. King understood economics. We have gone from fighting for the right to sit on the bus, to the right to drive the bus, to the right to own the bus company. Legal obstacles to black entrepreneurship have been removed. The Lorraine Motel was black-owned and during segregation offered blacks a nice place to stay. Dr. King demonstrated that just because we had the right to stay where we wanted, we should not forsake businesses in our own neighborhoods. The "Mountaintop" and "I Have a Dream" speeches are his most quoted, but Dr. King preached black economic empowerment long before it was fashionable. Not only did he preach it, his stay at the Lorraine Motel shows me he lived it.

Although Room 306 is the centerpiece of the museum, there are many other exhibits ranging from the slave trade to a chronicle of lynching. I learn something new each time I visit. On one visit I looked closely at some pictures and saw a woman hanging from a tree. I never knew women were lynched, and her picture haunts me. I feel a kinship with this black woman and wonder about her life. There is a replica of the Montgomery bus where Rosa Parks was arrested. I knew black people had to sit in the back, but I didn't know that blacks had to pay their money, then get off the bus and go to the back door to get on. I get mad just thinking about it. Maybe this is why I took so long to visit the museum. I didn't want to get all stirred up, then have to go to work and smile at white folks.

But this isn't a place that will leave African Americans upset and depressed. The exhibits generate a sense of pride. I am proud to be part of a legacy of people who endured so much, yet survived and thrived. I am proud, but I also feel a little guilty. When I see what others have gone through, I feel guilty that I am not doing more. When I see the Rosa Parks exhibit and see how the Montgomery residents walked and carpooled, in heels, for months, rather than ride segregated buses, I feel guilty that I won't drive an extra few miles to patronize a black business because it is out of my way. When I see the Freedom Riders exhibit and the sacrifices made for the right to vote, I feel guilty about the times I skipped voting because it was "just a primary," or I had to work late. When I see the sparse room that this great man stayed in, I think about how he sacrificed time with his children and spent time in rooms like this, and I feel guilty that I don't spend more time reviewing the civil rights struggle with my own children.

Each visit to the museum is a wake-up call for me. It's like the sense of renewal you feel after an inspiring church service. I enjoy taking visiting friends and relatives. I have gained an appreciation for the humanity of Dr. King and the contributions of "regular people" to the civil rights movement. After each visit to the museum, I wake up from complacency and recommit myself not to take things such as voting, public education or even my job for granted. I recommit myself not just to remembering the past, but trying to improve the present and the future. I make a special effort to patronize black businesses. I donate time and money to worthy causes. I hope my efforts will serve as a tribute to the lynched black woman in the picture. These are things a "regular person" like me can do to make Dr. King's dream a reality.

Phyllis R. Dixon

Shades of Black and White

It doesn't matter what you've been through, where you come from, who your parents are— nor your social or economic status. None of that matters. What matters is how you choose to love, how you choose to express that love through your work, family and what you have to give the world . . . own your power and your glory.

Oprah Winfrey

Tied down, my arms outstretched, I lay motionless on the gurney. I thought to myself, *I came into this world stretched out on a cross, maybe that's how I will die.* Helpless and afraid, being prepped for surgery, the events of my life began to replay in my mind.

I remembered my mama telling me stories about my birth. I had been strapped down before when my mother first received me. I was literally tied to a cross because, during my birth, both of my collarbones were broken as I was yanked out of the birth canal.

My Negro mama was significantly overweight, but her chocolate skin and dazzling good looks revealed a fiery and attractive woman. It was a long while before my mama could hold me. She didn't know at the time that the doctors were patching me up. Finally, the nurse brought in two Caucasian redheaded twin girls and handed them to her. Naturally Mama put them to her breast and they suckled. Perhaps a half hour or so had gone by when a nurse frantically returned to the room red-faced and apologizing. "Oh, Mother Roberts," she cried. "I'm so sorry. These are not your babies. Please forgive me—and please don't tell the mother across the hall that you nursed them," she pleaded.

The mother across the hall was a white woman, and the hospital did not want to be liable if the woman were to adamantly protest. They could imagine that even litigation might occur.

Mama agreed. "Okay," she said. "But don't bring me no *black* baby," she insisted.

A few minutes later I was brought in, white-skinned and tied to a cross.

My mama's reply was, "Well, she's all broke-up, but she's pretty." As my mother recounted the story, I couldn't imagine how confused that nurse must have been. My mother, the oldest girl of five siblings, had the darkest skin color of the girls in her family. Her father would irately address her as "Black Gal."

When I grew up, and you called somebody "black," them was "fightin'" words.

It was not until her father was sick and on his deathbed that he asked for his daughter's forgiveness. But by then, it was too late. My mama had already determined that there was something very wrong with her skin color and that having dark skin was a curse—a curse big enough to make even your own father treat you differently.

As I lay on the gurney waiting to be cut open, my mind's eye quickly flashed to the Detroit race riots of 1943. The riot of '67 was pale in comparison. It was reported that a pregnant woman on a streetcar was shot and killed through the window because they thought she was a white woman. She wasn't. And a white woman aboard another streetcar discreetly hid a black man under the skirt of her dress to keep him from being killed. What courage and tenacity this woman demonstrated.

This color thing is insane. Where did this notion come from? I pondered as I lay motionless. Blacks killing whites, whites killing blacks, skin color judged by both blacks and whites—it all seemed crazy to me.

I turned my reminiscence from my mother's childhood to my own. At the turn of the twentieth century my immigrant father traveled by water from Sicily to New York's Ellis Island. Eventually he came to Detroit, where he owned a neighborhood grocery store. Even though my parents were not married nor did they live together, we were never hungry.

I was born in 1924 to a single-parent Negro mother and an Italian father. In those days it was, without a doubt, a disgrace to give birth to a child out of wedlock. It was equally shameful for the child. Even though growing up mulatto and without a true father-daughter relationship brought me pain, there were many times that I'd say, "Mama, I don't care how I got here. I am glad I'm here."

I was happy she chose to have me and that I was alive regardless of the circumstances, but I hated school. The name-calling was cruel. I have been called every derogatory name you can think of and, thank God, I am now immune to all of them.

Even though I was light-skinned, dark-skinned colored girls were my best friends because, like me, they were ostracized and considered outcasts of society. The so-called respectable children (born in marriage) could not stay outside when I was out playing. Their mothers would call them inside.

My mind began to wander from the more painful memories to thoughts of the many good things about growing up in those times. Flickering images of growing up on Hastings and St. Antoine danced in my mind. Reverend Franklin (Aretha Franklin's father) had his church at that time on Hastings and Willis. We had many prayerful and singing good times in that church.

I smiled as I remembered the story Mama had told me about the time she was nursing me on the streetcar, and the conductor was so engrossed looking through his rear view mirror at a large Negro woman nursing a white baby that he missed his switchover. He had to back up the streetcar and reconnect his switch exchange.

And then there was the time she and I were in the ten-cent store, and I loudly cried and acted out for a doll. The store clerk implored my mother to buy the doll for me saying, "I'm sure her mother will be happy to repay you."

"I *am* her mother," Mama indignantly answered the clerk.

I tell people all the time, "I'm glad I came through those years." I reminisce and tell folks things like, "We could sleep all night on Belle Isle, and nobody would bother us." And I tell them about the times when Joe Louis was the upcoming champion in the world of heavyweight boxing. His mother lived in the neighborhood. She was such a nice woman. Most of us didn't have televisions, so when her son Joe was fighting, and it was televised, she would put the TV on the front porch, and we would walk around to her house on McDougall Street to watch the fights. We would all be cheering for the "Brown Bomber"!

When Hudson's department store began to hire colored girls as elevator operators they had to be light-skinned girls. I think part of my mother's healing was her refusal to buy anything from Hudson's.

As I lay spread out on that gurney I relived the aftermath of Pearl Harbor when Detroit's Ford Motor Company was hiring more factory workers. I set out one bright, brisk early morning looking for work and I stood in the long line marked "Colored." When I approached the clerk at the desk he abruptly snapped at me asserting, "We're *not* hiring!"

I was so disappointed; I was counting on that job to help our family make ends meet. Sadly, I turned around and went back home. My minister heard of the incident and encouraged me to go back, but this time he urged me to stand in the line marked "White." I did, and the response at that window was markedly different. A woman with a handheld apparatus stamped my application with a loud and deliberate motion and announced, "Hired!" I stood there startled and speechless.

Perhaps, it was in that astonishing moment when I realized that another world of opportunities could open for me if I went with the white side of my heritage and was quiet about the colored side. I looked white, so I learned to do what was necessary to survive. My father was white, so I was, indeed, both black *and* white. I was never ashamed of myself or felt like I was "passing." I was just using my challenging racial mixture to my benefit for a change.

I worked at Ford during the war as a riveter on the wings of the B29 bomber airplanes. Then, after the war, I took a job as a dance instructor at the renowned Arthur Murray Dance Studio. Considered beautiful by society's standards and compared by some to the likes of Rita Hayworth and Susan Hayward, I stood about 5-feet 6-inches tall, a brunette with long, flowing hair and a slender build, with a flair for glamour and style.

At the age of twenty-eight, married with two children, I lay on the table awaiting surgery to remove a lump from my breast, wondering if and praying that this will not be the last chapter of my life.

Somewhere between reminiscing about dancing at the

Elmwood Casino in Canada where my partner and I would waltz out and "take the dance floor," and being a finalist in Bob Hope's "My Favorite Brunette" contest . . . I remembered nothing more until I awoke from surgery.

What had looked like a tumor was really a milk clot from nursing my babies, and they removed it. I cried with relief and gratitude knowing how blessed I was to continue being with my family. And continue I would!

Today, I am eighty-one years old. I have been on both sides of the shades of black and white. The depth and the richness of being "colored" (it's still hard for me to say "black") has its roots in my soul. I have accepted and carried my crosses in the light and the dark of it. My spirit reigns free.

I love my mother for giving me birth and life. I'm glad I'm here. I don't care how I got here. Life is a gift no matter who we are, how we got here or what the color of our skin. I rejoice in all the shades of black and white in myself—and in you.

Dorothy Jackson As told to Hattie Mae Pembrook

Moving On from Militancy

I'm not a feminist. . . . I'm just a proud black woman.

Queen Latifah

"Hey, white girl! Hey, white girl! Damita, you look just like a white girl," said Johnny. Johnny was a fourth-grade classmate of mine. It was picture day, and my mother had pressed my hair real straight and made me some "Japanese bangs." I thought I looked fine, but Johnny said I looked white. My classmates began to laugh at me and make fun of me. I was downright mad.

"No I don't! I'm not white. Just because I'm not a tar baby like you! So there!" I stormed off, and when it was finally time for me to take my picture, I made sure that my hair was a mess. After all, I just did not want to be white. I wanted to look like everyone else in my class.

I had light hair, light eyes and a light complexion. Why me? Everyone else in my family was brown except me. My mocha-colored sister Kathy said that I was adopted! I didn't want to be adopted, either. My mother assured me that I was not adopted and that I was her baby. So there!

I grew up always trying to prove my ethnicity. When I got to high school in Los Angeles I decided to join a militant organization. It was called the Black Youth Alliance. I changed my name to Tamu Impanduzy, Sweetest of the Revolution. My boyfriend was a senior, and he had an African name also. Now I was so black—or so I thought. We also became involved with a ragtag organization outside of the school. They talked about "offing the pig," but I knew I wasn't going to "off" anything. I was a nonviolent black girl who happened to look white. I was just sitting in those meetings questioning my commitment to the movement. I didn't think that I had what it takes to be a full-fledged revolutionary. The following events confirmed it.

When I arrived home one day my mother met me at the door. Her face was red and swollen like a big beach ball, and her eyes were bulging like Kermit the Frog! I could have sworn that I saw steam coming out of the top of her head and drool peeking out of the corners of her mouth. *Oh God, what happened to her? What did my siblings do to her?* Well, I quickly found out that it wasn't the other kids that had caused her face to blow up—it was *me*!

The Federal Bureau of Investigation had visited my neighborhood. Can you believe it? Looking for *me*! They asked my neighbors questions about me and about my militant behavior. I couldn't believe it. All I did was wear a big Afro, dashikis, sandals and ethnic jewelry. Well, okay, I did *talk* a lot of mess, but I sure wasn't going to back it up!

And they had visited my mother.

"Who do you think you are? Didn't I raise you to be a law-abiding citizen? You are not Angela Davis, you're Damita Kelly, and you'd better start acting like it! The FBI! Well, somebody better call the FBI to get me off of you!" my mother ranted. I saw my entire life flash before my eyes, and suddenly looking like a white girl just didn't seem that important.

There was a funeral that day. Tamu Impanduzy was laid to rest. My mother "offed" her! I was told to excuse myself from that organization, press my hair, put on some "American" clothes and get myself some real friends. She informed me that as long as I lived under her roof, I was to answer only to the name "Damita."

I went to my last meeting to inform the brothers and sisters that I was no longer a member and why. It seemed as though each member had a story similar to mine. One of our new members was a spy. He was actually a member of the FBI and had gotten all of our information and turned it over. This was all too heavy for me. I didn't want to tangle with the FBI—or worse yet with my mother!

Oddly enough, I wasn't that upset about it. In retrospect, it is probably because the "establishment" was never my issue in the first place. My issue was wanting to feel like I belonged. Somehow my mother's lecture and the wake-up call about the direction my life was taking caused me to take another look in the proverbial mirror. This time when I looked in the mirror, I softened my critical eyes and worked on just accepting myself "as is."

I made a decision then and there to go to college. I even decided I'd try out for the cheerleading squad—a gang with a lighter purpose.

Now, I really don't care that I look white. I know who I am, and I finally know that I have nothing to prove.

Damita Jo Johnson

Never, Ever Give Up

*Courage allows the successful woman to fail—
and to learn powerful lessons from the failure—so
that in the end, she didn't fail at all.*

Maya Angelou

Growing up against the odds in the Brewster projects of
Detroit, Michigan, was no day at the beach. Just ask diva
Diana Ross and world champion boxer Joe Louis whose
lives began there also. Getting into fights was a way of life,
and most girls got pregnant before they graduated from
high school.

I was often chased home from school by jealous girls
yelling, "You think you're so cute." I was called "Yellow
Banana," and accused of having a white daddy because
my skin tone was so light. I would get my hair pulled or
get a kick from behind by someone while standing in the
lunch line.

When I was in junior high school my family moved into
a much nicer neighborhood. I thought things would get
better for me socially, but they got worse. Being blessed
with a God-given athletic ability and natural good looks, I

walked tall with confidence. The boys jockeyed for my attention while the girls hated me. I was the talk of my new school. I was referred to as the tall, light-skinned girl with long hair.

One day after school as I was leaving the girls' locker room, exhausted from an intense track practice, I was attacked by a gang of girls. I literally began fighting for my life. A couple of girls held me down while one girl beat me, another pulled my hair and kicked me, and one began to slice my face, arms, neck, chest and legs with a razor. As she was cutting my body, she said, "Let's see what boy is going to like you now!"

This fight was nothing like the Brewster projects' fist-fighting days with hair pulling and a few punches! I could not believe this was happening to me. I felt like I was having a nightmare and could not wake up. The girls attacking me began to run away as they heard someone yell, "Call an ambulance!"

Someone else shouted, "Oh my God, look at her face!"

I was covered in blood from head to toe and felt faint as I ran back into the locker room to look in the mirror. I cried so hard! I could not believe that I was looking at a cut so deep that I could see the inside of my flesh hanging out. It made me weak in the knees, and sobbing I screamed, "My face! Look at my face!" The face I once took pride in was now mangled and dripping with blood.

The tragic event that I had hoped no one would find out about became the headline news. I wondered how I would ever go back to school to face everyone. I was given over one hundred stitches and stayed home from school for the next fourteen days. While I was home recovering, I experienced many different emotions and had several conversations in my head about why someone would try to hurt me like that. I felt alone, embarrassed and helpless. I was very angry with my parents for not protecting me. I built an invisible wall between the outside world and myself, and I no longer trusted anyone. I kept pondering what I could have done to prevent this. Maybe on that particular day I should have run away as fast as I could instead of trying to defend myself.

The authorities became involved, and our case went to court. After a few days of hearings and witnesses taking the stand, the jury decided that the defendant was guilty of a misdemeanor crime and would have to serve 90 days in the county jail. The others involved were not charged at all. I was so glad that the girl who used the razor had to go to jail, but I felt cheated because it was for such a short period of time. I wanted her to serve ten or fifteen years in prison. In just a short period of time she could choose to erase the memory forever while I would have to spend the rest of my life with physical scars to remind me. Justice did not seem fair.

How could I return to school with everyone knowing my private business? For the first time I realized how humiliated celebrities must feel when their personal lives are publicly exposed without their permission. I went back to school nervously and with caution. I was very ashamed but determined to hold my head up high, even when I saw students staring at me. Where were those so-called "role models" when I needed them most? I wanted to hear how they would have dealt with this situation.

I was now referred to as the girl who got beat up and cut in the fight. I entered friendships with apprehension because I wasn't sure whom to trust. I began to have self-esteem issues and major problems with my family. I felt no one really understood what I was going through and that it was time for me to move on. I planned to run away from home. I packed up and off to school I went one day, never to return home again.

The thought of going somewhere new and leaving my past behind seemed like a great idea, but I realized that the hidden emotional scars would never be erased because of the visible scars that I wore daily as a constant reminder of what took place at school that day.

I lived with a friend's family for a while and eventually moved in with a relative who lived in another city. I wanted someone to hold me by the hand and shield me from my pain, but no one did. I was told to "be a big girl" or to "get over it." I talked to myself a lot and learned to talk to God through prayer.

My self-esteem was not the same after this event, and it took a while to learn to deal with my emotional pain. My teachers were the inspiration that got my life back on track. They gave me good, solid words of wisdom. They even gave me "tough love" when necessary, and I learned to trust them and take their advice. Through their unending commitment, I began to believe in myself. I forgot about my "physical handicap" and began to focus on my inner strength and beauty. I gradually went from walking with my shoulders slumped over and hair covering my face to hide the scars to wearing my hair pulled back and standing tall again.

One day, during my college career, while I was working in a department store, I got a visit from the woman who caused me this life of pain. She stood a few feet away, and when my eyes came into contact with hers my heart began to pound uncontrollably. I felt the same rush of adrenaline that I had experienced that awful day at school, and I wasn't sure why she was there. Did she come to assess the damage she had done, or was she there to finish the job?

She immediately began telling me about what she had been doing with her life, as if I cared, and then she asked me to forgive her for what she had done. This was a shock!

A million thoughts rushed through my head. I even thought that she was a bit insane. Our conversation ended with me answering "yes" to her request. Then she walked away, disappearing into the crowd of shoppers as suddenly as she had appeared, never to be seen by me again.

It was at that moment I realized my life had a purpose that was bigger than the scars on my body and the hatred in my heart. It took many, many years for me to regain my confidence and self-esteem. I learned to find inner peace by surrounding myself with positive people and reading a lot of great books to help me understand why bad things happen to good people—more specifically, what I could do to overcome the bad things that had happened to me. I forgave—and learned to respect—my parents, realizing that they had done the best that they knew how at that time.

Many years later as I stood at the podium ready to deliver my acceptance speech for being inducted into the Highland Park High School Hall of Fame, I was overcome with emotion and humbled to tears. No one knew that the woman being honored for her accomplishments as a college graduate, international fashion model, beauty queen, NFL cheerleader, Star Search television spokesmodel and successful entrepreneur was once too humiliated and embarrassed to show her face in public. Finally, I felt the courage to tell my story publicly for the first time.

I wanted the audience to know what built my character and gave me purpose. I wanted them to know the power of forgiveness. I wanted them to know that running away from home was not the answer to problems because when you run away from things, the problem is still there, and eventually you must deal with the problem in order for it to go away. I wanted them to know that you could overcome anything; to reach out to those who want to help you. I wanted them to know *me*, all of me, not just the "success story" they saw before them. I decided to *be* a role model so that kids like me would have someone to guide them if and when horrible things happened to them. So standing there in front of that audience, I said, "Let me tell you my story. . . ."

Tanya Hutchison

Queen Charlene

In the fall of 1973, I was a fourteen-year-old girl on my way to my first day of high school. I wasn't going to a school that was familiar to me. My parents hadn't registered me in time to attend any of the Catholic high schools in Newark, where I lived. As a result, they had to scramble to get me into the closest available Catholic high school, which was St. Cecilia's in Kearny, New Jersey.

That first day I sat on the public bus with sweaty palms and a jittery stomach. I reached into my bag and pulled out a small hand mirror. The cloud of my curly Afro surrounding my face looked a little lopsided, so I patted and shaped it into a neat dome. I stared at the round, full cheeks of my face and sighed. I hoped no one would tease me about my weight and quickly decided I would go in smiling, cheerful and chatting away like always, so they wouldn't even think about it.

I was feeling a little better as I got off the bus and walked through the doors of the high school. As instructed by the material I'd received over the summer, I made my way to the auditorium for freshman orientation.

"Hi," I said to a boy with curly red hair and freckles sprinkled across his face. He looked at me and turned away. I scanned the small crowd of no more than fifty students, mainly female, for a glimpse of brown skin like mine or another curly-kinky Afro. It was a small group. I could find no match to myself in the whole room. I noticed a few students looking at me and turning quickly away. I smiled widely and waved at a girl who didn't turn away fast enough and she nodded an acknowledgment. No smile, though.

Okay, I thought to myself, *these kids are not that friendly.*

I went through two or three classes, feeling the subtle chill from the students but glad to see that the nuns and other teachers were treating me with kindness and warmth. Stopping at my locker to drop off a book, I saw a note taped to it. I peeled it off and read three words: "Go home." The third word is too disgusting to repeat. My heart rate tripled, and I felt a weight in my stomach like I'd swallowed a brick for breakfast.

I bit my bottom lip, using the discomfort to distract me from the urge to cry, crumpled up the note and let it drop on the hallway floor. I'd never experienced anything like this before.

Fine, I told myself. *Okay, so this is how it is in this school.* I shoved my book into my locker and walked to my next class, chin up and eyes straight ahead. In my mind I repeated over and over, *They will not see me cry. They will not see me cry. They will not see me cry. . . .*

Lunchtime let me know that there was not one student willing to break through the invisible barrier around me. I sat at the table completely alone, ignored by them all. I didn't bother to try to talk or befriend anyone else. I moved through the rest of the day focusing on my schoolwork and trying not to feel anything.

Finally, the school day was over. Seated on the bus on my way back to Newark, I pulled out my hand mirror again. My curly hair was peppered with spitballs. I picked them all out before I arrived home. I didn't tell my parents the details of my day. I knew that my dad would insist that I stay in that school anyway and stand up for myself. I saw no point in saying anything about it.

The next few weeks were a repeat of that first day with only slight variations. Lunchtime improved somewhat as the cafeteria workers began to join me at my table during my lunch hour. I sat at the table, a caramel drop in the midst of milky whiteness, joking, chatting and glad for the company of those older women.

Still, the animosity of my classmates was wearing me down. I remember overhearing someone loudly ask another student, "Where does she live, anyway? Why is she going to our school?" I just ignored it.

But one day, about a month into the school year, I entered the girls' locker room, sweaty and tired from gym class. I spotted the white paper taped to my locker from a few feet away. I placed one foot slowly in front of the other until I was standing right in front of the note.

It read, "You are not welcome here."

With a shaky hand I snatched the note from the locker door and whipped around to face the girls.

"Who did this?!" I shouted as loudly as I could.

I waved the torn piece of notebook paper at the closest girl.

"Did you put this here?" I demanded.

She just looked at me, eyes wide. I glared around at the other faces all silently wearing the same expression.

"Listen up, all of you. I have just as much right to be here as any of you!"

I ripped the note into tiny pieces and flung it at them. They flinched as the pieces flew at them, fell short and fluttered to the floor.

"My parents are paying for me to go to this school just like yours."

One of the girls made a sound, and I turned to her.

"I'll take you on one by one if I have to. You know where I'm from? Huh?! I'm from Newark, and I will bring my gang up here, and we will kick your butts!"

Quickly my mind flashed to my girlfriends, soft-spoken Tasha in her thick glasses, and tall, lanky Debbie who'd never had a fight in her whole life. But my classmates were looking scared, so I ran with it.

"Yeah, that's what I'll do. I . . . have . . . had . . . enough, and the next person who messes with me is gonna get it. And I mean it!"

I turned away from them and pulled my locker door open so hard that it banged against the wall, ignoring them as I prepared for my next class.

For the rest of the day no one said a word to me or about me. They didn't even look my way. But for the first time since school started, I didn't have to pick spitballs out of my hair at the end of the day.

The next morning I took a deep breath before pushing through the school doors. My chin was up, and I was ready to do battle.

"Hi, Charlene!"

I whipped my head around in surprise, nodded and flashed a small smile to a girl with straight brown hair hanging down her back.

"Good morning, Charlene," said another student. She was one of the girls I'd yelled at in the locker room the previous day. "We're really sorry, Charlene."

My smile was bigger this time as I accepted her apology. The rest of the day was a blur. The girls had made a 180-degree turnaround overnight. At lunchtime, I sat with three of my fellow students and winked at one of the cafeteria ladies behind the counter. She smiled back.

The students joked and chatted with me, and we asked each other questions, getting to know each other better.

As the year went on, I became very close friends with three of the girls. We studied together after school, went to each other's homes and went to the school dances. The music and the dance moves at the school parties were different than what I was used to, but I joined right in and had a good time. Eventually, I joined the choir and the drama club. By the end of that freshman year I "stood out" in the best kind of way—a participant in school activities, friendly to all, talkative and social.

I decided to stay with St. Cecilia's for the next three years. And they were good years. As accepted as I was, I was still a bit surprised when my classmates nominated me for student council president in my junior year. I was even prouder when I actually won.

By the time I was a senior at the school, I strutted down the halls of St. Cecilia's Catholic High School like a queen.

Graduation day found me with a mix of emotions. My tears flowed freely that day. I looked around at the faces of my fellow students, and I was overwhelmed by their love. They'd taught me so much—how to stand up for myself, how to forgive, that I should always be true to myself and to go for what I want. Finally, their ability and willingness to change their attitude and behavior from hatred to love and acceptance taught me the value of seeing beyond the barriers of race, color or creed, through to the real person—through to the friend.

Charlene Copeland
As told to Sonya Simpson

Reclaiming My Soul

You must love and care for yourself because that's when the best comes out.

Tina Turner

The weather was reflective of my mood on this particular autumn day. The sky was gray and full of clouds, with no chance of sunshine in the forecast. For five months I had been battling a serious blood disorder, but I realized that my physical illness was the least of my problems. It was my emotional state that was killing me.

For the preceding twelve months, it was as if my life had been nothing but a showering downpour of rain. I was caught in "the perfect storm" and felt as if I had nowhere to run for shelter.

I had never felt so alone in my entire life. My older daughter was in Utah attending the RedCliff Ascent Wilderness Therapy Program for struggling teens. My younger daughter was at school. I was supposed to be at work, but I had called my assistant that morning and informed her that I was extremely ill. I told her to cancel all of my meetings and appointments for that day and inform my manager of my absence. My then-husband was in Atlanta; we had separated.

He had left two weeks earlier, the morning our septic tank backed up, and we had raw sewage backing up in the toilets, the bathtubs and even the washing machine. He simply called a plumber and a septic tank company and left before they arrived.

Now, still clad in my pajamas, I simply picked up my car keys, walked into my closed garage, sat in my car and cranked it on. I had decided to choose death over life. I wanted to close my eyes, peacefully fall asleep and never wake up again.

As I sat in my car with the engine running, two prevailing thoughts entered my mind. I thought of my younger daughter and the fact that she would be the one to come home from school to find me slumped over the steering wheel in the front seat of my car. I couldn't imagine the traumatic effect it would have on her for the rest of her life. My second thought, as stupid as it may be, was about IBM, the company where I was a vice president at the time. I couldn't help but think what all of my colleagues would say about me. My legacy would be, "The bright and shining star who self-destructed—maybe she didn't have what it takes after all."

I turned the engine off and sat there for about thirty minutes. I couldn't even cry. I was totally numb. I knew that I was seriously ill—physically, emotionally and spiritually. I felt as if I were just some insignificant item that had been tossed into the lost and found, waiting for its owner to come back and reclaim it. This was the defining moment for me as I realized that my *soul* was in the lost and found, and I decided *I* was going back to reclaim it.

I got out of my car, went into the house and picked up the phone. I made a call that saved my life. I called an employee assistance program (EAP) hotline. I had the number memorized because I had used it often in the preceding months when I was trying to find help for my daughter. That day, I spoke for an hour with a clinician. I told her I had just tried to commit suicide by carbon monoxide poisoning but couldn't go through with it. I was almost incoherent, rambling in my thoughts and words. I recall telling her, "I need help. I've been trying to get an appointment with a psychiatrist for over a week, but no one can see me for at least three weeks. I can't wait that long—I may be dead by then."

During my conversation with the clinician, I started to have small feelings of hope. She stayed on the phone with me and used her other line to try to set up an appointment with a psychiatrist for me right away. She was able to get an appointment for me for 4:00 that afternoon. It was about 11:00 A.M. when we finished our call, and she called me back every thirty minutes to check on me and see how I was doing.

I was so weak physically and emotionally that I could barely manage to take a shower and get dressed. The most mundane and ordinary tasks felt monumental to me, but I was driven by the thought that all of my life I had been perceived as this "strong and determined black woman" who would let nothing bring her down.

I watched the clock tick minute by minute for four and a half hours. As I waited for the time to come for me to leave for my appointment, I began thinking about my life. I reached deep into the memory bank of my childhood. I remembered that I had been raised with a very solid foundation of love, understanding, great values and principles, and a strong sense of spirituality and faith. I was not raised to be a coward or to give up. I was raised believing that I could do anything I put my mind to and that no obstacles were insurmountable.

I finally left for my appointment. During the twenty-minute drive, I was almost fixated on the beauty of the fall leaves changing colors and floating to the ground. It was somewhat symbolic—I too was shedding my leaves. My visit to the psychiatrist, filled with hope, increased my desire to live and that desire was validated by the second stranger of the day who would help save my life. It was the beginning of the healing process for me. I was finally reaching out for help. My mind, body and soul had completely shut down, but I knew with time, they would be back in synch. I was determined to do whatever work was necessary to ensure that happened. I was ready to grow new leaves.

I started out that gloomy autumn day making a choice of death. But by the end of the day, I had decided to choose life. If I had followed through on the first choice, I would have never seen all the bright days that I have since lived to see. I couldn't fathom then that there would be sunshine once again in my life. Even though it still pours rain some days, I just imagine that I'm Annie in the Broadway musical singing, "The sun will come out tomorrow." And it always does.

Today, I feel a glow around me every time I hear my daughters' voices, see their faces, or get hugs from them that fill my soul with a warmth that not even a blazing fire could replace. My older daughter survived her troubled youth and is blossoming like a beautiful flower. When I look into her eyes, I see my own reflection and am reminded that we indeed are both strong women who will let no obstacles keep us down. We've both learned to get back up, brush ourselves off and keep moving forward. My younger daughter fundamentally saved my life—the thought of her was my motivation to live—as if she breathed air into my lungs keeping me alive on that dreary day. Life is precious, and I now savor each and every moment of it. I have my soul back, reclaimed with a new sense of meaning and purpose. I now understand just how blessed I was, am and will always be.

Lisa J. Whaley

Greatness by Design

Our greatest problems in life come not so much from situations we confront as from our doubts about our ability to handle them.

Susan Taylor

I clenched his tiny hand in mine as we made our way to the top of the escalator. I was getting ready to do the unthinkable. My worst nightmare was here, and I was wide awake. As we walked closer to the gate, I began to feel overwhelmed, almost panic-stricken, because I knew in minutes he would be gone.

As the pain welled up inside me, the last year and a half flashed before my eyes—a mind movie of all the decisions I'd made leading to this moment. I'd sold my home in Florida, left everything and everyone I knew to follow a man I thought, without a doubt, loved my son and me. Yet now here I was, standing at the gates of hell, at least in my mind, getting ready to send my three-year-old son, Kwaku, on a plane without me to stay with my best friend, Suluki, and her husband, Saleem.

The night before, I had told her I was leaving my

husband. I told her I didn't know where I would be after tomorrow, my things would be in storage, and I needed to ask a huge favor. Before the words came out of my mouth, she said, "We'll be there tomorrow to pick up our godson. Don't worry. We'll get you through this."

Guilt and disappointment consumed my body and soul for putting my precious son through this. Would I ever forgive myself for what I was about to do? Were there signs, or was I just blinded by the idea of love and "happily ever after"? Ironically, we had just gotten really settled in our new life in Virginia. Kwaku was going to have a father for the first time, and my business was starting to thrive. I thought we were doing fine until the touches stopped, the kisses became void of affection and then anger became more prevalent than kindness. Before I knew it, I was planning to leave. *But where will I go, and how will I regroup from this?* I couldn't believe I was going to essentially be homeless and loveless all in one fell swoop. I refused to drag my baby around like a piece of furniture; my child must have a home and feel safe, even if his mother doesn't have one for a while. I kept chanting silently, *I can suffer, but my child will not feel this pain; that is not an option,* while I came closer and closer to completing the single most difficult task thus far in my life, sending my son away.

Kwaku and I watched the planes arriving on the runway. He pointed and cheered as they landed and took off. I hugged him knowing that these would be our last moments together for a while. It was gut-wrenching; my emotions were all over the place. I felt my anger, my sadness, and even my joy that I had someone in my life who loved me and I loved my son enough to stand up for him. Suluki had always been that kind of sista.

When "Uncle" Saleem arrived, Kwaku ran and greeted him. It was just another adventure as far as he was concerned.

When it was time to say good-bye, Kwaku turned and said, "Mom-me, the plane, big, go bye-bye. See you right back." Kwaku grabbed his godfather's hand and turned to get on the airplane. I waved and blew kisses and crumbled inside. I kept saying to myself, *It's temporary, and it's for the best.* I didn't know yet if I even believed my own words.

Then came the second most difficult task in my life, surviving this seeming eternity of pain and disillusionment. *Oh my God, what have I done? My baby is gone. I'm alone. Why me? Why now?*

In the midst of all this, I had a show to do. God had just blessed me, one month prior, with the launch of my own national radio talk show, sharing a message and a mindset reinforced by the inspirational lives and achievements of some of the most extraordinary women and men of our time. I believed God allowed me to host the show because, at this moment, I needed that inspiration the most. Many times I felt as if the guests showed up just to help me continue to push through. Every night I had the opportunity to have conversations with guests who had faced challenges, setbacks and fears and had persevered to phenomenal heights of achievement. It was clear that while my show was providing inspiration across the country, it was also saving me. One special night, Nikki Giovanni took me out of my pain while taking my breath away when she performed a favorite poem of hers, "The Song of Feet." She spoke of wiggling her toes in the sands of time, trusting and once again feeling the warmth of the embrace, celebrating being a black woman. I held tightly onto her words, filling my heart with spirit.

Kwaku is in good hands, I would constantly say to myself. *Suluki and Saleem love that "little critter,"* as they affectionately called him.

"Mom-me, Christopher is my new best friend," Kwaku shared during one of our daily phone calls. He had become instant buddies with the son of Suluki's niece. They went to school together, played together, got their first bikes together, shared a room together, and became brothers.

I got through my first month without Kwaku in the refuge of my sista-friend Dyan's home. She had *literally* created a space for me where I could heal, simply because she knew I had nowhere else to go. I was able to focus on allowing myself to cry out loud, pray, heal all the hurt and to transform my pain, my loneliness and my anger into forgiveness. First, I forgave myself for allowing and accepting less than what God had in store for me, and then I forgave myself for doubting myself as a mother. Then it happened, I didn't even see it coming—one day I felt my own toes begin to wiggle again. Then another day I felt a warm embrace all over my body; this hug was like no other I'd ever experienced. I looked around only to find that it was me, hugging myself, loving myself, singing and even dancing again. The tears I was shedding now were not from pain but in gratitude for the positive people God had put in my path; people who had made my journey meaningful and manageable.

Today is Kwaku's fourth birthday, a celebration, a home-coming and a renewal of the spirit of family. Unfortunately, I couldn't have a big party with all his classmates so far away, but as he walked into our new home he was greeted by trumpets of joy, a red carpet of balloons, and a cake lit with candles and wishes for new memories still to come. Today, after three months of missing and praying to be with Kwaku again, I'm just going to hold his little hand and watch both of our toes as they wiggle, together, again.

Blanche Williams

Kwanzaa on the Prairie

Sometimes I feel discriminated against, but it does not make me angry. It merely astonishes me. How can any deny themselves the pleasure of my company? It's beyond me.

Zora Neale Hurston

Two years of uninterrupted work time and a master's of fine arts from the nation's top creative writing program—that's what I was promised, and so I left behind a boyfriend I loved dearly, a three-bedroom Manhattan apartment and the most lucrative job I'd ever had to move halfway across the country to Iowa City, Iowa. I hadn't researched much about the workshop program beyond the writing time and the degree, and so I was pleasantly surprised at how good it felt to finally be thinking creatively again after years of working in law firms. I was thrilled with my classes, and I marveled at the insights of my teachers.

I was also surprised by the bitterly cold subzero days and the necessity of driving in snow that accumulated in feet rather than in inches. But I was scandalized at the fact that the town's black population was less than 3 percent.

And right from the beginning, I was aghast at the fact that out of one hundred students in my program, I was the only African American. The workshop, it seemed, had an unwritten rule that only one African American student be admitted at a time, and this had long been an issue: One of the last black students to go through the program had been so miserable he'd arranged to complete his degree in three semesters instead of the requisite four. Like the African American alums before me, I began to feel the pain and isolation of being the program's lone black writer. My characters, a fellow student insisted, didn't "talk like black people really would." An entire workshop of people averred that they didn't understand the significance of my protagonist's Afro. And an overheard discussion about Toni Morrison ended with, "I know she won the affirmative action Nobel, but is she really any good?" I began to avoid the campus, insuring that the only day I spent there was the Tuesday I had workshop. According to tradition, each workshop group went to a bar afterwards. I never went with mine.

Every couple of months I'd drive to Chicago, where I'd get my hair braided and eat at a soul food restaurant. Every black person I saw on the street was a jewel, proof that I wasn't crazy, that I didn't have to live by the script my classmates wanted to write for me, that I was more than a figment of some white writer's imagination. But then I'd recross the Illinois-Iowa border, and the black radio stations would fade out, and I'd return to feeling terribly alone. Every few days in Iowa City, I'd see another black person on the street. I would strike up frantic conversations—I'm sure some of them thought I was crazy. But others lingered and stayed in touch, no doubt as lonely as I was.

By Thanksgiving, my sense of isolation had peaked. My sister had given me a kinara for Christmas the year before, and I had looked forward to celebrating Kwanzaa with the friends I'd make in my new city. But as the weeks wore on, I realized I'd probably just be taking my kinara home to celebrate with my family. Meanwhile, school churned forward: I went to speak to the department secretary about my fellowship application for the following year. At the end of our conversation, she gave me a jolt. "How do you like it here?" she asked.

"I love it," I lied. But the tears were hot in my eyes, the lump rising in my throat.

"We don't see you around much," she said, continuing to prod.

"Well, it's just that . . . I feel so . . ." I had never been one to let myself cry in front of strangers, but as I choked out the word "alone," I couldn't help myself.

She handed me a tissue and watched me try, unsuccessfully, to regain my composure. Then she spoke. "It must be difficult," she said.

But how could she understand? Having been the only black child in my school for many years, I still smarted at the painful memories of the teasing and exclusion I endured, and I'd promised myself that as an adult I'd never put myself back into the "pioneer" situation. But there I was, a pioneer again by accident, trapped for two long years on the prairie. Knowing I could never fully explain, I bit my lip and left her office. I decided to go grocery shopping because it always put me in a better mood. As soon as I walked through the automatic door I saw a black woman with a full head of gorgeous braids. "Where did you get those done?" I gasped.

"Sylvia. She lives near campus."

"Really? Wow. And here I've been going to Chicago."

The woman chuckled. "Did you just move here?"

"A few months ago."

She held out her hand. "Irene."

"Jacinda."

It turned out Irene was also doing her M.F.A., in drama, and she also felt isolated. Irene gave me not only Sylvia's number but her own, and insisted that we get together for dinner.

"Cool. I'll call you soon," I said, "and hey . . . why don't you come to my Kwanzaa party?" I didn't know where the idea had come from, but Irene nodded vigorously.

"A Kwanzaa party? I've never been to one. Neat!"

I said good-bye to Irene and finished my shopping. I rushed home and called some of the black people I'd met on the street over the past few months. The following day, I called the minority graduate students' office and tracked down all the black students who were doing M.F.A.s at the university. There were about fifteen of us in all—more than I'd thought—and they were all glad to hear from me. The following Tuesday was a workshop day, but I was overjoyed that it had come, because it was also the day of my Kwanzaa party. I bought new red, green and black candles for my kinara, cooked up some greens and okra, and baked cornbread. I decorated my apartment with symbols of the harvest. And that evening, when workshop was over, I rushed home to finish my eggnog.

My classmates were no doubt out drinking after workshop, but I was partying into the night with my new friends. I will never forget how we boogied to my mother's old James Brown albums, or how, as we lit the seven candles, we each read the principle ours stood for and said what we'd do in the coming year to live that principle. I'll never forget how much we smiled at one another's jokes that night, or how the unattended kinara candles melted onto the hardwood floor. Eventually, someone looked out the window and noticed that it had snowed about five inches since the party started. Folks began to pile out my door into the coming blizzard, but they still looked warm from the friendships they'd forged. "Thank you so much for doing this," Irene said. "I've been here two years, and no one has ever gotten us all together like this." I was glad for everyone, and glad for myself, because the only thing that was lonely that night was the streetlamp outside my window that illuminated a perfect winter snow.

Having spent the night in the company of my black brothers and sisters, I felt as strong as that steel pole, as unburdened as the lightest flake of snow falling from its cloud. Spending an evening with folks who looked like me, joked like me, and understood me deeply had given me the strength and the calm to reenter a world I had formerly shunned. The following evening, I went to workshop. And I went out to the bar afterwards with my classmates, for the first of many Tuesdays.

Jacinda Townsend

The Bus Stop

*M*emories *of our lives, of our works and our deeds will continue in others.*

Rosa Parks

This particular day began as usual. I got up, got dressed and headed for work.

I walked the usual four long blocks to the bus stop.

As I arrived, the same old faces were in the old same places. I kept to myself and attempted to avoid all eye contact. I was determined not to engage any of them in conversation. In the past, nothing any one of them had said was truly of any consequence. So I stood in back of the bus bench and leaned against the wall.

I didn't have to look for the bus because the others each took turns leaning over to look for it.

Late again, I thought to myself.

So there I was at the bus stop with all those losers who didn't have lives or cars. I justified my place among this particular crowd: *I would have had a car and a better job, if my dad hadn't run out on us, making it impossible for me to go to college. If I had gone to college, then I wouldn't be at this bus stop.*

I looked around and noticed the white couple in their early sixties, who dressed alike every day. They sat ex-tremely close together. They were probably afraid of us.

They spoke constantly in some foreign language.

I looked over at the man I referred to as the "Dirty Old Man." He always made dirty remarks. No one paid attention to him. Besides, he still wore leisure suits. I'm sure he was Mr. Personality back in the day. He and the older couple who appeared to be joined at the hip always sat in the exact same seats.

Daily I could count on a variety of strangely dressed, loud, ignorant-acting teenage boys at the bus stop. These teenagers made a point to speak loudly enough for everyone within a block to hear every word of their conversation. I don't know why someone didn't tell them to shut up.

Then there was the "Book Worm," a girl with thick glasses. Daily she wore an oversized jacket that probably belonged to her brother. She never spoke to anyone, and she never looked up from her book and that was fine with me.

There was the "Music Man," a man in his early thirties. He wore the largest sunglasses on the planet and some kind of uniform. His earphones appeared to be attached to his head. He would blast the music so loud that you could hear it five feet away.

Lastly, there was an older woman about seventy-five. She wore a purple scarf over her head every day rain or shine. She and I leaned against the wall. She stared at me, but we never spoke. I was sure that she was a domestic worker.

Now on this particular day, I wondered why the bus people couldn't be as well groomed as I was. I wondered if they were Christians like me. I wondered if there was a reason we were always there together.

My thoughts were interrupted by the terrifying screech of skidding tires; the sound appeared to come from out of nowhere. My eyes frantically searched back and forth attempting to determine the source. Suddenly, there was a loud, horrific crash. The impact felt like a bomb, it shook everyone. Right in front of our eyes two cars collided, and one began to spin in a circle, totally out of control. The screeching became louder and louder. Everyone began to scream as the car came out of the spin and headed directly toward the bus bench and all of us.

Within a flash and without a thought for their welfare, the teenage boys, who just moments before I had called ignorant, grabbed the old man and the couple sitting on the bench and pulled them to safety. The Music Man, instead of running to get out of the way of the speeding car himself, risked his life by running over and pulling the girl reading the book out of the path of the oncoming car.

As the car jumped the curb, barely missing the teenage boys, it plowed through the cement bus bench and debris flew into the air. All I could see was a cloud of smoke heading right toward me. I closed my eyes and said, "Lord, please save me." I felt someone tugging on my right arm; I felt my feet fly off the ground. The back of my head was smashed into the wall, and I lost consciousness for a few moments.

When I finally opened my eyes, all I could see was the hood of a car right in my face, and I could feel the bumper pressing against me. The car was so close that I could see the face of the unconscious driver behind the steering wheel.

One of the teenage boys was holding my arm. He was pinned against the wall by the bumper of the car. He had risked his life to pull me from the fatal path of the car.

Immediately, I looked to my left and I saw a hole in the wall. Then I remembered the old lady who was standing next to me. I looked for her and saw that she had been hit by the car and smashed through the wall. I reached over to touch her. She looked at me and reached for my hand.

She asked, "Are you okay, honey?" as sweetly as if she were my grandmother instead of a familiar stranger at the bus stop. I said, "Yes," somewhat disbelievingly as I was certainly in shock and had not yet performed an overall assessment of my well-being.

She smiled and said, "Thank God." This was the first time we had ever spoken, in all our days at the bus stop.

Then, in a soft voice just above a whisper, she said to me, "I have watched you for months, and it made me so proud to see you looking so sharp and going to your important job. I'm so happy that you are safe."

I told her that help was on the way, but it was too late. She tenderly squeezed my hand, drew her last breath, and I felt her hand slowly slip away from mine. She closed her eyes as her head lowered. She looked so peaceful; I knew she was gone.

A pain shot through my heart. I couldn't breathe. We couldn't have been more than a foot away from each other. I was spared while she was taken. I kept asking myself why I hadn't spoken to her while I had the chance. She was proud of me even though I never even bothered to say hello or wish her a good morning. *What kind of person am I? What kind of Christian am I? I didn't even know her name.*

All the bus people, who just moments before I had called unintelligent and losers in my mind, had all clearly displayed genuine character and heroics. Without giving any thought to their own safety, they all responded, put their lives on the line and helped each other to safety. They literally saved the day.

Since then, I have learned to respect and love people, no matter what their station is in life—or what I may *think* their station is.

I continue to walk the four long blocks to the bus daily. Only the walk doesn't seem as long because I know when I get there my friends at the bus stop will be waiting for me.

DeAnna Blaylock

Who Is Jack Canfield?

Jack Canfield is the co-creator and editor of the *Chicken Soup for the Soul®* series, which *Time* magazine has called "the publishing phenomenon of the decade." The series now has 105 titles with more than 100 million copies in print in forty-one languages. Jack is also the co-author of eight other bestselling books including *The Success Principles™: How to Get from Where You Are to Where You Want to Be*, *Dare to Win*, *The Aladdin Factor*, *You've Got to Read This Book* and *The Power of Focus: How to Hit Your Business, Personal and Financial Targets with Absolute Certainty*.

Jack has recently developed a telephone coaching program and an on-line coaching program based on his most recent book, *The Success Principles*. He also offers a seven-day Breakthrough to Success seminar every summer, which attracts 400 people from fifteen countries around the world.

Jack is the CEO of Chicken Soup for the Soul Enterprises and the Canfield Training Group in Santa Barbara, California, and founder of the Foundation for Self-Esteem in Culver City, California. He has conducted intensive personal and professional development seminars on the principles of success for more than 900,000 people in twenty-one countries around the world. He has spoken to hundreds of thousands of others at numerous conferences and conventions and has been seen by millions of viewers on national television shows such as *The Today Show*, *Fox and Friends*, *Inside Edition*, *Hard Copy*, *CNN's Talk Back Live*, *20/20*, *Eye to Eye*, the *NBC Nightly News* and the *CBS Evening News*.

Jack is the recipient of many awards and honors, including three honorary doctorates and a Guinness World Records Certificate for having seven *Chicken Soup for the Soul* books appearing on the New York Times bestseller list on May 24, 1998.

To write to Jack or for inquiries about Jack as a speaker, his coaching programs or his seminars, use the following contact information:

Jack Canfield
The Canfield Companies
P.O. Box 30880
Santa Barbara, CA 93130
phone: 805-563-2935 • fax: 805-563-2945
E-mail: *info@jackcanfield.com*
Web site: *www.jackcanfield.com*

Who Is Mark Victor Hansen?

In the area of human potential, no one is more respected than Mark Victor Hansen. For more than thirty-years, Mark has focused solely on helping people from all walks of life reshape their personal vision of what's possible. His powerful messages of possibility, opportunity and action have created powerful change in thousands of organizations and millions of individuals worldwide.

He is a sought-after keynote speaker, bestselling author and marketing maven. Mark's credentials include a lifetime of entrepreneurial success and an extensive academic background. He is a prolific writer with many bestselling books, such as *The One Minute Millionaire, The Power of Focus, The Aladdin Factor* and *Dare to Win,* in addition to the *Chicken Soup for the Soul* series. Mark has made a profound influence through his library of audios, videos and articles in the areas of big thinking, sales achievement, wealth building, publishing success, and personal and professional development.

Mark is the founder of the MEGA Seminar Series. MEGA Book Marketing University and Building Your MEGA Speaking Empire are annual conferences where Mark coaches and teaches new and aspiring authors, speakers and experts on building lucrative publishing and speaking careers. Other MEGA events include MEGA Marketing Magic and My MEGA Life.

He has appeared on television (*Oprah,* CNN and *The Today Show*), in print (*Time, U.S. News & World Report, USA Today, New York Times* and *Entrepreneur*) and on countless radio interviews, assuring our planet's people that "You can easily create the life you deserve."

As a philanthropist and humanitarian, Mark works tirelessly for organizations such as Habitat for Humanity, American Red Cross, March of Dimes, Childhelp USA and many others. He is the recipient of numerous awards that honor his entrepreneurial spirit, philanthropic heart and business acumen. He is a lifetime member of the Horatio Alger Association of Distinguished Americans, an organization that honored Mark with the prestigious Horatio Alger Award for his extraordinary life achievements.

Mark Victor Hansen is an enthusiastic crusader of what's possible and is driven to make the world a better place.

Mark Victor Hansen & Associates, Inc.
P.O. Box 7665
Newport Beach, CA 92658
phone: 949-764-2640 • fax: 949-722-6912
Web site: *www.markvictorhansen.com*

Who Is Lisa Nichols?

Lisa Nichols is a dynamic motivational speaker and the founder and CEO of Motivating the Teen Spirit, LLC, a company committed to teaching teens emotional healthiness so they may fall back in love with themselves and begin to make integrity-based decisions. Her world-class curriculum has impacted the lives of more than 60,000 teens internationally, prevented more than 1,100 teen suicides, reunited thousands of teens with their parents, and influenced more than 950 teen dropouts to return to school. Her clients include the educational system, the juvenile justice system, faith-based organizations and youth serving agencies. Her transformational outcomes with teens ranks her company #1 by many experts.

Lisa Nichols is both a personal and professional coach and has appeared on NBC's daytime show *Starting Over* as a guest expert on life coaching. Her track record of getting entrepreneurs, writers and professionals clear on their vision, their roadblocks and their possibilities is exemplary. There is always a waiting list of people to receive her "breakthrough" coaching services.

Her no-holds-barred messages delivered to standing room only audiences are felt with powerful energy through her personal testimonies of turning her breakdowns into breakthroughs. She is known not to leave a dry eye in the house.

Lisa has been recognized for her work and dedication by receiving the 2006 Rising Star award, 2006 Best Story Telling Award, 2003 Trail Blazers Entrepreneurs award, Lego Land Heart of Learning award, Emotional Literacy award and having November 20th proclaimed by the Mayor of Henderson, Nevada as Motivating the Teen Spirit Day.

Born and raised in Los Angeles, California, she loves to dance, swim, skate, play laser tag and read. She and her son Jelani currently live in Southern California.

Lisa is available for keynote speaking, professional development workshops, teen empowerment workshops and professional or personal coaching.

www.Lisa-Nichols.com, www.AfricanAmericanSoul.com
info@lisa-nichols.com
858-376-3700

Who Is Eve Eschner Hogan?

Eve Eschner Hogan, senior editor of *Chicken Soup for the African American Woman's Soul* and *Chicken Soup for the African American Soul*, is an inspirational speaker, relationship specialist and writing coach.

She is the author of *How to Love Your Marriage: Making Your Closest Relationship Work, Way of the Winding Path: A Map for the Labyrinth of Life, Intellectual Foreplay: Questions for Lovers and Lovers-to-Be, Virtual Foreplay: Making Your Online Relationship a Real-Life Success,* and co-author of *Rings of Truth.* She is also a contributor to *Chicken Soup for the Ocean Lover's Soul.*

Founder of Wings to Wisdom: Tools for Self-Mastery, Eve facilitates personal and spiritual growth workshops nationally. She writes a regular Q and A relationship advice column for newspapers and web sites guiding readers to create healthier relationships. She possesses a rare and deep understanding of human behavior and is a true example of the principles she shares. Her charismatic style captivates listeners, igniting people's enthusiasm and joy for life.

Eve has been featured as a relationship expert on Lifetime TV, *Iyanla, The Other Half,* and in *Cosmopolitan, Men's Health* and *Bride* magazines. Her special interest is in helping people discover their own inner resources, thus expanding their strengths and life skills. She leaves her audiences empowered with the skills to effect positive change in their lives.

Together, Eve and her husband, Steve, own Makena Coast Dive Charters (*www.MauiUnderwater.com*) and The Sacred Gardens where she offers personal growth and writing retreats, facilitates labyrinth walks and performs weddings on Maui.

For information about Eve Eschner Hogan, her workshops, retreats, coaching and books, contact her at:

Wings to Wisdom: Tools for Self-Mastery
P.O. Box 943, Puunene, Maui, HI 96784
phone: (808) 573-6521 • fax: (808) 879-8201
E-mail: *Eve@HeartPath.com*
www.HeartPath.com or *www.EveHogan.com*

Contributors

H. Renay Anderson has an M.A. in organizational management and a B.S. in management/marketing. Her first book was *Why Women Wear Shoes They Know Will Eventually Hurt Their Feet*. In 2005 she won a national ad contest for ADCandy. She reviews books for Bella Online, EuroReviews and BBW Reviews. Her Web site is: *http://clix.to/renay*.

Marvin V. Arnett is the author of *Pieces from Life's Crazy Quilt*, a childhood memoir of growing up black in Detroit, Michigan, during the 1930s and '40s. Winner of the American Library Association Best of the Best for 2004, and AAA-HA Best Nonfiction Award for 2003, Marvin is in demand as a motivational speaker when not involved with the lives of her children, grandchildren and great-grandchildren. You may contact her at *mvarnett@hotmail.com*.

Lindale Banks received her B.A. in English writing from Missouri Western State College. She was born and raised in Kansas City, Missouri and attends Emmanuel Church. Lindale is single with no children, but adores her three beautiful godchildren. She enjoys long walks, laughing with friends, but most of all praying and writing. She contributes her drive to people who said it couldn't be done and her best friend, Dr. Zelema Horris.

Lisa Bartley-Lacey graduated cum laude with B.A. in English/theatre and a master's of holistic counseling from Salve Regina University in 2003. She's CEO of SOULutions for Dynamic Living, has a holistic consulting practice, is coauthor of *100 Words of Wisdom for Women*, and Co-Producer/Artist of: *The Pakoli Project*.

Connie Bennett is an ACSM certified fitness professional and a twenty-seven-year industry veteran. Her specialty is happiness education through movement. Her hobbies are laughing long and hard, baking chocolate chip cookies and anything iPod. Connie has a joyous African Dance DVD available. Contact her at: *yes.connie@yahoo.com*.

Rita Billbe is a retired high school principal whose passions are singing in the church choir and writing stories to inspire others. She and her husband own a resort called Angels Retreat on the White River in Arkansas, where she is learning to fly-fish. Their Web site is *www.whiteriver.net/angels-retreat*.

Andrea Blackstone attended Morgan State University and earned an M.A. from St. John's College. She is the author of *Schemin': Confessions of a Gold Digger* and *Short Changed*. Andrea is working on a nonfiction project outside of the urban genre, as well as a new novel. Please e-mail her at: *dreamweaverpress@aol.com*.

DeAnna Blaylock is a retired bank manager with thirty years of people-oriented experience. The years have provided knowledge and understanding of people in crisis. Her passion for writing is apparent in her stories and poems of people facing challenges and how character is formed by life-defining moments.

Karla Brown writes African American children's, paranormal, romantic and young adult novels. Her short story "The Trophy" will be published in an upcoming anthology titled *Color Him Father* to be released in June 2006. She lives with her two daughters in a suburb of Philadelphia.

Sanyika Calloway Boyce is an author, speaker and columnist for *Young Money* magazine. Sanyika's mission is to help as many students as possible understand the importance of managing their money, protecting their credit and handling debt properly. Sanyika now travels to high schools, colleges and universities nation-wide with a uniquely "edu-taining" and timely message of financial literacy and credit responsibility. Please contact her at *info@financialfitnesscoach.com* or visit *www.sanyika.com*.

Brenda Caperton first became interested in putting her life experiences on paper in high school. A requirement for senior English class was completion of a creative writing course. Her love of literature and self-expression through the creative writing process has continued throughout her life.

Tracy Clausell-Alexander is a financial analyst who possesses a love for writing. Her stories have been published in *Chicken Soup for the African American Soul, Conscious Women—Conscious Lives, Woman's World* magazine, and *Adoptive Families* magazine. She is currently working on her first novel. Tracy is the mother of six children, one of whom lives only in her heart. Please contact her at *tdclausell@comcast.net*.

Linda Coleman-Willis is a professional speaker, author of several books and a per-formance improvement coach. She is the 2002-2003 president of the National Speakers Association–Los Angeles Chapter. Linda enjoys spending "fun" time with her family and friends. The story *Just Like Mom* is a tribute to her mom, Helen Brown. Please e-mail Linda at *Lindaspeak@aol.com*.

Jerry Craft is a contributor to *Chicken Soup for the African American Soul,* winner of the African American Literary Awards Show Open Book Award, a National Cartoonists Society Award Nominee (2000) and graduate of the School of Visual Arts. *Mamas Boyz: As American As Sweet Potato Pie!* was named a Great Book For African American Children. See *www.mamasboyz.com*.

Antonio Crawford is a Christian, a husband, a father, a teacher and an entrepreneur who is proudly serving his country in the United States Navy. He is a gifted and dedicated writer, contributing from the farthest reaches of Southern California, San Diego.

Michelle Cummins wrote articles for *Garage Band Magazine* in Orange County, California. She's written, directed, produced and edited music videos. Her produc-tion company in Hemet, California, Chez Michelle Production, produced a short film.

Jeanine DeHoney is a freelance writer and a family services coordinator in a Brooklyn daycare center. She has had her essays, articles and stories published in several magazines, such as *Black Secrets, Black Romance, Essence, Upscale, Sisters In Style, Emerge, Radiance, Today's Black Woman, TimbookTu* and *Bahiyah Woman Magazine.* Currently she is writing a novel about a family who lives in a Brooklyn brownstone. She owes her love of writing to her mother, Evelyn Rushing, who always had a notebook and a pen beside her when Jeanine was growing up.

Betty DeRamus is a newspaper columnist and a 1993 Pulitzer Prize finalist. The Detroiter is the author of *Forbidden Fruit: Love Stories from the Underground Railroad,* true stories about free and enslaved nineteenth-century black couples who went to extraordinary lengths to stay together. Please contact her at *bjderamus@aol.com*.

Phyllis R. Dixon is a native of Milwaukee, Wisconsin and graduated from the University of Wisconsin. She is the author of *Let the Brother Go If* and the novel *Forty Acres.* She currently lives in Memphis, Tennessee.

Adiya Dixon–Sato received her B.A. on East Asian studies from Yale University and worked as a writer and teacher in Tokyo. Returning to New York for law school, she is currently penning a collection of essays on Japan. Please e-mail her at *adiya.dixon@gmail.com*.

RuNett Nia Ebo entertains, educates, ministers and motivates. That's her purpose. RuNett Nia Ebo (Gray), Philadelphia author and poet, established "Nia's Purpose" to teach black History in Rhyme while entertaining audiences of all ages. She has eight books of poetry. For more information, visit her Web site at *http://poetebo.expage.com*.

Lorraine M. Elzia is an editor, author and literary artist. She is co-owner of Eve's Literary Services and co-moderates Essentially Women, a writing group for African American women. She has previously been published in *Chicken Soup for the Single Parent's Soul*. Lorraine can be reached at *LorrainesZone@gmail.com* and *www.evesliteraryservice.com*.

Michelle Fitzhugh-Craig is the founder and editor-in-chief of *Shades Magazine*; a reporter with the Tri-Valley Herald in Pleasanton, California; has worked as an editor and reporter for several publications; and is the coauthor of *Living in the Moment: A Guide to Living a Full and Spiritual Life*.

Leslie Ford is a self-taught trumpeter, arranger, composer and lecturer, CEO of Leslie Ford & Group, LLC, and founder of the Jazz Institute of New Jersey, Inc., helping children connect to the power of music. Leslie is writing his autobiography. To contact Mr. Ford visit his Web site: *http://lesliefordandgroup.org*.

E. Claudette Freeman is an award-winning playwright/author and a twenty-plus year radio veteran. She is the station manager of Gospel AM 1490 WMBM in Miami. She is currently working on a screenplay version of her novel *Sheltered Deliverance*, while developing theatre for radio. E-mail her at *eclaudettecreative@yahoo.com*.

Nancy Gilliam is a 2005 Who's Who Among America's Teachers honoree. She teaches English at Greater Hope Christian Academy in Philadelphia. She has authored the companion study guide to *B.J. Robinson's Lebron James: King of the Court* and was included in *Chicken Soup for the African American Soul*. Visit her on the Web at *www.nancygilliam.com*.

Elaine K. Green is a native New Orleanian, freelance writer, avid reader, married to husband, Eddie, and mother to daughter, Kelli. Please e-mail her at *ekgreen@hotmail.com*.

Kiana Green is currently in her junior year at Williams College. She is pursuing a degree in American studies with a concentration in African American Studies and Political Science. She enjoys writing short stories and poetry that explore black life and culture. She is a slamm poet, DJ and jazz vocalist. She plans on becoming a playwright.

Joe Gurneak has worked in the oil industry his whole life and served as police commissioner for his community. Joseph has experienced the gift of others that have come into his life and left him enriched in heart and soul. He is passing that gift on in *Chicken Soup* stories.

Emma Ransom Hayward is a former teacher and librarian. A well-known black-doll collector, she uses her dolls to profile and document the black experience in America from slavery to the present. She is completing a book, *Images in Black Spoken in Many Voices*, photostories with vintage pictures. E-mail her at *miblkdoll1@aol.com*.

Briana Hendrix is a recent high school graduate who is looking forward to her freshman year at a Michigan university. She enjoys playing basketball, socializing with friends and spending time with family—but mostly playing basketball.

Lolita Hendrix, APR is a professor of public relations at Eastern Michigan University in Ypsilanti, Michigan. She also consults regularly, assisting businesses and organizations with public relations, grant writing and other communication needs. She enjoys writing, exercising and spending time with her two children. Please e-mail her at *lhendrix@emiich.edu*.

Barbara Holt is a Chicago Urban League executive whose career has spanned service in the public and private sectors and included election as the first woman and first African American alderman of the Fifth Ward. She enjoys spending time with her children and grandchildren, writing, needlework, bowling, traveling and, of course, cooking and dancing.

Tanya Hutchison resides in California with her husband and five children. She founded Phenomenal Women, Inc., a nonprofit organization. Tanya's recent book, *Beauty! It's a Journey Not a Destination*, is a memoir about her life growing up against the odds.

Damita Jo Johnson taught middle school for twenty years. She holds several degrees and is currently pursuing her doctorate degree. She has been married to Pastor Gene Johnson for twenty-three years. They pastor a church in Carson, California. She enjoys singing, teaching, acting, writing, exercising and helping people.

Yvonda Johnson is a recent Habitat for Humanity homeowner. She works as a quality control representative. She enjoys reading, writing, spending time with her two sons, as well as attending church. She plans to continue her journey as a newfound writer. Please e-mail her at *vonjon23@aol.com*.

Linda Jones, a veteran journalist and freelance writer, is author of *Nappyisms: Affirmations for Nappy-Headed People and Wannabes!* She is founder of A Nappy Hair Affair, Inc., which promotes African American culture, and is owner of ManeLock Communications, a writing service. She lives in Dallas, Texas and her Web site is *www.lindaLjones.com*.

Berthena Kemp is a mother, grandmother and great grandmother who is active in church, writes, travels, swims and loves the Lord. She is a breast cancer survivor who spends her time lobbying on behalf of survivors. She is an amazing woman who earned her bachelor's degree at age seventy-three. Berthena inspires everyone she comes in contact with. Contact her by e-mail at *Berthena2@aol.com*.

T. Rhythm Knight is a native Floridian currently residing in Miami. Although she works as a computer systems analyst, she's a writer at heart. She recently completed her first novel, *On the Wings of Angels*, and is currently working on the second one, *The Master Plan*. You can e-mail her at *ms_t_2u@yahoo.com*.

Sherie Labedis is a Berkeley graduate, civil rights worker, teacher, speaker, mountain climber, black belt and writer. In her book, *You Came Here to Die*, she chronicles her fears, loneliness and jubilation as an eighteen-year-old voter registration volunteer in South Carolina in 1965. Contact her at: *jslab@surewest.net*.

Anita S. Lane is the founder and editor of *Keeping Family First* online magazine (*http://KeepingFamilyFirst.org*). She earned her bachelor's and master's degrees from the University of Michigan in Ann Arbor. She lives in Detroit, Michigan, with her husband and four young children. Please e-mail her at *anita@keepingfamilyfirst.org*.

Margaret Lang is a published author of fourteen stories and a Christian speaker/teacher in the United States, Thailand, East Timor and Australia. Margaret's desire is to help the poor overseas. Margaret's daughter is a physician/missionary in Asia, her son is a worship leader and she has two granddaughters. Her e-mail address: *Contact@servingourworld.org.*

Evelyn K. Lemar is an Army veteran and mother of one daughter, Chantel, twelve. She is currently working on her first novel and is also a poetry/spoken word artist. In addition to writing, she enjoys books, live music and the beach. Please e-mail her at *YorHyness@aol.com.*

Susan Madison resides on St. Helena Island in South Carolina. Madison writes a column for the *Lowcountry Weekly* and has recently released a book entitled *if i can't sing the blues,* a collection of essays and poems. Susan can be e-mailed at *colorsofjoy@islc.net.*

Keith Mallett is a painter, etcher and ceramic artist, his subject matter ranges from still lifes to abstracts. In recent years, he has devoted his talents to themes that portray the beauty and strength of the African American experience. For more information, visit his Web site at *www.keithmallet.com* or write Keith Mallet Studios, Inc., P.O. Box 151378, San Diego, CA 92175.

Nadine McIlwain is a former Ohio public school educator, who has received numerous awards for excellence in the classroom including the prestigious National Educator Award from the Milken Family Foundation. Her first book, *From Ghetto to God: The Incredible Journey of NFL Star Reggie Rucker* was published in 2001.

Charles Stanley McNeal is a student of American Sign Language at Mount San Antonio, Walnut, California. He is an employee of AT&T in the city of Pasadena, California. Charles's love for poetry and writing developed when he was a child. His goal is to become a licensed interpreter.

Monica Montgomery was born and raised in East St. Louis, Illinois. She has been writing short stories and poetry for personal enjoyment since she was ten years old. She is currently pursuing a bachelor's degree in mass communications at a local university. Monica likes to spend her free time bowling, skating, at the movies or on road trips. Her dream is to see the world and then write about it.

Evelyn Palfrey writes romantic suspense for the "Marvelously Mature." Her novels, *The Prince of Passion, Dangerous Dilemmas* and *Everything in Its Place* have appeared on the Essence Best Seller List. She is an attorney in Texas. Find out more about her at *www.evelynpalfrey.com.*

Dawn Nicole Patterson earned her B.A. and Juris Doctor from Washburn University. She is a wife, mother and educational consultant who speaks Spanish and enjoys research and helping others. Her book, *God's Leaders Leading God's People,* is available through Cushani Publishing, Inc., 913-299-4144. Please contact her at *dawn_n_patterson@yahoo.com.*

Hattie Mae Pembrook has written her first book, *Messages to Awaken yourSelf,* which is the companion text to her sister's original and inspirational CD, *A Musical Messenger.* She enjoys writing, facilitating wake-shops™ with her sister and being a champion for children. You can visit her Web site at *www.hattiemae.com.*

Ruthell Cook Price received her bachelor of science degree from California State University, Los Angeles. She is an administrative assistant in banking for HTC International Ministry. Ruth is a wife and the mother of three sons and has one grandson. A professional singer for several decades, writing has become her current passion. E-mail her at: *marstepri@yahoo.com.*

Swannee Rivers received her Bachelor of Arts degree from the University of Washington in 1987. She lives with her family in Renton, Washington. Swannee is the author of three literary works: *Healthcare Under Dress: An Inside Look at the University of Washington Billing Scandal,* a cancer journal, and a teen journal. Please e-mail her at swanneerivers@mindspring.com.

Bari-Ellen Ross graduated from Loyola University in Chicago where she received a B.A. in business. Bari and her husband, Charles, own and operate a seafood/soul-food restaurant, Ross' Hooked & Cooked, in Phoenix, Arizona. She is the proud mother of two daughters, Brooke and Staci.

Carol Ross-Burnett is a gospel artist, songwriter and producer with Mighty Power Productions and H.I.S. Records, founded with her husband, Ron. A Berkeley graduate, she is also a dynamic speaker, trainer and published author who travels nationally through her company, CRB Consulting. Carol resides in Los Angeles with her husband and two sons. For booking and information, contact her at *crburnett@prodigy.net.*

Jerilyn Upton Sanders lives outside Chattanooga, Tennessee, with her husband and infant son. She currently directs an inner-city educational enrichment program. She hopes to follow in her grandmother's footsteps to encourage all children to work hard, educate themselves and make their ancestors proud. E-mail her at *rookiemom1@hotmail.com.*

Sophfronia Scott, "The Book Sistah," wrote for *Time* and *People* magazines before publishing her first novel, *All I Need to Get By* and being hailed by Henry Louis Gates, Jr. as potentially "one of the best writers of her generation." Sophfronia provides workshops and coaching for aspiring authors at *www.TheBookSistah.com.*

Angel V. Shannon, poet, writer and activist, is the author of *. . . And Then There Were Butterflies* (2004). Committed to social change, she balances a career in medicine with motherhood, writing, and lecturing on human rights and environmental justice. Ms. Shannon is currently completing her first novel. Visit her Web site at: *www.angelvshannon.typepad.com.*

Nikki D. Shearer-Tilford is a writer and owns a business, The Sacred Mind. Her story, "I Am My Sister's Keeper," appeared in *Chicken Soup for the African American Soul.* She enjoys encouraging the expression of unresolved emotions through gifts, talents and strengths, and creating healing messages that speak to the heart/Spirit. She can be reached at *thesacredmind@cinci.rr.com.*

Sonya Simpson received her bachelor of arts in psychology from the University of Notre Dame. She is transitioning her career from the financial industry to teaching preschool children and writing. Sonya enjoys cooking, live music, dancing, swimming and going to the theatre. Please e-mail her at *simpson6140@comcast.net.*

Dayciaa C. Smith is author of *The Godfamily Series* and *The Way of the Righteous.* Visit her Web site at *www.dayciaa.net* for more information about her and her novels. She has a doctor of education degree and teaches children's Bible study and Sunday school. Her son is Timothy Paul Smith.

Sheila P. Spencer created W.O.W. (Women of Words) and SistahFriend, an online newsletter. *He Is: A Lyrical Miracle* is her spoken word CD. She writes because that's what she was created to do! Sheila believes she's been blessed to be a blessing to you. Contact her at *SistahSpk@aol.com* or *www.SistahSheila.com.*

Kelly Starling Lyons, a North Carolina journalist, transforms relationships, memories and history into stories of discovery. Her children's books include *NEATE: Eddie's Ordeal* and the upcoming release, *A Million Men and Me* (Just Us Books). Find out more at *www.kellystarlinglyons.com*. This story is dedicated to her grandma, Ruth Starling, and her mother, husband and daughter.

Bernetta Thorne-Williams was born and raised in Washington, D.C. She received a B.A. in English and a B.S. in criminal justice from North Carolina Wesleyan College. Bernetta has written several romance novels. She resides in North Carolina with her husband and two sons. Please e-mail her at *Bernetta.Williams@ncmail.net*.

Jacinda Townsend a 2003–04 fiction fellow at the Wisconsin Institute of Creative Writing and a 2002 Hurston Wright Award finalist, has been published in numerous literary magazines and anthologies. A former Fulbright fellow and graduate of both Harvard University and the Iowa Writers' Workshop, she teaches at Southern Illinois University.

Karen Waldman, Ph.D., a licensed psychologist, is a frequent contributor to the *Chicken Soup* series. She enjoys writing, dancing, the theater, music, nature, spending time with relatives and friends, traveling with her husband, Ken, and playing with their children and grandchildren (Lana, Greta, and Natalie). Karen's e-mail is *krobens@aol.com*.

Patricia L. Watler Johnson earned a bachelor of business administration degree in real estate from Pace University in 1983 and is a housing and communications professional in New York State government. She is the proud mother of Theodore and Clifton Johnson and has received awards for her community service. Pat enjoys writing and motivational speaking and is writing a book on forgiveness as a path toward healing. She can be reached at *highlyfavored509@verizon.net*.

Carolyn West received her certification in Audix and Definity administration from Avaya University in Pasadena, California, in 2001. She is currently a telecommunications analyst with IBM Global Services. She enjoys singing, writing poetry and mentoring her grandson Derell. She plans to write a novel. Please e-mail her at *berrylovr1@yahoo.com*.

Lisa J. Whaley is president of Life Work Synergy, LLC. A highly sought-after speaker, she's the author of *Reclaiming My Soul from the Lost and Found* and *Prisoners of Technology: Time to Get UNPLUGGED*. Lisa received a bachelor of science degree from Hampton University in 1982. Contact Lisa at *www.lisawhaley.com*.

Mary Saxon Wilburn a retired R.N., has been writing since childhood. She currently lives near Atlanta, Georgia, where she is active in the writing community. One of her stories appeared in *Chicken Soup for the Nurse's Soul*, and her first mystery novel, *Blood Kin*, was published in 2005. E-mail her at: *mnsaxon@aol.com*.

Blanche Williams is the host of the nation's newest talk show sensation, Greatness by Design, broadcast live from coast-to-coast on XM Satellite Radio. She's an acclaimed author of *How to Design Your Mind for Greatness*, motivational speaker, business strategist, inspirational columnist, life coach and successful entrepreneur. Please e-mail her at *blanche@blanchewilliams.com*.

Permissions

We would like to acknowledge the following publishers and individuals for permission to reprint the following material. (Note: The stories that were penned anonymously, that are in the public domain, or that were written by Jack Canfield, Mark Victor Hansen or Lisa Nichols are not included in this listing.)

A Line in the Sand. Reprinted by permission of Sherie Labedis. ©2005 Sherie Labedis.

Legacy. Reprinted by permission of Jerilyn Upton Sanders. ©2002 Jerilyn Upton Sanders.

Letters of Love. Reprinted by permission of Lorraine M. Elzia. ©2005 Lorraine M. Elzia.

Walking the Lessons of Life. Reprinted by permission of H. Renay Anderson. ©2005 H. Renay Anderson.

These Precious Hands. Reprinted by permission of Sheila P. Spencer. ©2005 Sheila P. Spencer.

My Mother's Shoes. Reprinted by permission of Andrea Blackstone. ©2005 Andrea Blackstone.

What She Said. Reprinted by permission of Betty DeRamus. ©2005 Betty DeRamus.

Getting to Know Miss Gladys. Reprinted by permission of Bari-Ellen Ross. ©2004 Bari-Ellen Ross.

The Ring. Reprinted by permission of Monica Montgomery. ©2004 Monica Montgomery.

Just Like Mom. Reprinted by permission of Linda Coleman-Willis. ©2005 Linda Coleman-Willis.

Mama's Hands. Reprinted by permission of Evelyn Palfrey. ©2005 Evelyn Palfrey.

The Outfit. Reprinted by permission of Berthena Kemp. ©2005 Berthena Kemp.

Birthdays and Blessings. Reprinted by permission of Karen Waldman. ©2005 Karen Waldman.

Dancing in the Kitchen. Reprinted by permission of Barbara Holt. ©2002 Barbara Holt.

History Through Herstory. Reprinted by permission of Emma Ransom Hayward. ©2003 Emma Ransom Hayward.

Ninety-Pound Powerhouse. Reprinted by permission of Swannee Rivers. ©2003 Swannee Rivers.

My Womb's Butterfly. Reprinted by permission of E. Claudette Freeman. ©2005 E. Claudette Freeman.

The Wisdom of Motherhood. Reprinted by permission of Lolita and Briana Hendrix. ©2005 Briana Hendrix and Lolita Hendrix.

One Day, You'll Understand. Reprinted by permission of Kelly Starling Lyons. ©2005 Kelly Starling Lyons.

Even a Dancing Time. Reprinted by permission of Angel V. Shannon. ©2005 Angel V. Shannon.

Keeping Faith. Reprinted by permission of Tracy Clausell-Alexander. ©2004 Tracy Clausell-Alexander.

Handpicked to Nurture. Reprinted by permission of T. Rhythm Knight. ©2005 T. Rhythm Knight.

Single-Mommy Love. Reprinted by permission of Dayciaa C. Smith. ©2005 Dayciaa C. Smith.

The Christmas Sparrows. Reprinted by permission of Joe Gurneak. ©2005 Joe Gurneak.

Soul Food Rite of Passage. Reprinted by permission of Anita S. Lane. ©2005 Anita S. Lane.

Lesson for a New Life. Reprinted by permission of Evelyn K. Lemar. ©2005 Evelyn K. Lemar.

Bathed in Love. Reprinted by permission of Adiya Dixon-Sato. ©2005 Adiya Dixon-Sato.

My Cup Runneth Over. Reprinted by permission of Nikki Shearer-Tilford. ©2005 Nikki Shearer-Tilford.

Meet Me in the Middle. Reprinted by permission of Connnie Bennett. ©2005 Connie Bennett.

The Dreadful Story. Reprinted by permission of Lisa Bartley-Lacey. ©2005 Lisa Bartley-Lacey.

Gluttony to Glory. Reprinted by permission of Stacey Lindale Banks. ©2005 Stacey Lindale Banks.

Getting Real. Reprinted by permission of Elaine K. Green. ©2004 Elaine K. Green.

Crown of Splendor. Reprinted by permission of Sheila P. Spencer. ©2005 Sheila P. Spencer.

Birth of a Nappy Hair Affair. Reprinted by permission of Linda Jones. ©2003 Linda Jones.

A Cup of Tenderness. Reprinted by permission of Brenda Caperton. ©2005 Brenda Caperton.

Sistahood. Reprinted by permission of Jeanine DeHoney. ©2005 Jeanine DeHoney.

Who Is Helping Whom? Reprinted by permission of Margaret Lang. ©2005 Margaret Lang.

Merry Christmas, Emma. Reprinted by permission of Mary Saxon Wilburn. ©2001 Mary Saxon Wilburn.

Elegant Ladies . . . Again. Reprinted by permission of Karla Brown. ©2005 Karla Brown.

Friday Afternoon at the Beauty Shop. Reprinted by permission of Michelle Fitzhugh-Craig. ©2002 Michelle Fitzhugh-Craig.

Sisters' Song. Reprinted by permission of Rita Billbe. ©2000 Rita Billbe.

Divine Intervention. Reprinted by permission of Michelle Cummins. ©2005 Michelle Cummins.

Holy Ghost Filled. Reprinted by permission of Kiana Green. ©2002 Kiana Green.

God's Will. Reprinted by permission of Sophfronia Scott Gregory. ©2005 Sophfronia Scott Gregory.